Advanced C++ Programming Cookbook

Become an expert C++ programmer by mastering concepts like templates, concurrency, and type deduction

Dr. Rian Quinn

BIRMINGHAM - MUMBAI

Advanced C++ Programming Cookbook

Commissioning Editor: Richa Tripathi
Acquisition Editor: Shriram Shekhar
Content Development Editor: Tiksha Sarang
Senior Editor: Storm Mann
Technical Editor: Romy Dias
Copy Editor: Safis Editing
Project Coordinator: Francy Puthiry
Proofreader: Safis Editing
Indexer: Rekha Nair
Production Designer: Jyoti Chauhan

First published: January 2020

Production reference: 1290120

Published by Packt Publishing Ltd.
Livery Place
35 Livery Street
Birmingham
B3 2PB, UK.

ISBN 978-1-83855-991-5

www.packt.com

To my kids, embrace the challenges that others deem too hard to take on; be patient, strong, and confident, never letting anyone stand in your way.

– Dad

Packt>

Packt.com

Subscribe to our online digital library for full access to over 7,000 books and videos, as well as industry leading tools to help you plan your personal development and advance your career. For more information, please visit our website.

Why subscribe?

- Spend less time learning and more time coding with practical eBooks and Videos from over 4,000 industry professionals

- Improve your learning with Skill Plans built especially for you

- Get a free eBook or video every month

- Fully searchable for easy access to vital information

- Copy and paste, print, and bookmark content

Did you know that Packt offers eBook versions of every book published, with PDF and ePub files available? You can upgrade to the eBook version at www.packt.com and as a print book customer, you are entitled to a discount on the eBook copy. Get in touch with us at customercare@packtpub.com for more details.

At www.packt.com, you can also read a collection of free technical articles, sign up for a range of free newsletters, and receive exclusive discounts and offers on Packt books and eBooks.

Contributors

About the author

Dr. Rian Quinn is the **Chief Technology Officer (CTO)** in the Advanced Technologies Business Unit at Assured Information Security, Inc., having focused on trusted computing, hypervisor-related technologies, machine learning/artificial intelligence, and cybersecurity for more than 10 years, and has 9 years of technical management and business development experience. He holds a Ph.D. in computer engineering, with specializations in information assurance and computer architectures, from Binghamton University. He is the cofounder and lead developer of the Bareflank hypervisor, and is an active member of several open source projects, including Microsoft's **Guideline Support Library (GSL)** and OpenXT. Rian previously wrote *Hands-On System Programming with C++*.

About the reviewers

Sergey Gomon started his journey in IT 12 years ago at Belarus State University of Informatics and Radioelectronics, in the Artificial Intelligence department. He has about 8 years of industrial programming experience using C++ in several fields, such as network programming, information security, and image processing. He currently works at SolarWinds MSP and is an activist in the CoreHard C++ community.

Zhuo Qingliang (also known as KDr2 online) is presently working at paodingai.com, a start-up FinTech company in China that is dedicated to improving the financial industry by using artificial intelligence technologies. He has over 10 years of experience in Linux, C, C++, Python, Perl, and Java development. He is interested in programming, doing consulting work, and participating in and contributing to the open source community (including the Julia community, of course).

Packt is searching for authors like you

If you're interested in becoming an author for Packt, please visit authors.packtpub.com and apply today. We have worked with thousands of developers and tech professionals, just like you, to help them share their insight with the global tech community. You can make a general application, apply for a specific hot topic that we are recruiting an author for, or submit your own idea.

Table of Contents

Preface

In this book, you will learn advanced C++ techniques that you can use on your own C++ projects. This book teaches C++ using a recipe-style approach, complete with examples and screenshots for each recipe that you can download from GitHub and work with yourself. This book teaches C++ using the C++17 specification, with a sneak peek at the new features being added to C++20 at the end. In some recipes, we will even use a disassembler to better understand how C++ is compiled, and the impact certain decisions have on your applications. By the end of this book, you will have mastered the advanced concepts of C++ and will be able to solve everyday problems, which will take your C++ programming to the next level.

Who this book is for

This book is for intermediate C++ developers who are familiar with C++ and want to obtain expert skills and become a proficient C++ developer. A good understanding of the language is assumed, including a basic understanding of assembly.

What this book covers

Chapter 1, *Getting Started with Library Development*, teaches you how to develop your own libraries, including an explanation of the principle of least surprise, how to namespace everything, how to write header-only libraries, and how to ensure others will continue to use your libraries.

Chapter 2, *Using Exceptions for Error Handling*, covers more advanced topics of C++ exception and error handling, including a detailed explanation of the `noexcept` specifier and operator, how RAII supports resource management in the presence of exceptions, why throwing from a destructor should be avoided, and how to write your own exceptions.

Chapter 3, *Implementing Move Semantics*, provides a detailed explanation of C++ move semantics, including an explanation of the *Big Five*, how to make your class movable, how to write move-only (and non-move) non-copy style classes, how to properly implement a move constructor, why `const &&` makes no sense, and how to use reference qualification.

Chapter 4, *Using Templates for Generic Programming*, teaches you how to write template functions like an expert, including how to implement your own SFINAE, how to perform perfect forwarding, how to use `constexpr-if` statements, how to leverage tuples with parameter packs, how to loop over parameter packs at compile time, how to use type traits to implement different versions of the same function, how to use `template<auto>`, and how to leverage explicit type declarations in your own applications.

Chapter 5, *Concurrency and Synchronization*, teaches you how to use `std::mutex` (and friends), when to use atomic types, how to handle `const` classes with thread-safety using the `mutable` keyword, how to write a thread-safe class, how to write a thread-safe wrapper, as well as how to write asynchronous C++ including promises and futures.

Chapter 6, *Optimizing Your Code for Performance*, covers how to profile and benchmark your C++, how to disassemble your C++ to better understand how to optimize your code, how to locate and remove unneeded memory allocations, and why `noexcept` helps with optimizations.

Chapter 7, *Debugging and Testing*, walks you through how to use `Catch2` to unit test C++, how to use Google's ASAN and UBSAN sanitizers to dynamically analyze your code for memory corruption and undefined behavior, as well as how to use NDEBUG.

Chapter 8, *Creating and Implementing Your Own Container*, teaches you how to write your own container wrapper by creating a `std::vector` that is always sorted.

Chapter 9, *Exploring Type Erasure*, teaches you everything you need to know about type erasure, including how to erase types through inheritance and using template, how to implement the type erasure pattern, and how to implement the delegate pattern.

Chapter 10, *An In-Depth Look at Dynamic Allocation*, teaches you advanced topics in dynamic memory allocation, including how to properly use `std::unique_ptr` and `std::shared_ptr`, how to handle circular references, how to type cast smart pointers, and how the heap works behind the scenes to provide your application with dynamic memory.

Chapter 11, *Common Patterns in C++*, explains how different patterns in computer science are implemented in C++, including the factory pattern, the singleton pattern, the decorator pattern, and the observer pattern, as well as how to implement static polymorphism to write your own static interfaces without the need for virtual inheritance.

Chapter 12, *A Closer Look at Type Deduction*, provides a deep dive into how type deduction is performed in C++17, including how `auto`, `decltype`, and `template` deduce their types automatically. This chapter concludes with examples of how to write your own C++17 user-defined deduction guides.

Chapter 13, *Bonus: Using C++20 Features*, provides a sneak peek at the new features coming with C++20, including concepts, modules, ranges, and coroutines.

To get the most out of this book

We assume that you have written C++ before and are already familiar with some modern C++ features.

This book uses Ubuntu to provide examples that you can compile and run yourself as you read the book. We assume you have some basic knowledge of Ubuntu, how to install it, and how to use a Linux terminal.

We use a disassembler in some of the recipes to better understand what the compiler is doing under the hood. Although you do not need to know how to read the assembly to understand what is being taught, a basic understanding of x86_64 assembly will help.

Download the example code files

You can download the example code files for this book from your account at `www.packt.com`. If you purchased this book elsewhere, you can visit `www.packtpub.com/support` and register to have the files emailed directly to you.

You can download the code files by following these steps:

1. Log in or register at `www.packt.com`.
2. Select the **Support** tab.
3. Click on **Code Downloads**.
4. Enter the name of the book in the **Search** box and follow the onscreen instructions.

Once the file is downloaded, please make sure that you unzip or extract the folder using the latest version of:

- WinRAR/7-Zip for Windows
- Zipeg/iZip/UnRarX for Mac
- 7-Zip/PeaZip for Linux

The code bundle for the book is also hosted on GitHub at https://github.com/ PacktPublishing/Advanced-CPP-Programming-CookBook. In case there's an update to the code, it will be updated on the existing GitHub repository.

We also have other code bundles from our rich catalog of books and videos available at https://github.com/PacktPublishing/. Check them out!

Code in Action

Visit the following link to check out videos of the code being run: https://bit.ly/2tQoZyW

Conventions used

There are a number of text conventions used throughout this book.

constexpr: Indicates code words in text, numbers, folder names, filenames, file extensions, pathnames, dummy URLs, and user input. Here is an example: "The noexcept specifier is used to tell the compiler whether a function may or may not throw a C++ exception."

A block of code is set as follows:

```
int main(void)
{
    the_answer is;
    return 0;
}
```

When we wish to draw your attention to a particular part of a code block, the relevant lines or items are set in bold:

```
int main(void)
{
    auto execute_on_exit = finally{[]{
        std::cout << "The answer is: 42\n";
    }};
}
```

Any command-line input or output is written as follows:

```
> mkdir build && cd build
> cmake ..
> make recipe04_examples
```

Bold: Indicates a new term, an important word, or words that you see onscreen. For example, important words appear in the text like this. Here is an example: "In this recipe, we will learn why throwing exceptions in a destructor is a **bad idea**."

Warnings or important notes appear like this.

Tips and tricks appear like this.

Sections

In this book, you will find several headings that appear frequently (*Getting ready*, *How to do it...*, *How it works...*, *There's more...*, and *See also*).

To give clear instructions on how to complete a recipe, use these sections as follows:

Getting ready

This section tells you what to expect in the recipe and describes how to set up any software or any preliminary settings required for the recipe.

How to do it...

This section contains the steps required to follow the recipe.

How it works...

This section usually consists of a detailed explanation of what happened in the previous section.

There's more...

This section consists of additional information about the recipe in order to make you more knowledgeable about the recipe.

See also

This section provides helpful links to other useful information for the recipe.

Get in touch

Feedback from our readers is always welcome.

General feedback: If you have questions about any aspect of this book, mention the book title in the subject of your message and email us at customercare@packtpub.com.

Errata: Although we have taken every care to ensure the accuracy of our content, mistakes do happen. If you have found a mistake in this book, we would be grateful if you would report this to us. Please visit www.packtpub.com/support/errata, selecting your book, clicking on the Errata Submission Form link, and entering the details.

Piracy: If you come across any illegal copies of our works in any form on the Internet, we would be grateful if you would provide us with the location address or website name. Please contact us at copyright@packt.com with a link to the material.

If you are interested in becoming an author: If there is a topic that you have expertise in and you are interested in either writing or contributing to a book, please visit authors.packtpub.com.

Reviews

Please leave a review. Once you have read and used this book, why not leave a review on the site that you purchased it from? Potential readers can then see and use your unbiased opinion to make purchase decisions, we at Packt can understand what you think about our products, and our authors can see your feedback on their book. Thank you!

For more information about Packt, please visit packt.com.

Getting Started with Library Development

1

In this chapter, we will cover some useful recipes for creating our own libraries, including an explanation of the principle of least surprise, which encourages us to implement libraries using semantics that our users are already familiar with. We will also look at how to namespace everything to ensure our custom libraries don't conflict with others. In addition, we will look at how to create header-only libraries, as well as some best practices associated with library development. Finally, we will conclude this chapter with a demonstration of the boost libraries to show you what a large library looks like and how it can be used by users in their own projects.

In this chapter, we will cover the following recipes:

- Understanding the principle of least surprise
- How to namespace everything
- Header-only libraries
- Learning library development best practices
- Learning how to use the boost APIs

Let's get started!

Technical requirements

To compile and run the examples in this chapter, you must have administrative access to a computer running Ubuntu 18.04 with a functional internet connection. Prior to running these examples, you must install the following packages using the following command:

```
> sudo apt-get install build-essential git cmake
```

If this is installed on any operating system other than Ubuntu 18.04, then GCC 7.4 or higher and CMake 3.6 or higher will be required.

Understanding the principle of least surprise

When either using existing C++ libraries or creating your own, understanding the **principle of least surprise** (also called the **principle of least astonishment**) is critical to developing source code efficiently and effectively. This principle simply states that any feature that a C++ library provides should be intuitive and should operate as the developer expects. Another way of saying this is that a library's APIs should be self-documenting. Although this principle is critically important when designing libraries, it can and should be applied to all forms of software development. In this recipe, we will explore this principle in depth.

Getting ready

As with all of the recipes in this chapter, ensure that all of the technical requirements have been met, including installing Ubuntu 18.04 or higher and running the following in a Terminal window:

```
> sudo apt-get install build-essential git cmake
```

This will ensure your operating system has the proper tools to compile and execute the examples in this recipe. Once you've done this, open a new Terminal. We will use this Terminal to download, compile, and run our examples.

How to do it...

Perform the following steps to complete this recipe:

1. From a new Terminal, run the following code to download the source code:

```
> cd ~/
> git clone
https://github.com/PacktPublishing/Advanced-CPP-CookBook.git
> cd Advanced-CPP-CookBook/chapter01
```

2. To compile the source code, run the following code:

```
> mkdir build && cd build
> cmake ..
> make recipe01_examples
```

3. Once the source code has been compiled, you can execute each example in this recipe by running the following commands:

```
> ./recipe01_example01
The answer is: 42

> ./recipe01_example02
The answer is: 42

> ./recipe01_example03
The answer is: 42

> ./recipe01_example04
The answer is: 42
The answer is: 42

> ./recipe01_example05
The answer is: 42
The answer is: 42

> ./recipe01_example06
The answer is: 42
The answer is: 42

> ./recipe01_example07
```

```
The answer is: 42

> ./recipe01_example08
The answer is: 42

> ./recipe01_example09
The answer is: 42
```

In the next section, we will step through each of these examples and explain what each example program does and how it relates to the lessons being taught in this recipe.

How it works...

As stated in the previous section, the principle of least surprise states that a library's APIs should be intuitive and self-documenting and this principle generally applies to all forms of software development and not just library design. To understand this, we'll look at some examples.

Example 1

Example 1 demonstrates the principle of least surprise as follows:

```cpp
#include <iostream>

int sub(int a, int b)
{ return a + b; }

int main(void)
{
    std::cout << "The answer is: " << sub(41, 1) << '\n';
    return 0;
}
```

As shown in the preceding example, we have implemented a library API that adds two integers and returns the results. The problem is that we named the function `sub`, which most developers would associate with subtraction and not addition; although the API functions as designed, it breaks the principle of least surprise because the API's name is not intuitive.

Example 2

Example 2 demonstrates the principle of least surprise as follows:

```
#include <iostream>

void add(int a, int &b)
{ b += a; }

int main(void)
{
    int a = 41, b = 1;
    add(a, b);

    std::cout << "The answer is: " << b << '\n';
    return 0;
}
```

As shown in the preceding example, we have implemented the same library API that we implemented in the previous exercise; it is designed to add two numbers and return the result. The issue with this example is that the API is implementing the following:

```
b += a;
```

In this example, the principle of least surprise is being violated in two different ways:

- The add function's arguments are a and then b, even though we would write this equation as b += a, meaning that the order of the arguments is intuitively backward.
- It is not immediately obvious to the user of this API that the result would be returned in b without reading the source code.

A function's signature should document how the function will execute using semantics the user is already accustomed to, thus reducing the probability of causing the user to execute the API incorrectly.

Example 3

Example 3 demonstrates the principle of least surprise as follows:

```
#include <iostream>

int add(int a, int b)
{ return a + b; }
```

```
int main(void)
{
    std::cout << "The answer is: " << add(41, 1) << '\n';
    return 0;
}
```

As shown in the preceding example, we're adhering to the principle of least surprise here. The API is designed to add two integers and return the result, and the API intuitively performs this action as expected.

Example 4

Example 4 demonstrates the principle of least surprise as follows:

```
#include <stdio.h>
#include <iostream>

int main(void)
{
    printf("The answer is: %d\n", 42);
    std::cout << "The answer is: " << 42 << '\n';
    return 0;
}
```

As shown in the preceding example, another great example of the principle of least surprise is the difference between `printf()` and `std::cout`. The `printf()` function requires the addition of format specifiers to output integers to `stdout`. There are many reasons why `printf()` is not intuitive:

- To a beginner, the `printf()` function's name, which stands for print formatted, is not intuitive (or in other words, the function's name is not self-documenting). Other languages avoid this issue by picking more intuitive names for a print function, such as `print()` or `console()`, which do a better job of adhering to the principle of least surprise.
- The format specifier symbol for an integer is `d`. Once again, to a beginner this is unintuitive. In this specific case, `d` stands for decimal, which is another way of saying *signed integer*. A better format specifier might have been `i` to match the language's use of `int`.

Contrast this with `std::cout`, which stands for character output. Although this is less intuitive compared to `print()` or `console()`, it is more intuitive than `printf()`. Furthermore, to output an integer to `stdout`, the user doesn't have to memorize a table of format specifiers to complete their task. Instead, they can simply use the << operator. Then, the APIs handle formatting for you, which is not only more intuitive but also safer (especially when working with `std::cin` as opposed to `scanf()`).

Example 5

Example 5 demonstrates the principle of least surprise as follows:

```
#include <iostream>

int main(void)
{
    auto answer = 41;

    std::cout << "The answer is: " << ++answer << '\n';
    std::cout << "The answer is: " << answer++ << '\n';

    return 0;
}
```

As shown in the preceding example, the ++ operators uphold the principle of least surprise. Although a beginner would have to learn that ++ represents the increment operator, which means the variable is incremented by 1, the position of ++ with respect to the variable is quite helpful.

To understand the difference between `++variable` and `variable++`, all the user has to do is read the code left to right as normal. When ++ is on the left, the variable is incremented and then the contents of the variable are returned. When ++ is on the right, the contents of the variable are returned and then the variable is incremented. The only issue with respect to the position of ++ is the fact that ++ on the left is generally more efficient (as the implementation doesn't require extra logic to store the value of the variable prior to the increment operation).

Example 6

Example 6 demonstrates the principle of least surprise as follows:

```cpp
#include <iostream>

int add(int a, int b)
{ return a + b; }

int Sub(int a, int b)
{ return a - b; }

int main(void)
{
    std::cout << "The answer is: " << add(41, 1) << '\n';
    std::cout << "The answer is: " << Sub(43, 1) << '\n';

    return 0;
}
```

As shown in the preceding code, we have implemented two different APIs. The first adds two integers and returns the results while the second subtracts two integers and returns the results. The issue with the subtract function is two-fold:

- The addition function is in lowercase while the subtraction function is in uppercase. This is not intuitive and users of the APIs would have to learn which APIs are in lowercase and which are in uppercase.
- The C++ standard APIs are all in snake case, meaning they leverage lowercase words with the use of _ to denote a space. In general, it is better to design C++ library APIs with snake case as a beginner is more likely to find this intuitive. It should be noted that, although this is generally the case, the use of snake case is highly subjective and there are several languages that do not adhere to this guidance. The most important thing is to pick a convention and stick to it.

Once again, ensuring your APIs mimic existing semantics ensures the user can quickly and easily learn to use your APIs, while reducing the probability of the user writing your APIs incorrectly, leading to compile errors.

Example 7

Example 7 demonstrates the principle of least surprise as follows:

```cpp
#include <queue>
#include <iostream>

int main(void)
{
    std::queue<int> my_queue;

    my_queue.emplace(42);
    std::cout << "The answer is: " << my_queue.front() << '\n';
    my_queue.pop();

    return 0;
}
```

As shown in the preceding example, we are showing you how a `std::queue` can be used to add integers to a queue, output the queue to `stdout`, and remove elements from the queue. The point of this example is to highlight the fact that C++ already has a standard set of naming conventions that should be leveraged during C++ library development.

If you are designing a new library, it is helpful to the user of your library to use the same naming conventions that C++ has already defined. Doing so will lower the barrier to entry and provide a more intuitive API.

Example 8

Example 8 demonstrates the principle of least surprise as follows:

```cpp
#include <iostream>

auto add(int a, int b)
{ return a + b; }

int main(void)
{
    std::cout << "The answer is: " << add(41, 1) << '\n';
    return 0;
}
```

As shown in the preceding example, we are demonstrating how the use of `auto`, which tells the compiler to figure out what the return type of the function is automatically, does not uphold the principle of least surprise. Although `auto` is extremely helpful for writing generic code, its use should be avoided as much as possible when designing a library API. Specifically, for the user of the API to understand what the inputs and outputs of the API are, the user must read the API's implementation as `auto` does not specify the output type.

Example 9

Example 9 demonstrates the principle of least surprise as follows:

```
#include <iostream>

template <typename T>
T add(T a, T b)
{ return a + b; }

int main(void)
{
    std::cout << "The answer is: " << add(41, 1) << '\n';
    return 0;
}
```

As shown in the preceding example, we are demonstrating a more appropriate way to uphold the principle of least surprise while simultaneously supporting generic programming. Generic programming (also called template meta-programming or programming with C++ templates) provides the programmer with a way to create an algorithm without stating the types that are being used in the algorithm. In this case, the `add` function doesn't dictate the input type, allowing the user to add two values of any type (in this case, the type is called `T`, which can take on any type that supports the `add` operator). Instead of returning an `auto`, which would not state the output type, we return a type `T`. Although `T` is not defined here as it represents any type, it does tell the user of the API that any type we input into this function will also be returned by the function. This same logic is used heavily in the C++ standard library.

How to namespace everything

When creating a library, it is important to namespace everything. Doing so ensures that of the APIs provided by the library cause name collisions with the user's code or with facilities provided by other libraries. In this recipe, we will demonstrate how to do this in our own libraries.

Getting ready

As with all of the recipes in this chapter, ensure that all of the technical requirements have been met, including installing Ubuntu 18.04 or higher and running the following in a Terminal window:

```
> sudo apt-get install build-essential git cmake
```

This will ensure your operating system has the proper tools to compile and execute the examples in this recipe. Once you have done this, open a new Terminal. We will use this Terminal to download, compile, and run our examples.

How to do it...

You need to perform the following steps to complete this recipe:

1. From a new Terminal, run the following to download the source code:

```
> cd ~/
> git clone
https://github.com/PacktPublishing/Advanced-CPP-CookBook.git
> cd Advanced-CPP-CookBook/chapter01
```

2. To compile the source code, run the following code:

```
> mkdir build && cd build
> cmake ..
> make recipe02_examples
```

3. Once the source code has been compiled, you can execute each example in this recipe by running the following commands:

```
> ./recipe02_example01
The answer is: 42

> ./recipe02_example02
The answer is: 42
```

In the next section, we will step through each of these examples and explain what each example program does and how it relates to the lessons being taught in this recipe.

How it works...

C++ provides us with the ability to wrap code in a `namespace`, which simply adds the `namespace` name to all functions and variables inside the `namespace` code (it should be noted that C style macros are not included in the `namespace` and should be used with care because C macros are a preprocessor feature that does not contribute to the code's compiled syntax). To explain why we should `namespace` everything when creating our own libraries, we'll look at some examples.

Example 1

Example 1 demonstrates how to wrap your library's APIs in a C++ `namespace`:

```cpp
// Contents of library.h

namespace library_name
{
    int my_api() { return 42; }
    // ...
}

// Contents of main.cpp

#include <iostream>

int main(void)
{
    using namespace library_name;

    std::cout << "The answer is: " << my_api() << '\n';
    return 0;
}
```

As shown in the preceding example, the contents of the library are wrapped in a `namespace` and stored in the header (this example demonstrates a header-only library, which is an extremely useful design approach as the end user doesn't have to compile libraries, install them on his/her system, and then link against them). The library user simply includes the library header file and uses the `using namespace library_name` statement to unwrap the library's APIs. If the user has more than one library with the same API names, this statement can be omitted to remove any ambiguity.

Example 2

Example 2 expands upon the previous example and demonstrates how to wrap your library's APIs in a C++ namespace header-only library while still including global variables:

```
// Contents of library.h

namespace library_name
{
    namespace details { inline int answer = 42; }

    int my_api() { return details::answer; }
    // ...
}

// Contents of main.cpp

#include <iostream>

int main(void)
{
    using namespace library_name;

    std::cout << "The answer is: " << my_api() << '\n';
    return 0;
}
```

As shown in the preceding example, C++17 was leveraged to create an `inline` global variable that is wrapped in our library's `namespace`. `inline` variables are needed as header-only libraries don't have a source file to define global variables; without the `inline` keyword, defining a global variable in a header would result in the variable being defined multiple times (that is, the result would be a linking error during compilation). C++17 resolved this issue by adding `inline` global variables, which allows a header-only library to define global variables without the need for tricky magic (such as returning a pointer to a static variable from a singleton style function).

In addition to the library's `namespace`, we wrapped the global variable in a `details` namespace. This is done to create a `private` place within your library in case the user of the library declares `using namespace library_name`. If the user does this, all of the APIs and variables that are wrapped by the `library_name` namespace become globally accessible within the scope of the `main()` function. For this reason, any private APIs or variables that are not meant to be accessible by the user should be wrapped by a second `namespace` (typically called `details`) to prevent their global accessibility. Finally, leveraging C++17's `inline` keyword allows us to create a global variable for use in our library while still supporting a header-only design.

Header-only libraries

Header-only libraries are exactly as they sound; an entire library is implemented using header files (usually a single header file). The benefit of header-only libraries is that they are easy to include in your project as you simply include the header and you are done (there is no need to compile the library as there are no source files to compile). In this recipe, we will learn about some issues that arise when attempting to create a header-only library and how to overcome them. This recipe is important because, if you plan to create your own library, a header-only library is a great place to start and will likely increase your adoption rates as downstream users will have less trouble integrating your library into their code base.

Getting ready

As with all of the recipes in this chapter, ensure that all of the technical requirements have been met, including installing Ubuntu 18.04 or higher and running the following in a Terminal window:

```
> sudo apt-get install build-essential git cmake
```

This will ensure your operating system has the proper tools to compile and execute the examples in this recipe. Once you have done this, open a new Terminal. We will use this Terminal to download, compile, and run our examples.

How to do it...

You need to perform the following steps to complete this recipe:

1. From a new Terminal, run the following to download the source code:

```
> cd ~/
> git clone
https://github.com/PacktPublishing/Advanced-CPP-CookBook.git
> cd Advanced-CPP-CookBook/chapter01
```

2. To compile the source code, run the following code:

```
> mkdir build && cd build
> cmake ..
> make recipe03_examples
```

3. Once the source code has been compiled, you can execute each example in this recipe by running the following commands:

```
> ./recipe03_example01
The answer is: 42

> ./recipe03_example02
The answer is: 42

> ./recipe03_example03
The answer is: 42

> ./recipe03_example04
The answer is: 42
The answer is: 2a

> ./recipe03_example05

> ./recipe03_example06
The answer is: 42

> ./recipe03_example07
The answer is: 42
```

In the next section, we will step through each of these examples and explain what each example program does and how it relates to the lessons being taught in this recipe.

How it works...

To create a header-only library, simply ensure that all of your code is implemented in header files, as follows:

```
#ifndef MY_LIBRARY
#define MY_LIBRARY

namespace library_name
{
    int my_api() { return 42; }
}

#endif
```

The preceding example implements a simple library with a single function. The entire implementation of this library can be implemented in a single header file and included in our code as follows:

```
#include "my_library.h"
#include <iostream>

int main(void)
{
    using namespace library_name;

    std::cout << "The answer is: " << my_api() << '\n';
    return 0;
}
```

Although creating header-only libraries seems simple enough, there are some issues that arise when attempting to create a header-only library that should be taken into account.

How to handle includes

In the preceding example, you might have noticed that, when we used our custom header-only library, we included the library first. This is an essential first step to writing a header-only library. When writing examples or tests for header-only libraries, our library should be the first thing we include to ensure that all of the header's dependencies are defined in the header-only library and not in our example or test.

For example, suppose we change our library as follows:

```
#ifndef MY_LIBRARY
#define MY_LIBRARY

namespace library_name
{
    void my_api()
    {
        std::cout << "The answer is: 42" << '\n';
    }
}

#endif
```

As shown in the preceding code snippet, instead of returning an integer our API now outputs to `stdout`. We can use our new API as follows:

```
#include <iostream>
#include "my_library.h"

int main(void)
{
    library_name::my_api();
    return 0;
}
```

Although the preceding code compiles and runs as expected, there is a bug in the code that would likely only be identified by the user of your library. Specifically, if the user of your library swaps the order of the includes or doesn't `#include <iostream>`, the code will fail to compile and produce the following error:

This is because the header-only library itself doesn't include all of its dependencies. Since our example put the library after other includes, our example accidentally hides this issue. For this reason, when creating your own header-only library, always include the library first in your tests and examples to ensure this type of issue never happens to your users.

Global variables

One of the biggest limitations with header-only libraries is that, prior to C++17, there was no way to create global variables. Although global variables should be avoided whenever possible, there are situations where they are needed. To demonstrate this, let's create a simple API that outputs to stdout as follows:

```
#ifndef MY_LIBRARY
#define MY_LIBRARY

#include <iostream>
#include <iomanip>

namespace library_name
{
    void my_api(bool show_hex = false)
    {
        if (show_hex) {
            std::cout << std::hex << "The answer is: " << 42 << '\n';
        }
        else {
            std::cout << std::dec << "The answer is: " << 42 << '\n';
        }
    }
}

#endif
```

The preceding example creates an API that will output to stdout. If the API is executed with true instead of the default false, it will output integers in hexadecimal instead of decimal format. In this example, the change from decimal to hexadecimal is really a configuration setting in our library. Without global variables, however, we would have to resort to other mechanisms to make this work, including macros or, in the preceding example, function parameters; the latter choice is even worse as it couples the configuration of the library to its API, which means any additional configuration options would alter the API itself.

One of the best ways to address this is to use global variables in C++17, as follows:

```
#ifndef MY_LIBRARY
#define MY_LIBRARY

#include <iostream>
#include <iomanip>

namespace library_name
```

```
{
    namespace config
    {
        inline bool show_hex = false;
    }

    void my_api()
    {
        if (config::show_hex) {
            std::cout << std::hex << "The answer is: " << 42 << '\n';
        }
        else {
            std::cout << std::dec << "The answer is: " << 42 << '\n';
        }
    }
}

#endif
```

As shown in the preceding example, we added a new namespace to our library called `config`. Our API no longer needs any parameters and determines how to function based on an inline global variable instead. Now, we can use this API as follows:

```
#include "my_library.h"
#include <iostream>

int main(void)
{
    library_name::my_api();
    library_name::config::show_hex = true;
    library_name::my_api();

    return 0;
}
```

The results in the following output:

It should be noted that we placed the configuration setting in a `config` namespace to ensure that our library's namespace isn't polluted with name collisions, which ultimately ensures that the intent of the global variable is obvious.

Issues with C-style macros

The biggest issue with C-style macros is that, if you place them in a C++ namespace, their name is not decorated by the namespace. This means that macros always pollute the global namespace. For example, suppose you are writing a library that needs to check the value of a variable, as follows:

```
#ifndef MY_LIBRARY
#define MY_LIBRARY

#include <cassert>

namespace library_name
{
    #define CHECK(a) assert(a == 42)

    void my_api(int val)
    {
        CHECK(val);
    }
}

#endif
```

As shown in the preceding code snippet, we have created a simple API that uses a C-style macro to check an integer value in its implementation. The problem with the preceding example is that, if you attempt to use a unit test library with your own library, you will likely end up with a namespace collision.

C++20 could fix this using C++20 modules and is a topic we will discuss in more detail in Chapter 13, *Bonus – Using C++20 Features*. Specifically, C++20 modules do not expose C-style macros to the user of the library. The positive side of this is you will be able to use macros without namespace issues as your macros will not be exposed to the user. The downside to this approach is that a lot of library authors use C-style macros to configure a library (for example, they define a macro prior to including the library to change its default behavior). This type of library configuration will not work with C++ modules unless the macros are defined on the command line when the library is compiled.

Until C++20 is available, if you need to use macros make sure you manually add decorations to the macro names, as follows:

```
#define LIBRARY_NAME__CHECK(a) assert(a == 42)
```

The preceding line of code would do the same thing as having the macro were inside the C++ namespace, ensuring your macro doesn't collide with macros from other libraries or macros the user might define.

How to implement a large library as header-only

Ideally, a header-only library is implemented using a single header. That is, the user only has to copy a single header to their source code to use the library. The problem with this approach is that, for really big projects, a single header can get really large. A great example of this is a popular JSON library for C++ located here: `https://github.com/nlohmann/json/blob/develop/single_include/nlohmann/json.hpp`.

At the time of writing, the preceding library is more than 22,000 lines of code. Attempting to make modifications to a file that is 22,000 lines of code would be awful (if your editor could even handle it). Some projects overcome this problem by implementing their header-only library using several header files with a single header file that includes the individual header files as needed (for example, Microsoft's Guideline Support Library for C++ is implemented this way). The problem with this approach is that the user must copy and maintain multiple header files, which starts to defeat the purpose of a header-only library as its complexity increases.

Another way to handle this problem is to use something such as CMake to autogenerate a single header file from multiple header files. For example, in the following, we have a header-only library with the following headers:

```cpp
#include "config.h"

namespace library_name
{
    void my_api()
    {
        if (config::show_hex) {
            std::cout << std::hex << "The answer is: " << 42 << '\n';
        }
        else {
            std::cout << std::dec << "The answer is: " << 42 << '\n';
        }
    }
}
```

As shown in the preceding code snippet, this is the same as our configuration example, with the exception that the configuration portion of the example has been replaced with an include to a `config.h` file. We can create this second header file as follows:

```
namespace library_name
{
    namespace config
    {
        inline bool show_hex = false;
    }
}
```

This implements the remaining portion of the example. In other words, we have split our header into two headers. We can still use our headers as follows:

```
#include "apis.h"

int main(void)
{
    library_name::my_api();
    return 0;
}
```

However, the problem is that users of our library would need a copy of both headers. To remove this problem, we need to autogenerate a header file. There are many ways to do this, but the following is one way to do so with CMake:

```
file(STRINGS "config.h" CONFIG_H)
file(STRINGS "apis.h" APIS_H)

list(APPEND MY_LIBRARY_SINGLE
    "${CONFIG_H}"
    ""
    "${APIS_H}"
)

file(REMOVE "my_library_single.h")
foreach(LINE IN LISTS MY_LIBRARY_SINGLE)
    if(LINE MATCHES "#include \"")
        file(APPEND "my_library_single.h" "// ${LINE}\n")
    else()
        file(APPEND "my_library_single.h" "${LINE}\n")
    endif()
endforeach()
```

The preceding code reads both headers into CMake variables using the `file()` function. This function converts each variable into a CMake list of strings (each string is a line in the file). Then, we combine both files into a single list. To create our new, autogenerated single header file, we loop through the list and write each line to a new header called `my_library_single.h`. Finally, if we see a reference to a local include, we comment it out to ensure that there are no references to our additional headers.

Now, we can use our new single header file as follows:

```
#include "my_library_single.h"

int main(void)
{
    library_name::my_api();
    return 0;
}
```

Using the preceding method, we can develop our library using as many includes as we like and our build system can autogenerate our single header file, which will be used by the end user, giving us the best of both worlds.

Learning library development best practices

When writing your own library, there are certain best practices that all library authors should adhere to. In this recipe, we will explore some higher-priority best practices and conclude with some information about a project dedicated to defining these best practices, including a registration system that provides your library with a grade as to how well it compiles. This recipe is important as it will teach you how to make the highest-quality library, ensuring a strong and vibrant user base.

Getting ready

As with all of the recipes in this chapter, ensure that all of the technical requirements have been met, including installing Ubuntu 18.04 or higher and running the following in a Terminal window:

```
> sudo apt-get install build-essential git cmake clang-tidy valgrind
```

This will ensure your operating system has the proper tools to compile and execute the examples in this recipe. Once you have done this, open a new Terminal. We will use this Terminal to download, compile, and run our examples.

How to do it...

You need to perform the following steps to complete this recipe:

1. From a new Terminal, run the following to download the source code:

```
> cd ~/
> git clone
https://github.com/PacktPublishing/Advanced-CPP-CookBook.git
> cd Advanced-CPP-CookBook/chapter01
```

2. To compile the source code, run the following code:

```
> mkdir build && cd build
> cmake  ..
> make recipe04_examples
```

3. Once the source code has been compiled, you can execute each example in this recipe by running the following commands:

```
> ./recipe04_example01
21862
```

In the next section, we will step through each of these examples and explain what each example program does and how it relates to the lessons being taught in this recipe.

How it works...

Every library author should ensure their library is easy to use and incorporate into their users' own projects. Doing so will ensure your users continue to use your library, resulting in a growing user base over time. Let's look at a few of these best practices.

What about warnings?

The lowest possible hanging fruit for any library author is ensuring your code compiles with as many warnings enabled as possible. Sadly, GCC does not make this process simple as there is no one warning flag to rule them all, specifically because GCC has many warning flags that are not useful for modern versions of C++ (in other words, they are, in a sense, mutually exclusive). The best place to start is with the following warnings:

```
-Wall -Wextra -pedantic -Werror
```

This turns on most of the important warnings while ensuring that any warnings that your examples or tests compile will generate an error. For some libraries, however, this will not be enough. At the time of writing, the following are the flags that Microsoft's Guideline Support Library uses:

```
-Wall -Wcast-align -Wconversion -Wctor-dtor-privacy -Werror -Wextra -
Wpedantic -Wshadow -Wsign-conversion
```

One additional warning that the GSL uses is conversion warnings, which will tell you when you convert between different integer types. If you are using Clang, this process can be a lot easier as it provides -Weverything. If weeding through all of the warnings that GCC provides is too much work, one approach to solving this issue is to make sure that your library compiles with the Clang compiler with this warning turned on, which will ensure your code compiles with most of the warnings that GCC provides. This way, your users will not have trouble with your library when they have to ensure specific warnings are enabled in their code as you will have tested as many of them as possible.

Static and dynamic analysis

In addition to testing for warnings, libraries should also be tested with static and dynamic analysis tools. Once again, as an author of a library, you must assume your users might use static and dynamic analysis tools to shore up the quality of their own applications. If your library triggers these tools, your users are more likely to look for alternatives that have been tested more thoroughly.

For C++, there is a large number of tools that can be used to analyze your libraries. In this recipe, we will focus on Clang Tidy and Valgrind, which are both free to use. Let's look at the following simple example:

```cpp
#include <iostream>

int universe()
{
    auto i = new int;
    int the_answer;
    return the_answer;
}

int main()
{
    std::cout << universe() << '\n';
    return 0;
}
```

In the preceding example, we created a function called `universe()` that returns an integer and allocates an integer. In our main function, our `universe()` function output the results to `stdout`.

To statically analyze the preceding code, we can use CMake as follows:

```
set(CMAKE_CXX_CLANG_TIDY clang-tidy)
```

The preceding line of code tells CMake to use `clang-tidy` when compiling the preceding example. When we compile the code, we get the following result:

If a user of your library has turned on static analysis using Clang Tidy, this is the error they might receive, even though their code is perfectly fine. If you are using someone else's library and run into this issue, one way to overcome the problem is to include the library as a system include, which tells tools such as Clang Tidy to ignore these errors. This, however, doesn't always work as some libraries require the use of macros, which expose the library's logic to your own code, resulting in chaos. In general, if you are a library developer, statically analyze your library as much as you can afford to as you don't know how your users might use your library.

The same goes for dynamic analysis. The preceding analysis didn't detect the obvious memory leak. To identify this, we can use `valgrind`, as follows:

```
[~/book/chapter01/build]: valgrind ./recipe04_example01
==965771== Memcheck, a memory error detector
==965771== Copyright (C) 2002-2017, and GNU GPL'd, by Julian Seward et al.
==965771== Using Valgrind-3.15.0 and LibVEX; rerun with -h for copyright info
==965771== Command: ./recipe04_example01
==965771==
==965771== Conditional jump or move depends on uninitialised value(s)
==965771==    at 0x497C25F: std::ostreambuf_iterator<char, std::char_traits<char> > std::num_put<char, std::ostreambuf_i
terator<char, std::char_traits<char> > >::_M_insert_int<long>(std::ostreambuf_iterator<char, std::char_traits<char> >, s
td::ios_base&, char, long) const (in /usr/lib64/libstdc++.so.6.0.27)
==965771==    by 0x498B5B9: std::ostream& std::ostream::_M_insert<long>(long) (in /usr/lib64/libstdc++.so.6.0.27)
==965771==    by 0x4011A5: main (in /home/user/book/chapter01/build/recipe04_example01)
==965771==
==965771== Use of uninitialised value of size 8
==965771==    at 0x497C10B: ??? (in /usr/lib64/libstdc++.so.6.0.27)
==965771==    by 0x497C288: std::ostreambuf_iterator<char, std::char_traits<char> > std::num_put<char, std::ostreambuf_i
terator<char, std::char_traits<char> > >::_M_insert_int<long>(std::ostreambuf_iterator<char, std::char_traits<char> >, s
td::ios_base&, char, long) const (in /usr/lib64/libstdc++.so.6.0.27)
==965771==    by 0x498B5B9: std::ostream& std::ostream::_M_insert<long>(long) (in /usr/lib64/libstdc++.so.6.0.27)
==965771==    by 0x4011A5: main (in /home/user/book/chapter01/build/recipe04_example01)
==965771==
==965771== Conditional jump or move depends on uninitialised value(s)
==965771==    at 0x497C11E: ??? (in /usr/lib64/libstdc++.so.6.0.27)
==965771==    by 0x497C288: std::ostreambuf_iterator<char, std::char_traits<char> > std::num_put<char, std::ostreambuf_i
terator<char, std::char_traits<char> > >::_M_insert_int<long>(std::ostreambuf_iterator<char, std::char_traits<char> >, s
td::ios_base&, char, long) const (in /usr/lib64/libstdc++.so.6.0.27)
==965771==    by 0x498B5B9: std::ostream& std::ostream::_M_insert<long>(long) (in /usr/lib64/libstdc++.so.6.0.27)
==965771==    by 0x4011A5: main (in /home/user/book/chapter01/build/recipe04_example01)
==965771==
==965771== Conditional jump or move depends on uninitialised value(s)
==965771==    at 0x497C2BB: std::ostreambuf_iterator<char, std::char_traits<char> > std::num_put<char, std::ostreambuf_i
terator<char, std::char_traits<char> > >::_M_insert_int<long>(std::ostreambuf_iterator<char, std::char_traits<char> >, s
td::ios_base&, char, long) const (in /usr/lib64/libstdc++.so.6.0.27)
==965771==    by 0x498B5B9: std::ostream& std::ostream::_M_insert<long>(long) (in /usr/lib64/libstdc++.so.6.0.27)
==965771==    by 0x4011A5: main (in /home/user/book/chapter01/build/recipe04_example01)
==965771==
0
==965771==
==965771== HEAP SUMMARY:
==965771==     in use at exit: 4 bytes in 1 blocks
==965771==   total heap usage: 3 allocs, 2 frees, 73,732 bytes allocated
==965771==
==965771== LEAK SUMMARY:
==965771==    definitely lost: 4 bytes in 1 blocks
==965771==    indirectly lost: 0 bytes in 0 blocks
==965771==      possibly lost: 0 bytes in 0 blocks
==965771==    still reachable: 0 bytes in 0 blocks
==965771==         suppressed: 0 bytes in 0 blocks
==965771== Rerun with --leak-check=full to see details of leaked memory
==965771==
==965771== Use --track-origins=yes to see where uninitialised values come from
==965771== For lists of detected and suppressed errors, rerun with: -s
==965771== ERROR SUMMARY: 4 errors from 4 contexts (suppressed: 0 from 0)
[~/book/chapter01/build]:
```

As shown in the preceding screenshot, `valgrind` is able to detect the memory leak in our code. Actually, `valgrind` also detects the fact that we never initialize our temporary variable in the `universe()` function, but the output is far too verbose to show here. Once again, if you fail to identify these types of problem with your libraries, you will end up exposing these bugs to your users.

Documentation

Documentation is an absolute must for any good library. Besides buggy code, a lack of documentation will absolutely prevent others from using your library. Libraries should be easy to set up and install, and even easier to learn and incorporate into your own applications. One of the most frustrating aspects of using existing C++ libraries is the lack of documentation.

CII Best Practices

In this recipe, we have touched on a couple of common best practices that all library developers should incorporate into their projects. In addition to these best practices, a more complete list of best practices is provided by the CII Best Practices program here: `https://bestpractices.coreinfrastructure.org/en`.

The CII Best Practices program provides a comprehensive list of best practices that are updated over time and that library developers (and any application in general) can leverage. These best practices are grouped into passing, silver, and gold, with the gold practices being the hardest to achieve. The higher your score, the more likely users are to use your library as it shows commitment and stability.

Learning how to use the boost APIs

The boost libraries are a set of libraries designed to work in conjunction with the standard C++ libraries. In fact, a lot of the libraries that are currently being provided by C++ originated from the boost libraries. The boost libraries provide everything from containers, clocks, and timers to more complicated mathematical APIs such as graphs and CRC calculations. In this recipe, we will learn how to use the boost libraries, specifically to demonstrate what a large library looks like and how such a library would be included in a user's project. This recipe is important as it will demonstrate just how complicated a library can get, teaching you how to write your own libraries accordingly.

Getting ready

As with all of the recipes in this chapter, ensure that all of the technical requirements have been met, including installing Ubuntu 18.04 or higher and running the following in a Terminal window:

```
> sudo apt-get install build-essential git cmake libboost-all-dev
```

This will ensure your operating system has the proper tools to compile and execute the examples in this recipe. Once you have done this, open a new Terminal. We will use this Terminal to download, compile, and run our examples.

How to do it...

You need to perform the following steps to complete this recipe:

1. From a new Terminal, run the following to download the source code:

```
> cd ~/
> git clone
https://github.com/PacktPublishing/Advanced-CPP-CookBook.git
> cd Advanced-CPP-CookBook/chapter01
```

2. To compile the source code, run the following code:

```
> mkdir build && cd build
> cmake ..
> make recipe05_examples
```

3. Once the source code has been compiled, you can execute each example in this recipe by running the following commands:

```
> ./recipe05_example01
Date/Time: 1553894555446451393 nanoseconds since Jan 1, 1970
> ./recipe05_example02
[2019-03-29 15:22:36.756819] [0x00007f5ee158b740] [debug] debug
message
[2019-03-29 15:22:36.756846] [0x00007f5ee158b740] [info] info
message
```

In the next section, we will step through each of these examples and explain what each example program does and how it relates to the lessons being taught in this recipe.

How it works...

The boost libraries provide a set of user APIs that implement commonly needed functionality in most programs. These libraries can be included in your own projects to simplify your code and provide an example of what a finished library might look like. To explain how your own libraries could be leveraged by others, let's look at some examples of how to use the boost libraries.

Example 1

In this example, we are using the boost APIs to output the current date and time to `stdout`, as follows:

```
#include <iostream>
#include <boost/chrono.hpp>

int main(void)
{
    using namespace boost::chrono;

    std::cout << "Date/Time: " << system_clock::now() << '\n';
    return 0;
}
```

As shown in the preceding example, the current date and time are outputted to `stdout` as the total number of nanoseconds since the Unix Epoch (January 1, 1970). In addition to including boost in your source code, you must also link your application against the boost libraries. In this case, we needed to link against the following:

-lboost_chrono -lboost_system -lpthread

An example of how this is done can be seen in the `CMakeLists.txt` file that was downloaded with this recipe. Once these libraries have been linked to your project, your code will be able to leverage the APIs inside them. This extra step is why header-only libraries can be so useful when creating your own libraries as they obviate the need for additional linking.

Example 2

In this example, we're demonstrating how to log to the console using boost's trivial logging APIs, as follows:

```
#include <boost/log/trivial.hpp>

int main(void)
{
    BOOST_LOG_TRIVIAL(debug) << "debug message";
    BOOST_LOG_TRIVIAL(info) << "info message";
    return 0;
}
```

As shown in the preceding example, the "debug message" and "info message" messages were outputted to stdout. In addition to linking against the proper boost libraries, we also had to include the following definition during compilation:

```
-DBOOST_LOG_DYN_LINK -lboost_log -lboost_system -lpthread
```

Once again, linking these libraries ensures that the APIs you are using in your code (as shown in the preceding example) exist in the executable.

See also

For more information on the boost libraries, please check out https://www.boost.org/.

2
Using Exceptions for Error Handling

In this chapter, we will learn some advanced C++ exception handling techniques. We assume here that you have a basic understanding of how to throw as well as catch a C++ exception. Instead of focusing on the basics of C++ exceptions, this chapter will teach you some of the more advanced techniques of C++ exception handling. This includes the proper use of the `noexcept` specifier and the `noexcept` operator so that you can properly mark your APIs as either possibly throwing an exception or explicitly not throwing a C++ exception, instead of calling `std::terminate()` when an error occurs that cannot be handled.

This chapter will also explain what the term **Resource Acquisition is Initialization (RAII)** is and how it complements C++ exception handling. We will also discuss why you should never throw a C++ exception from a class's destructor and how to handle these types of issues. Finally, we will look at how to create your own custom C++ exceptions including providing some basic guidelines on what to do and what not to do when creating your own exceptions.

From the information provided in this chapter, you will gain a better understanding of how C++ exceptions work under the hood and the types of things that can be done with C++ exceptions to build more robust and reliable C++ programs.

The recipes in this chapter are as follows:

- Using the noexcept specifier
- Using the noexcept operator
- Using RAII
- Learning why to never throw exceptions in destructors
- Easily creating your own exception classes

Technical requirements

To compile and run the examples in this chapter, you must have administrative access to a computer running Ubuntu 18.04 with a functional internet connection. Before running these examples, you must install the following:

```
sudo apt-get install build-essential git cmake
```

If this is installed on any operating system other than Ubuntu 18.04, then GCC 7.4 or higher and CMake 3.6 or higher will be required.

Using the noexcept specifier

The noexcept specifier is used to tell the compiler whether a function may or may not throw a C++ exception. If a function is marked with the noexcept specifier, it is not allowed to throw an exception and, if it does, std::terminate() will be called when the exception is thrown. If the function doesn't have the noexcept specifier, exceptions can be thrown as normal.

In this recipe, we will explore how to use the noexcept specifier in your own code. This specifier is important because it is a contract between the API that you are creating and the user of the API. When the noexcept specifier is used, it tells the user of the API that they do not need to consider exceptions when using the API. It also tells the author that if they add the noexcept specifier to their API, they have to ensure that no exceptions are thrown, which, in some cases, requires the author to catch all possible exceptions and either handle them or call std::terminate() if the exception cannot be handled. Also, there are certain operations, such as std::move, where exceptions cannot be thrown without the fear of corruption as a move operation oftentimes cannot be safely reversed if an exception is thrown. Finally, with some compilers, adding noexcept to your APIs will reduce the overall size of the function, resulting in a smaller overall application.

Getting ready

Before beginning, please ensure that all of the technical requirements are met, including installing Ubuntu 18.04 or higher and running the following in a Terminal window:

```
> sudo apt-get install build-essential git cmake
```

This will ensure your operating system has the proper tools to compile and execute the examples in this recipe. Once this is complete, open a new Terminal. We will use this Terminal to download, compile, and run our examples.

How to do it...

To try this recipe, perform the following steps:

1. From a new Terminal, run the following to download the source code:

```
> cd ~/
> git clone
https://github.com/PacktPublishing/Advanced-CPP-CookBook.git
> cd Advanced-CPP-CookBook/chapter02
```

2. To compile the source code, run the following:

```
> mkdir build && cd build
> cmake ..
> make recipe01_examples
```

3. Once the source code is compiled, you can execute each example in this recipe by running the following commands:

```
> ./recipe01_example01
The answer is: 42

> ./recipe01_example02
terminate called after throwing an instance of 'std::runtime_error'
what(): The answer is: 42
Aborted

> ./recipe01_example03
The answer is: 42

> ./recipe01_example04
terminate called after throwing an instance of 'std::runtime_error'
what(): The answer is: 42
Aborted

> ./recipe01_example05
foo: 18446744069414584320
foo: T is too large
```

In the next section, we will step through each of these examples and explain what each example program does and how it relates to the lessons being taught in this recipe.

How it works...

First, let's briefly review how C++ exceptions are thrown and caught. In the following example, we will throw an exception from a function and then catch the exception in our `main()` function:

```cpp
#include <iostream>
#include <stdexcept>

void foo()
{
    throw std::runtime_error("The answer is: 42");
}

int main(void)
{
    try {
        foo();
    }
    catch(const std::exception &e) {
        std::cout << e.what() << '\n';
    }

    return 0;
}
```

As shown in the preceding example, we created a function called `foo()` that throws an exception. This function is called in our `main()` function inside a `try/catch` block, which is used to catch any exceptions that might be thrown by the code executed inside the `try` block, which in this case is the `foo()` function. When the exception is thrown by the `foo()` function, it is successfully caught and outputted to `stdout`.

All of this works because we did not add the `noexcept` specifier to the `foo()` function. By default, a function is allowed to throw an exception, just as we did in this example. In some cases, however, we do not want to allow exceptions to be thrown, depending on how we expect a function to execute. Specifically, how a function handles exceptions can be defined as the following (known as exception safety):

- **No-throw guarantee**: The function cannot throw an exception, and if an exception is thrown internally, the exception must be caught and handled, including allocation failures.
- **Strong exception safety**: The function can throw an exception, and if an exception is thrown, any state that was modified by the function is rolled back or undone with no side effects.

- **Basic exception safety**: The function can throw an exception, and if an exception is thrown, any state that was modified by the function is rolled back or undone, but side effects are possible. It should be noted that these side effects do not include invariants, meaning the program is in a valid, non-corrupted state.
- **No exception safety**: The function can throw an exception, and if an exception is thrown, the program could enter a corrupted state.

In general, if a function has a no-throw guarantee, it is labeled with `noexcept`; otherwise, it is not. An example of why exception safety is so important is with `std::move`. For example, suppose we have two instances of `std::vector` and we wish to move one vector into another. To perform the move, `std::vector` might move each element of the vector from one instance to the other. If the object is allowed to throw when it is moved, the vector could end up with an exception in the middle of the move (that is, half of the objects in the vector are moved successfully). When the exception occurs, `std::vector` would obviously attempt to undo the moves that it has already performed by moving these back to the original vector before returning the exception. The problem is, attempting to move the objects back would require `std::move()`, which could throw and exception again, resulting in a nested exception. In practice, moving one `std::vector` instance to another doesn't actually perform an object-by-object move, but resizing does, and, in this specific issue, the standard library requires the use of `std::move_if_noexcept` to handle this situation to provide exception safety, which falls back to a copy when the move constructor of an object is allowed to throw.

The `noexcept` specifier is used to overcome these types of issues by explicitly stating that the function is not allowed to throw an exception. This not only tells the user of the API that they can safely use the function without fear of an exception being thrown and potentially corrupting the execution of the program, but it also forces the author of the function to safely handle all possible exceptions or call `std::terminate()`. Although `noexcept`, depending on the compiler, also provides optimizations by reducing the overall size of the application when defined, its main use is to state the exception safety of a function such that other functions can reason about how a function will execute.

In the following example, we add the `noexcept` specifier to our `foo()` function defined earlier:

```
#include <iostream>
#include <stdexcept>

void foo() noexcept
{
    throw std::runtime_error("The answer is: 42");
}
```

```
int main(void)
{
    try {
        foo();
    }
    catch(const std::exception &e) {
        std::cout << e.what() << '\n';
    }

    return 0;
}
```

When this example is compiled and executed, we get the following:

```
[~/book/chapter02/build]: ./recipe01_example02
terminate called after throwing an instance of 'std::runtime_error'
  what():  The answer is: 42
Aborted (core dumped)
[~/book/chapter02/build]:
```

As shown in the preceding example, the `noexcept` specifier was added, which tells the compiler that `foo()` is not allowed to throw an exception. Since, however, the `foo()` function does throw an exception, when it is executed, `std::terminate()` is called. In fact, in this example, `std::terminate()` will always be called, which is something the compiler is able to detect and warn about.

Calling `std::terminate()` is obviously not the desired outcome of a program. In this specific case, since the author has labeled the function as `noexcept`, it is up to the author to handle all possible exceptions. This can be done as follows:

```
#include <iostream>
#include <stdexcept>

void foo() noexcept
{
    try {
        throw std::runtime_error("The answer is: 42");
    }
    catch(const std::exception &e) {
        std::cout << e.what() << '\n';
    }
}

int main(void)
```

```
{
    foo();
    return 0;
}
```

As shown in the preceding example, the exception is wrapped in a `try`/`catch` block to ensure the exception is safely handled before the `foo()` function completes its execution. Also, in this example, only exceptions that originate from `std::exception()` are caught. This is the author's way of saying which types of exceptions can be safely handled. If, for example, an integer was thrown instead of `std::exception()`, `std::terminate()` would still be executed automatically since `noexcept` was added to the `foo()` function. In other words, as the author, you are only required to handle the exceptions that you can, in fact, safely handle. The rest will be sent to `std::terminate()` for you; just understand that, by doing this, you change the exception safety of the function. If you intend for a function to be defined with a no-throw guarantee, the function cannot throw an exception at all.

It should also be noted that if you mark a function as `noexcept`, you need to not only pay attention to exceptions that you throw but also to the functions that may throw themselves. In this case, `std::cout` is being used inside the `foo()` function, which means the author has to either knowingly ignore any exceptions that `std::cout` could throw, which would result in a call to `std::terminate()` (which is what we are doing here), or the author needs to identify which exceptions `std::cout` could throw and attempt to safely handle them, including exceptions such as `std::bad_alloc`.

The `std::vector.at()` function throws an `std::out_of_range()` exception if the provided index is out of bounds with respect to the vector. In this case, the author can catch this type of exception and return a default value, allowing the author to safely mark the function as `noexcept`.

The `noexcept` specifier is also capable of acting as a function, taking a Boolean expression, as in the following example:

```
#include <iostream>
#include <stdexcept>

void foo() noexcept(true)
{
    throw std::runtime_error("The answer is: 42");
}

int main(void)
{
    try {
```

```
        foo();
    }
    catch(const std::exception &e) {
        std::cout << e.what() << '\n';
    }

    return 0;
}
```

This results in the following when executed:

As shown in the preceding example, the `noexcept` specifier was written as `noexcept(true)`. If the expression evaluates to true, it is as if `noexcept` was provided. If the expression evaluates to false, it is as if the `noexcept` specifier was left out, allowing exceptions to be thrown. In the preceding example, the expression evaluates to true, which means that the function is not allowed to throw an exception, which results in `std::terminate()` being called when `foo()` throws an exception.

Let's look at a more complicated example to demonstrate how this can be used. In the following example, we will create a function called `foo()` that will shift an integer value by 32 bits and cast the result to a 64-bit integer. This example will be written using template metaprogramming, allowing us to use this function on any integer type:

```
#include <limits>
#include <iostream>
#include <stdexcept>

template<typename T>
uint64_t foo(T val) noexcept(sizeof(T) <= 4)
{
    if constexpr(sizeof(T) <= 4) {
        return static_cast<uint64_t>(val) << 32;
    }

    throw std::runtime_error("T is too large");
}

int main(void)
{
```

```
    try {
        uint32_t val1 = std::numeric_limits<uint32_t>::max();
        std::cout << "foo: " << foo(val1) << '\n';

        uint64_t val2 = std::numeric_limits<uint64_t>::max();
        std::cout << "foo: " << foo(val2) << '\n';
    }
    catch(const std::exception &e) {
        std::cout << e.what() << '\n';
    }

    return 0;
}
```

This results in the following when executed:

As shown in the preceding example, the issue with the `foo()` function is that if the user provides a 64-bit integer, it cannot shift by 32 bits without generating an overflow. If the integer provided, however, is 32 bits or less, the `foo()` function is perfectly safe. To implement the `foo()` function, we used the `noexcept` specifier to state that the function is not allowed to throw an exception if the provided integer is 32 bits or less. If the provided integer is greater than 32 bits, an exception is allowed to throw, which, in this case, is an `std::runtime_error()` exception stating that the integer is too large to be safely shifted.

Using the noexcept operator

The `noexcept` operator is a compile-time check that is used to ask the compiler whether a function is labeled `noexcept` or not. With C++17, this can be paired with a compile-time `if` statement (that is, an `if` statement that is evaluated at compile time and that can be used to add/remove code from an executable during compilation) to change the semantics of a program based on whether or not a function is allowed to throw an exception.

In this recipe, we will explore how to use the `noexcept` operator in your own code. This operator is important because, in some cases, you may not know whether a function is capable of throwing an exception by simply looking at its definition. For example, if a function uses the `noexcept` specifier, your code might not be able to determine whether the function will throw, as you might not know—based on the function's inputs—what the `noexcept` specifier will evaluate to. The `noexcept` operator provides you with a mechanism to handle these types of scenarios, which is essential, especially when metaprogramming.

Getting ready

Before beginning, please ensure that all of the technical requirements are met, including installing Ubuntu 18.04 or higher and running the following in a Terminal window:

```
> sudo apt-get install build-essential git cmake
```

This will ensure your operating system has the proper tools to compile and execute the examples in this recipe. Once this is complete, open a new Terminal. We will use this Terminal to download, compile, and run our examples.

How to do it...

Perform the following steps to try the recipe:

1. From a new Terminal, run the following to download the source code:

   ```
   > cd ~/
   > git clone
   https://github.com/PacktPublishing/Advanced-CPP-CookBook.git
   > cd Advanced-CPP-CookBook/chapter02
   ```

2. To compile the source code, run the following:

   ```
   > mkdir build && cd build
   > cmake ..
   > make recipe02_examples
   ```

3. Once the source code is compiled, you can execute each example in this recipe by running the following commands:

```
> ./recipe02_example01
could foo throw: true

> ./recipe02_example02
could foo throw: true
could foo throw: true
could foo throw: false
could foo throw: false

> ./recipe02_example03
terminate called after throwing an instance of 'std::runtime_error'
what(): The answer is: 42
Aborted

> ./recipe02_example04

> ./recipe02_example05
terminate called after throwing an instance of 'std::runtime_error'
what(): The answer is: 42
Aborted

> ./recipe02_example06
could foo throw: true
could foo throw: true
```

In the next section, we will step through each of these examples and explain what each example program does and how it relates to the lessons being taught in this recipe.

How it works...

The noexcept operator is used to determine whether a function can throw. Let's start with a simple example:

```cpp
#include <iostream>
#include <stdexcept>

void foo()
{
    std::cout << "The answer is: 42\n";
}

int main(void)
{
```

```
    std::cout << std::boolalpha;
    std::cout << "could foo throw: " << !noexcept(foo()) << '\n';
    return 0;
}
```

This results in the following:

As shown in the preceding example, we defined a `foo()` function that outputs to `stdout`. We don't actually execute `foo()` but, instead, we use the `noexcept` operator to check to see whether the `foo()` function could throw. As you can see, the answer is yes; this function can throw. This is because we did not label the `foo()` function with `noexcept`, and, as stated in the previous recipe, functions can throw by default.

It should also be noted that we added `!` to the `noexcept` expression. This is because `noexcept` returns `true` if the function is labeled `noexcept`, which means that the function is not allowed to throw. However, in our example, we are not asking whether the function cannot throw, but instead we are asking whether the function can throw, hence the logical Boolean reversal.

Let's expand upon this by adding a couple more functions to our example. Specifically, in the following example, we will add some functions that throw as well as some functions that are labeled `noexcept`:

```
#include <iostream>
#include <stdexcept>

void foo1()
{
    std::cout << "The answer is: 42\n";
}

void foo2()
{
    throw std::runtime_error("The answer is: 42");
}

void foo3() noexcept
{
    std::cout << "The answer is: 42\n";
}
```

```
void foo4() noexcept
{
    throw std::runtime_error("The answer is: 42");
}

int main(void)
{
    std::cout << std::boolalpha;
    std::cout << "could foo throw: " << !noexcept(foo1()) << '\n';
    std::cout << "could foo throw: " << !noexcept(foo2()) << '\n';
    std::cout << "could foo throw: " << !noexcept(foo3()) << '\n';
    std::cout << "could foo throw: " << !noexcept(foo4()) << '\n';
    return 0;
}
```

This results in the following:

As shown in the preceding example, if a function is labeled with noexcept, the noexcept operator returns true (which, in our example, outputs false). More importantly, a keen observer would notice that the functions that throw exceptions do not change the output of the noexcept operator. That is, the noexcept operator returns false if a function *can* throw an exception, not if it *will* throw an exception. This is important as the only way to know whether a function *will* throw an exception is to execute it. The only thing the noexcept specifier states is whether or not an exception is allowed to be thrown by the function. It doesn't state whether or not an exception *will* be thrown. By extension, the noexcept operator doesn't tell you whether the function *will* throw or not but instead tells you whether the function is labeled with the noexcept specifier (and, more importantly, what the noexcept specifier evaluates to).

Before we attempt to use the noexcept specifier in a more realistic example, let's look at the following example:

```
#include <iostream>
#include <stdexcept>

void foo()
{
    throw std::runtime_error("The answer is: 42");
```

```
    }

    int main(void)
    {
        foo();
    }
```

As shown in the preceding example, we have defined a `foo()` function that throws, and then we call this function from our main function, resulting in `std::terminate()` being called because we didn't handle the exception before leaving the program. In a more complicated setting, we might not know whether `foo()` throws or not, and, as a result, we may not want to add the additional overhead of exception handling if it is not needed. To better explain this, let's examine the resulting assembly code for the `main()` function for this example:

```
user@localhost:~/book/chapter02/build
[~/book/chapter02/build]: objdump -d recipe02_example03 | grep "main>:" -A 7
0000000000004011ff <main>:
    4011ff:    55                      push    %rbp
    401200:    48 89 e5                mov     %rsp,%rbp
    401203:    e8 ae ff ff ff          callq   4011b6 <_Z3foov>
    401208:    b8 00 00 00 00          mov     $0x0,%eax
    40120d:    5d                      pop     %rbp
    40120e:    c3                      retq

[~/book/chapter02/build]:
```

As you can see, the `main` function is simple and doesn't contain any additional logic outside of calling the `foo` function. Specifically, the `main` function doesn't have any catch logic in it.

Now, let's use the `noexcept` operator in a more concrete example:

```
#include <iostream>
#include <stdexcept>

void foo()
{
    throw std::runtime_error("The answer is: 42");
}

int main(void)
{
    if constexpr (noexcept(foo())) {
        foo();
    }
    else {
        try {
```

```
        foo();
    }
    catch (...)
    { }
  }
}
```

As shown in the preceding example, we use the `noexcept` operator in conjunction with the `constepxr` operator in the `if` statement that was added in C++17. This allows us to ask the compiler whether `foo()` is allowed to throw. If it is, we execute the `foo()` function inside a `try/catch` block so that we can handle any possible exceptions as needed. If we examine the assembly of this function, as shown in the following screenshot, we can see that some additional `catch` logic was added to the resulting binary to handle the exceptions as needed:

```
user@localhost:~/book/chapter02/build                                    □   X
[~/book/chapter02/build]: objdump -d recipe02_example04 | grep "main>:" -A 12
000000000040121f <main>:
  40121f:    55                push    %rbp
  401220:    48 89 e5          mov     %rsp,%rbp
  401223:    e8 ae ff ff ff    callq   4011d6 <_Z3foov>
  401228:    b8 00 00 00 00    mov     $0x0,%eax
  40122d:    eb 0f             jmp     40123e <main+0x1f>
  40122f:    48 89 c7          mov     %rax,%rdi
  401232:    e8 09 fe ff ff    callq   401040 <__cxa_begin_catch@plt>
  401237:    e8 64 fe ff ff    callq   4010a0 <__cxa_end_catch@plt>
  40123c:    eb ea             jmp     401228 <main+0x9>
  40123e:    5d                pop     %rbp
  40123f:    c3                retq

[~/book/chapter02/build]:
```

Now, let's take this same example one step further by stating that the `foo()` function is not allowed to throw using the `noexcept` specifier:

```cpp
#include <iostream>
#include <stdexcept>

void foo() noexcept
{
    throw std::runtime_error("The answer is: 42");
}

int main(void)
{
    if constexpr (noexcept(foo())) {
        foo();
    }
    else {
```

```
        try {
            foo();
        }
        catch (...)
        { }
    }
}
```

As shown in the preceding example, the program calls `std::terminate()` since the `foo()` function was labeled `noexcept`. Furthermore, if we look at the resulting assembly, we can see that the `main()` function no longer contains the additional `try`/`catch` logic, which means that our optimization worked:

Finally, we might possibly not know how to label our own function if we do not know whether a function that was called can throw or not. Let's look at the following example to demonstrate this issue:

```cpp
#include <iostream>
#include <stdexcept>

void foo1()
{
    std::cout << "The answer is: 42\n";
}

void foo2() noexcept(noexcept(foo1()))
{
    foo1();
}

int main(void)
{
    std::cout << std::boolalpha;
    std::cout << "could foo throw: " << !noexcept(foo1()) << '\n';
    std::cout << "could foo throw: " << !noexcept(foo2()) << '\n';
}
```

This results in the following:

As shown in the preceding example, the foo1() function is not labeled with the noexcept specifier, which means it is allowed to throw an exception. In foo2(), we want to ensure that our noexcept specifier is correct but we call foo1(), and, in this example, we assume that we don't know whether foo1() is noexcept or not.

To ensure foo2() is labeled properly, we combine the lessons learned in this recipe and the previous one to mark the function properly. Specifically, we use the noexcept operator to tell us whether the foo1() function will throw, and then we use the noexcept specifier's Boolean expression syntax to use the results of the noexcept operator to label foo2() as noexcept or not. If foo1() is labeled with noexcept, the noexcept operator will return true, resulting in foo2() being marked as noexcept(true), which is the same as simply stating noexcept. If foo1() is not labeled as noexcept, the noexcept operator will return false, in which case the noexcept specifier will be labeled as noexcept(false), which is the same as not adding the noexcept specifier (that is, the function is allowed to throw an exception).

Using RAII

RAII is a programming principle that states that a resource is tied to the lifetime of the object that acquired the resource. RAII is a powerful feature of the C++ language that really helps to set C++ apart from C, helping to prevent resource leaks and general instability.

In this recipe, we will dive into how RAII works and how RAII can be used to ensure that C++ exceptions do not introduce resource leaks. RAII is a critical technology for any C++ application and should be used whenever possible.

Getting ready

Before beginning, please ensure that all of the technical requirements are met, including installing Ubuntu 18.04 or higher and running the following in a Terminal window:

```
> sudo apt-get install build-essential git cmake
```

This will ensure your operating system has the proper tools to compile and execute the examples in this recipe. Once this is complete, open a new Terminal. We will use this Terminal to download, compile, and run our examples.

How to do it...

You need to perform the following steps to try the recipe:

1. From a new Terminal, run the following to download the source code:

```
> cd ~/
> git clone
https://github.com/PacktPublishing/Advanced-CPP-CookBook.git
> cd Advanced-CPP-CookBook/chapter02
```

2. To compile the source code, run the following:

```
> mkdir build && cd build
> cmake ..
> make recipe03_examples
```

3. Once the source code is compiled, you can execute each example in this recipe by running the following commands:

```
> ./recipe03_example01
The answer is: 42

> ./recipe03_example02
The answer is: 42

> ./recipe03_example03
The answer is not: 43

> ./recipe03_example04
The answer is: 42

> ./recipe03_example05
step 1: Collect answers
The answer is: 42
```

In the next section, we will step through each of these examples and explain what each example program does and how it relates to the lessons being taught in this recipe.

How it works...

To better understand how RAII works, we must first examine how a class in C++ works as C++ classes are used to implement RAII. Let's look at a simple example. C++ classes provide support for both constructors and destructors as follows:

```cpp
#include <iostream>
#include <stdexcept>

class the_answer
{
public:
    the_answer()
    {
        std::cout << "The answer is: ";
    }

    ~the_answer()
    {
        std::cout << "42\n";
    }
};

int main(void)
{
    the_answer is;
    return 0;
}
```

This results in the following when compiled and executed:

In the preceding example, we create a class with both a constructor and a destructor. When we create an instance of the class, the constructor is called, and, when the instance of the class loses scope, the class is destroyed. This is a simple C++ pattern that has been around since the initial versions of C++ were created by Bjarne Stroustrup. Under the hood, the compiler calls a construction function when the class is first instantiated, but, more importantly, the compiler has to inject code into the program that executes the destruction function when the instantiation of the class loses scope. The important thing to understand here is that this additional logic is inserted into the program automatically by the compiler for the programmer.

Before the introduction of the classes, the programmer had to add construction and destruction logic to the program manually, and, while construction is a fairly simple thing to get right, destruction is not. A classic example of this type of issue in C is storing a file handle. The programmer will add a call to an `open()` function to open the file handle and, when the file is done, will add a call to `close()` to close the file handle, forgetting to execute the `close()` function on all possible error cases that might crop up. This is inclusive of when the code is hundreds of lines long and someone new to the program adds another error case, forgetting also to call `close()` as needed.

RAII solves this issue by ensuring that, once the class loses scope, the resource that was acquired is released, no matter what the control-flow path was. Let's look at the following example:

```cpp
#include <iostream>
#include <stdexcept>

class the_answer
{
public:

    int *answer{};

    the_answer() :
        answer{new int}
    {
        *answer = 42;
    }

    ~the_answer()
    {
        std::cout << "The answer is: " << *answer << '\n';
        delete answer;
    }
};

int main(void)
{
    the_answer is;

    if (*is.answer == 42) {
        return 0;
    }

    return 1;
}
```

In this example, we allocate an integer and initialize it in the constructor of a class. The important thing to notice here is that we do not need to check for `nullptr` from the `new` operator. This is because the `new` operator will throw an exception if the memory allocation fails. If this occurs, not only will the rest of the constructor not be executed, but the object itself will not be constructed. This means if the constructor successfully executed, you know that the instance of the class is in a valid state and actually contains a resource that will be destroyed when the instance of the class loses scope

The destructor of the class then outputs to `stdout` and deletes the previously allocated memory. The important thing to understand here is that, no matter what control path the code takes, this resource will be released when the instance of the class loses scope. The programmer only needs to worry about the lifetime of the class.

This idea that the lifetime of the resource is directly tied to the lifetime of the object that allocated the resource is important as it solves a complicated issue for the control flow of a program in the presence of C++ exceptions. Let's look at the following example:

```cpp
#include <iostream>
#include <stdexcept>

class the_answer
{
public:

    int *answer{};

    the_answer() :
        answer{new int}
    {
        *answer = 43;
    }

    ~the_answer()
    {
        std::cout << "The answer is not: " << *answer << '\n';
        delete answer;
    }
};

void foo()
{
    the_answer is;

    if (*is.answer == 42) {
        return;
    }
```

```
        throw std::runtime_error("");
}

int main(void)
{
    try {
        foo();
    }
    catch(...)
    { }

    return 0;
}
```

In this example, we create the same class as the previous example, but, in our `foo()` function, we throw an exception. The `foo()` function, however, doesn't need to catch this exception to ensure that the memory allocated is properly freed. Instead, the destructor handles this for us. In C++, many functions might throw and, without RAII, every single function that could throw would need to be wrapped in a `try/catch` block to ensure that any resources that were allocated are properly freed. We, in fact, see this pattern a lot in C code, especially in kernel-level programming where `goto` statements are used to ensure that, within a function, if an error occurs, the function can properly unwind itself to release any resources might have previously been acquired. This result is a nest of code dedicated to checking the result of every function call within the program and the logic needed to properly handle the error.

With this type of programming model, it's no wonder that resource leaks are so common in C. RAII combined with C++ exceptions remove the need for this error-prone logic, resulting in code that is less likely to leak resources.

How RAII is handled in the presence of C++ exceptions is outside the scope of this book as it requires a deeper dive into how C++ exception support is implemented. The important thing to remember is that C++ exceptions are faster than checking the return value of a function for an error (as C++ exceptions are implemented using a no overhead algorithm) but are slow when an actual exception is thrown (as the program has to unwind the stack and properly execute each class destructor as needed). For this reason, and others such as maintainability, C++ exceptions should never be used for valid control flow.

Another way that RAII can be used is the `finally` pattern, which is provided by the C++ **Guideline Support Library** (**GSL**). The `finally` pattern leverages the destructor-only portion of RAII to provide a simple mechanism to perform non-resource-based cleanup when the control flow of a function is complicated or could throw. Consider the following example:

```
#include <iostream>
#include <stdexcept>

template<typename FUNC>
class finally
{
    FUNC m_func;

public:
    finally(FUNC func) :
        m_func{func}
    { }

    ~finally()
    {
        m_func();
    }
};

int main(void)
{
    auto execute_on_exit = finally{[]{
        std::cout << "The answer is: 42\n";
    }};
}
```

In the preceding example, we create a class that is capable of storing a lambda function that is executed when an instance of the `finally` class loses scope. In this particular case, we output to `stdout` when the `finally` class is destroyed. Although this uses a pattern similar to that of RAII, this technically is not RAII as no resource has been acquired.

Also, if a resource does need to be acquired, RAII should be used instead of the `finally` pattern. The `finally` pattern, instead, is useful when you are not acquiring a resource but want to execute code when a function returns no matter what control flow path the program takes (a conditional branch or C++ exception).

To demonstrate this, let's look at a more complicated example:

```cpp
#include <iostream>
#include <stdexcept>

template<typename FUNC>
class finally
{
    FUNC m_func;

public:
    finally(FUNC func) :
        m_func{func}
    { }

    ~finally()
    {
        m_func();
    }
};

int main(void)
{
    try {
        auto execute_on_exit = finally{[]{
            std::cout << "The answer is: 42\n";
        }};

        std::cout << "step 1: Collect answers\n";
        throw std::runtime_error("???");
        std::cout << "step 3: Profit\n";
    }
    catch (...)
    { }
}
```

When executed, we get the following:

In the preceding example, we want to ensure that we always output to `stdout` no matter what the code does. In the middle of execution, we throw an exception, and even though the exception was thrown, our `finally` code is executed as intended.

Learning why to never throw exceptions in destructors

In this recipe, we will discuss the issues with C++ exceptions, specifically in regard to throwing exceptions within a class destructor, something that should be avoided at all costs. The lessons learned in this recipe are important because, unlike other functions, a C++ class destructor is marked as `noexcept` by default, which means that if you accidentally throw an exception inside a class destructor, your program will call `std::terminate()`, even though the destructor my not be overtly labeled `noexcept`.

Getting ready

Before beginning, please ensure that all of the technical requirements are met, including installing Ubuntu 18.04 or higher, and run the following in a Terminal window:

```
> sudo apt-get install build-essential git cmake
```

This will ensure your operating system has the proper tools to compile and execute the examples in this recipe. Once this is complete, open a new Terminal. We will use this Terminal to download, compile, and run our examples.

How to do it...

Perform the following steps to try the recipe:

1. From a new Terminal, run the following to download the source code:

    ```
    > cd ~/
    > git clone
    https://github.com/PacktPublishing/Advanced-CPP-CookBook.git
    > cd Advanced-CPP-CookBook/chapter02
    ```

2. To compile the source code, run the following:

```
> mkdir build && cd build
> cmake ..
> make recipe04_examples
```

3. Once the source code is compiled, you can execute each example in this recipe by running the following commands:

```
> ./recipe04_example01
terminate called after throwing an instance of 'std::runtime_error'
what(): 42
Aborted

> ./recipe04_example02
The answer is: 42

> ./recipe04_example03
terminate called after throwing an instance of 'std::runtime_error'
what(): 42
Aborted

> ./recipe04_example04
# exceptions: 2
The answer is: 42
The answer is: always 42
```

In the next section, we will step through each of these examples and explain what each example program does and how it relates to the lessons being taught in this recipe.

How it works...

In this recipe, we will learn why throwing exceptions in a destructor is a *bad* idea, and why class destructors are labeled as noexcept by default. To start, let's look at a simple example:

```cpp
#include <iostream>
#include <stdexcept>

class the_answer
{
public:
    ~the_answer()
    {
        throw std::runtime_error("42");
    }
```

```
};

int main(void)
{
    try {
        the_answer is;
    }
    catch (const std::exception &e) {
        std::cout << "The answer is: " << e.what() << '\n';
    }
}
```

When we execute this, we get the following:

In this example, we can see that if we throw an exception from a class destructor, `std::terminate()` is called. This is because, by default, a class destructor is marked as `noexcept`.

We can change this by explicitly allowing a class destructor to throw by marking the class's destructor as `noexcept(false)`, as shown in the next example:

```
#include <iostream>
#include <stdexcept>

class the_answer
{
public:
    ~the_answer() noexcept(false)
    {
        throw std::runtime_error("42");
    }
};

int main(void)
{
    try {
        the_answer is;
    }
    catch (const std::exception &e) {
        std::cout << "The answer is: " << e.what() << '\n';
```

```
        }
    }
```

As shown in the preceding example, when the class is destroyed, an exception is thrown and properly handled. Even though this was successfully handled, we have to ask ourselves, what is the state of the program after we catch this exception? The destructor didn't successfully complete. If this class was more complex and had state/resources that it was managing, can we conclude that the state/resources that we care about were properly handled/released? The short answer is no. This is the same as destroying a hard drive with a hammer. If you slam a hard drive with a hammer to destroy it, did you actually destroy the data on the hard drive? There is no way to know because, when you hit the hard drive with the hammer, you broke the electronics that would have been used to answer that very question. When you attempt to destroy a hard drive, you need a reliable process that ensures that, under no circumstance could the process of destroying the drive leave data in a recoverable state. Otherwise, you have no way of knowing what state you are in, with no way of going back.

The same applies to C++ classes. Destroying a C++ class needs to be an operation that must provide basic exception safety (that is, the state of the program is deterministic with some possible side effects). Otherwise, the only other logical course of action is to call std::terminate() since you cannot be sure what will happen if the program continues to execute.

Besides putting the program in an undefined state, the other issue with throwing an exception from a destructor is, what happens if an exception has already been thrown? What does the try/catch block catch? Let's look at an example of this type of issue:

```cpp
#include <iostream>
#include <stdexcept>

class the_answer
{
public:
    ~the_answer() noexcept(false)
    {
        throw std::runtime_error("42");
    }
};

int main(void)
{
    try {
        the_answer is;
        throw std::runtime_error("first exception");
    }
```

```
        catch (const std::exception &e) {
            std::cout << "The answer is: " << e.what() << '\n';
        }
    }
```

In the preceding example, we mark the destructor as noexcept(false) just like we did in the previous example, but we throw before the destructor is called, which means that, when the destructor is called, there is already an exception being processed. Now, when we attempt to throw, std::terminate() is called even though the destructor was marked as noexcept(false):

The reason for this is the C++ library has no way of handling this situation because the try/catch block cannot handle more than one exception. It is possible, however, to have more than one pending exception; we simply need a try/catch block to handle each exception. This situation occurs when we have nested exceptions, as in this example:

```
#include <iostream>
#include <stdexcept>

class nested
{
public:
    ~nested()
    {
        std::cout << "# exceptions: " << std::uncaught_exceptions() <<
'\n';
    }
};

class the_answer
{
public:
    ~the_answer()
    {
        try {
            nested n;
            throw std::runtime_error("42");
        }
        catch (const std::exception &e) {
```

```
        std::cout << "The answer is: " << e.what() << '\n';
    }
}
};
```

In this example, we will start by creating a class that outputs the results of calling `std::uncaught_exceptions()`, which returns the total number of exceptions currently being processed. We will then create a second class that creates the first class and then throws from its destructor, with the important note that all of the code in the destructor is wrapped in a `try/catch` block:

```
int main(void)
{
    try {
        the_answer is;
        throw std::runtime_error("always 42");
    }
    catch (const std::exception &e) {
        std::cout << "The answer is: " << e.what() << '\n';
    }
}
```

When this example is executed, we get the following:

```
user@localhost:~/book/chapter02/build
[~/book/chapter02/build]: ./recipe04_example04
# exceptions: 2
The answer is: 42
The answer is: always 42
[~/book/chapter02/build]:
```

Finally, we will create this second class and throw again with another `try/catch` block. Unlike the previous example, all of the exceptions are being properly handled, and, in fact, `noexcept(false)` is not needed to ensure that this code executes properly as, for each exception that is thrown, we have a `try/catch` block. Even though an exception was thrown inside a destructor, it was properly handled, which means that the destructor executes safely and remains `noexcept`-compliant, even though the second class is executing in the presence of the two exceptions being processed.

Easily creating your own exception classes

In this recipe, you will learn how to easily create your own exception types. This is an important lesson to learn as, although C++ exceptions are easy to create yourself, some guidelines should be followed to ensure this is done safely.

Getting ready

Before beginning, please ensure that all of the technical requirements are met, including installing Ubuntu 18.04 or higher and running the following in a Terminal window:

```
> sudo apt-get install build-essential git cmake
```

This will ensure your operating system has the proper tools to compile and execute the examples in this recipe. Once this is complete, open a new Terminal. We will use this Terminal to download, compile, and run our examples.

How to do it...

Perform the following steps to try the recipe:

1. From a new Terminal, run the following to download the source code:

   ```
   > cd ~/
   > git clone
   https://github.com/PacktPublishing/Advanced-CPP-CookBook.git
   > cd Advanced-CPP-CookBook/chapter02
   ```

2. To compile the source code, run the following:

   ```
   > mkdir build && cd build
   > cmake ..
   > make recipe05_examples
   ```

3. Once the source code is compiled, you can execute each example in this recipe by running the following commands:

   ```
   > ./recipe05_example01
   The answer is: 42

   > ./recipe05_example02
   The answer is: 42
   ```

```
> ./recipe05_example03
The answer is: 42
```

In the next section, we will step through each of these examples and explain what each example program does and how it relates to the lessons being taught in this recipe.

How it works...

Creating your own C++ exceptions allows you to filter out what type of exception you are getting. For example, did the exception come from your code or the C++ library? By creating your own C++ exceptions, you can easily answer these questions during runtime in your own code. Let's look at the following example:

```cpp
#include <iostream>
#include <stdexcept>

class the_answer : public std::exception
{
public:
    the_answer() = default;
    const char *what() const noexcept
    {
        return "The answer is: 42";
    }
};

int main(void)
{
    try {
        throw the_answer{};
    }
    catch (const std::exception &e) {
        std::cout << e.what() << '\n';
    }
}
```

As shown in the preceding example, we create our own C++ exception by inheriting `std::exception`. This is not a requirement. Technically, anything can be a C++ exception including an integer. Starting from `std::exception`, however, gives you a standard interface to work from including overriding the `what()` function, which describes the exception that was thrown.

In this preceding example, we return a hardcoded string in the `what()` function. This is the ideal type of exception (even more so than the exceptions that are provided by the C++ library). This is because this type of exception is `nothrow copy-constructable`. Specifically, this means that the exception itself can be copied without the copy generating an exception, for example, due to `std::bad_alloc`. The exception types provided by the C++ library support construction from `std::string()`, which could throw `std::bad_alloc`.

The issue with the preceding C++ exception is that you would need 1 exception type for every type of message you wish to provide. Another way to implement a safe exception type is to use the following:

```cpp
#include <iostream>
#include <stdexcept>

class the_answer : public std::exception
{
    const char *m_str;
public:

    the_answer(const char *str) :
        m_str{str}
    { }

    const char *what() const noexcept
    {
        return m_str;
    }
};

int main(void)
{
    try {
        throw the_answer("42");
    }
    catch (const std::exception &e) {
        std::cout << "The answer is: " << e.what() << '\n';
    }
}
```

In the preceding example, we store a pointer to `const char*` (that is, a C-style string). C-style strings are stored globally as constants within the program. This type of exception satisfies all of the same preceding rules, and no allocations are taking place during the construction of the exception. It should also be noted that, since the strings are stored globally, this type of operation is safe.

Many types of exceptions can be created using this approach, including things other than strings that are accessible through custom getters (that is, without having to use the `what()` function). If, however, these preceding rules are not an issue for you, the easiest way to create a custom C++ exception is to simply subclass an existing C++ exception such as `std::runtime_error()`, as in the following example:

```cpp
#include <iostream>
#include <stdexcept>
#include <string.h>

class the_answer : public std::runtime_error
{
public:
    explicit the_answer(const char *str) :
        std::runtime_error{str}
    { }
};

int main(void)
{
    try {
        throw the_answer("42");
    }
    catch (const the_answer &e) {
        std::cout << "The answer is: " << e.what() << '\n';
    }
    catch (const std::exception &e) {
        std::cout << "unknown exception: " << e.what() << '\n';
    }
}
```

When this example is executed, we get the following:

```
[~/book/chapter02/build]: ./recipe05_example03
The answer is: 42
[~/book/chapter02/build]:
```

In the preceding example, we create our own C++ exception in just a few lines of code by subclassing `std::runtime_error()`. We can then use different `catch` blocks to figure out what type of exception was thrown. Just remember that if you use the `std::string` version of `std::runtime_error()`, you could end up with `std::bad_alloc` being thrown during the construction of the exception itself.

Implementing Move Semantics

3

In this chapter, we will learn some advanced C++ move semantics. We will first discuss the Big Five, which is an idiom that simply encourages programmers to explicitly define the destruction and move/copy semantics of a class. Next, we will learn how to define a move constructor and move assignment operator; the different combinations of move semantics (including move-only and non-copyable); non-movable classes; and how to implement these classes and why they are important.

This chapter will also discuss some common pitfalls such as why a `const &&` move makes no sense, and how to overcome l-value versus r-value reference types. The recipes in this chapter are important because once you enable C++11 or higher, move semantics is enabled, which changes how C++ fundamentally handles classes in numerous situations. The recipes in this chapter provide the foundation for writing efficient code in C++ that behaves as intended.

The recipes in this chapter are as follows:

- Using compiler-generated special class member functions and the Big Five
- Making your class movable
- Moving only types
- Implementing the `noexcept` move constructor
- Learning to be wary of `const &&`
- Referencing qualified member functions
- Exploring objects that cannot be moved or copied

Technical requirements

To compile and run the examples in this chapter, you must have administrative access to a computer running Ubuntu 18.04 with a functional internet connection. Before running these examples, you must install the following:

```
> sudo apt-get install build-essential git cmake
```

If this is installed on any operating system other than Ubuntu 18.04, then GCC 7.4 or higher and CMake 3.6 or higher will be required.

Using compiler-generated special class member functions and the Big Five

When using C++11 or higher, the compiler will auto-generate certain functions for your C++ classes if you do not explicitly provide them in the class definition. In this recipe, we will explore how this works, which functions the compiler will create for you, and how this affects your program's performance and validity. In general, the goal of this recipe is to make the case that every class should, at a minimum, have the Big Five defined to ensure your class is explicit about how you wish to manage resources.

Getting ready

Before beginning, please ensure that all of the technical requirements are met, including installing Ubuntu 18.04 or higher, and run the following in a Terminal window:

```
> sudo apt-get install build-essential git
```

This will ensure your operating system has the proper tools to compile and execute the examples in this recipe. Once this is complete, open a new Terminal. We will use this Terminal to download, compile, and run our examples.

How to do it...

You need to perform the following steps to try this recipe:

1. From a new Terminal, run the following to download the source code:

    ```
    > cd ~/
    > git clone
    https://github.com/PacktPublishing/Advanced-CPP-CookBook.git
    > cd Advanced-CPP-CookBook/chapter03
    ```

2. To compile the source code, run the following:

    ```
    > cmake .
    > make recipe01_examples
    ```

3. Once the source code is compiled, you can execute each example in this recipe by running the following commands:

    ```
    > ./recipe01_example01
    The answer is: 42

    > ./recipe01_example02
    The answer is: 42

    > ./recipe01_example03
    The answer is: 42

    > ./recipe01_example04
    The answer is: 42
    ```

In the next section, we will step through each of these examples and explain what each example program does and how it relates to the lessons being taught in this recipe.

How it works...

In this recipe, we will explore the difference between a move and copy and how this relates to the Big Five, which is a reference to five functions that all classes should explicitly define. To start, let's first look at a simple example of a class that outputs an integer value in its constructor:

```
class the_answer
{
    int m_answer{42};

public:
```

```
    ~the_answer()
    {
        std::cout << "The answer is: " << m_answer << '\n';
    }
};
```

In the preceding example, the class will output to `stdout` when the class is destructed. The class also has an integer member variable that is initialized on construction. The problem with the preceding example is that the implicit copy and move semantics are suppressed because we defined the class's destructor.

The Big Five are the following functions, which every class should define if at least one of these functions are defined (that is, if you define one, you must define them all):

```
~the_answer() = default;

the_answer(the_answer &&) noexcept = default;
the_answer &operator=(the_answer &&) noexcept = default;

the_answer(const the_answer &) = default;
the_answer &operator=(const the_answer &) = default;
```

As shown, the Big Five includes the destructor, move constructor, move assignment operator, copy constructor, and copy assignment operator. The author of these classes need not implement these functions but instead should—at a minimum—*define* the functions, explicitly stating how deletions, copying, and moving should take place (if at all). This ensures that if one of these functions is defined, the rest of the class's move, copy, and destruction semantics are correct, as in this example:

```
class the_answer
{
    int m_answer{42};

public:

    the_answer()
    {
        std::cout << "The answer is: " << m_answer << '\n';
    }

public:

    virtual ~the_answer() = default;

    the_answer(the_answer &&) noexcept = default;
    the_answer &operator=(the_answer &&) noexcept = default;
```

```
        the_answer(const the_answer &) = default;
        the_answer &operator=(const the_answer &) = default;
    };
```

In the preceding example, the class is marked as `virtual` by defining a virtual destructor (meaning the class is capable of participating in runtime polymorphism). No implementation is needed (by setting the destructor to `default`), but the definition itself is explicit, which tells the compiler that we want the class to support virtual functions. This tells the user of the class that a pointer to this class can be used to delete an instance of any class that derives from it. It also tells the user that inheritance will leverage runtime polymorphism and not composition. This class also states that copies and moves are both allowed.

Let's look at another example:

```
    class the_answer
    {
        int m_answer{42};

    public:

        the_answer()
        {
            std::cout << "The answer is: " << m_answer << '\n';
        }

    public:

        ~the_answer() = default;

        the_answer(the_answer &&) noexcept = default;
        the_answer &operator=(the_answer &&) noexcept = default;

        the_answer(const the_answer &) = delete;
        the_answer &operator=(const the_answer &) = delete;
    };
```

In the preceding example, copies are explicitly deleted (which is the same as defining a move constructor without defining copy semantics). This defines a move-only class, which means that the class can only be moved; it cannot be copied. An example of such a class in the standard library is `std::unique_ptr`.

The next class implements the opposite:

```
    class the_answer
    {
        int m_answer{42};
```

```
public:

    the_answer()
    {
        std::cout << "The answer is: " << m_answer << '\n';
    }

public:

    ~the_answer() = default;

    the_answer(the_answer &&) noexcept = delete;
    the_answer &operator=(the_answer &&) noexcept = delete;

    the_answer(const the_answer &) = default;
    the_answer &operator=(const the_answer &) = default;
};
```

In the preceding example, we have explicitly defined a copy-only class.

There are many different combinations of the Big Five. The point of this recipe is to show that explicitly defining these five functions ensures that the author of the class is explicit about the intent of the class itself. This is with respect to how it should operate and how a user should use the class. Being explicit ensures the author of the class doesn't intend for one type of behavior, but instead gets another because of how the compiler will implicitly construct the class based on the compiler's implementation and how the C++ specification was defined.

Making your class movable

In C++11 or higher, objects can either be copied or moved, which can be used to dictate how your object's resources are managed. The big difference between a copy and a move is simple: a copy creates a copy of the resources an object manages, while a move transfers the resources from one object to another.

In this recipe, we will explain how to make a class movable, including how to properly add move constructors and move assignment operators. We will also explain some of the subtle details of a movable class and how to use them in your code. This recipe is important because, in a lot of cases, moving an object instead of copying an object increases the performance and reduces the memory consumption of your programs. However, the use of movable objects could introduce some instabilities if they are not used properly.

Getting ready

Before beginning, please ensure that all of the technical requirements are met, including installing Ubuntu 18.04 or higher and running the following in a Terminal window:

```
> sudo apt-get install build-essential git
```

This will ensure your operating system has the proper tools to compile and execute the examples in this recipe. Once this is complete, open a new Terminal. We will use this Terminal to download, compile, and run our examples.

How to do it...

You need to perform the following steps to try this recipe:

1. From a new Terminal, run the following to download the source code:

```
> cd ~/
> git clone
https://github.com/PacktPublishing/Advanced-CPP-CookBook.git
> cd Advanced-CPP-CookBook/chapter03
```

2. To compile the source code, run the following:

```
> cmake .
> make recipe02_examples
```

3. Once the source code is compiled, you can execute each example in this recipe by running the following commands:

```
> ./recipe02_example01
The answer is: 42
> ./recipe02_example02
The answer is: 42
The answer is: 42

The answer is: 42
```

In the next section, we will step through each of these examples and explain what each example program does and how it relates to the lessons being taught in this recipe.

How it works...

In this recipe, we will learn how to make a class movable. To start, let's examine a basic class definition:

```
#include <iostream>

class the_answer
{
    int m_answer{42};

public:

    the_answer() = default;

public:

    ~the_answer()
    {
        std::cout << "The answer is: " << m_answer << '\n';
    }
};

int main(void)
{
    the_answer is;
    return 0;
}
```

In the preceding example, we create a simple class with a private integer member that is initialized. We then define a default constructor and a destructor that outputs to `stdout` when an instance of the class is destroyed. By default, this class is movable, but the move operation mimics a copy (in other words, there is no difference between a move or a copy with this simple example).

To really make this class movable, we need to add both a move constructor and a move assignment operator as follows:

```
the_answer(the_answer &&other) noexcept;
the_answer &operator=(the_answer &&other) noexcept;
```

Once we add these two functions, we will be able to use the following to move our class from one instance to another:

```
instance2 = std::move(instance1);
```

To support this, in the preceding class, we will not only add the move constructor and assignment operator, but we will also implement a default constructor to provide a valid moved-from state to our example class, as follows:

```
#include <iostream>

class the_answer
{
    int m_answer{};

public:

    the_answer() = default;

    explicit the_answer(int answer) :
        m_answer{answer}
    { }
```

As shown, the class now has a default constructor and an explicit constructor that takes an integer argument. The default constructor initializes the integer memory variable, which represents our moved-from or invalid state:

```
public:

    ~the_answer()
    {
        if (m_answer != 0) {
            std::cout << "The answer is: " << m_answer << '\n';
        }
    }
```

As shown in the preceding example, we output the value of our integer member variable when the class is destroyed, but in this case, we first check to make sure the integer variable is valid:

```
    the_answer(the_answer &&other) noexcept
    {
        *this = std::move(other);
    }

    the_answer &operator=(the_answer &&other) noexcept
    {
        if (&other == this) {
            return *this;
        }
        m_answer = std::exchange(other.m_answer, 0);
        return *this;
```

```
    }

    the_answer(const the_answer &) = default;
    the_answer &operator=(const the_answer &) = default;
};
```

Finally, we implement the move constructor and assignment operators. The move constructor simply calls the move assignment operator to prevent the need for duplication (as they perform the same action). The move assignment operator first checks to make sure that we are not moving to ourselves. This is because doing so would lead to corruption as the user would expect the class to still contain a valid integer but in fact, the internal integer would inadvertently be set to 0.

We then exchange the integer value and set the original to 0. This is because, once again, a move is not a copy. A move transfers the value from one instance to another. In this case, the instance being moved to starts as 0 and is given a valid integer, while the instance being moved from starts with a valid integer and is set to 0 after the move, resulting in only 1 instance containing a valid integer.

It should also be noted that we have to define the copy constructor and assignment operator. This is because, by default, if you provide a move constructor and assignment operator, C++ will automatically delete the copy constructor and assignment operator if they are not explicitly defined.

In this example, we will compare a move versus a copy, so we define the copy constructor and assignment operator to ensure they are not implicitly deleted. In general, it is best practice to define your destructor, the move constructor, and assignment operator as well as the copy constructor and assignment operator for every class you define. This ensures that the copy/move semantics for every class you write are explicit and intentional:

```
int main(void)
{
    {
        the_answer is;
        the_answer is_42{42};
        is = is_42;
    }

    std::cout << '\n';

    {
        the_answer is{23};
        the_answer is_42{42};
        is = std::move(is_42);
```

```
    }

    return 0;
}
```

When the preceding code is executed, we get the following:

In our main function, we run two different tests:

- The first test creates two instances of our class and copies the contents of one instance to the other.
- The second test creates two instances of our class and then moves the contents of one instance to the other.

When this example is executed, we see the first test's output was written to twice. This is because the first instance of our class is given a copy of the second instance of our class, which has a valid integer value. The second test's output is only written to once because we are transferring the valid state of one instance to the other, resulting in only one instance having a valid state at any given moment.

There are some notable instances worth mentioning here:

- Move constructors and assignment operators should never throw exceptions. Specifically, a move operation transfers the valid state of an instance of a type to another instance of that type. At no point should this operation fail as no state is being created or destroyed. It is simply being transferred. Also, it is oftentimes difficult to *undo* a move operation part of the way through the move. For these reasons, these functions should always be labeled as noexcept (refer to https:/ /github.com/isocpp/CppCoreGuidelines/blob/master/CppCoreGuidelines. md#Rc-move-noexcept).
- Move constructors and assignment operators do not include const types in their function signature because the instance being moved from cannot be const since its internal state is being transferred, which implicitly assumes a write is occurring. More importantly, if you label a move constructor or assignment operator as const, it is possible that a copy would occur instead.

- Unless you intend to create a copy, a move should be used instead, especially for large objects. Just like passing `const T&` as a function argument to prevent a copy from occurring, when a function is called, a move should be used in place of a copy when a resource is being moved into another variable instead of being copied.
- The compiler will automatically generate move operations instead of copy operations when possible. For example, if you create an object in a function, configure the object, and then return the object, a move will be automatically performed by the compiler.

Now that you know how to make your classes movable, in the next recipe, we will learn what a move-only type is, and why you might want to use them in your applications.

Move-only types

In this recipe, we will learn how to make a class move-only. A great example of the difference between a copy and a move is the difference between `std::unique_ptr` and `std::shared_ptr`.

The point of `std::unique_ptr` is to enforce a single owner for dynamically allocated types while `std::shared_ptr` allows for multiple owners of dynamically allocated types. Both allow the user to move the contents of a pointer type from one instantiation to another, but only `std::shared_ptr` allows the user to make a copy of the pointer (as copying the pointer would create more than one owner).

In this recipe, we will use these two classes to show how to make a move-only class and to show why this type of class is used so heavily in C++ (as most of the time we wish to move and not copy).

Getting ready

Before beginning, please ensure that all of the technical requirements are met, including installing Ubuntu 18.04 or higher and running the following in a Terminal window:

```
> sudo apt-get install build-essential git
```

This will ensure your operating system has the proper tools to compile and execute the examples in this recipe. Once this is complete, open a new Terminal. We will use this Terminal to download, compile, and run our examples.

How to do it...

You need to perform the following steps to try this recipe:

1. From a new Terminal, run the following to download the source code:

```
> cd ~/
> git clone
https://github.com/PacktPublishing/Advanced-CPP-CookBook.git
> cd Advanced-CPP-CookBook/chapter03
```

2. To compile the source code, run the following:

```
> cmake .
> make recipe03_examples
```

3. Once the source code is compiled, you can execute each example in this recipe by running the following commands:

```
> ./recipe03_example01
The answer is: 42

> ./recipe03_example03
count: 2
The answer is: 42
The answer is: 42

count: 1
The answer is: 42
```

In the next section, we will step through each of these examples and explain what each example program does and how it relates to the lessons being taught in this recipe.

How it works...

A move-only class is a class that can be moved but cannot be copied. To explore this type of class, let's wrap std::unique_ptr, which itself is a move-only class, in the following example:

```
class the_answer
{
    std::unique_ptr<int> m_answer;

public:

    explicit the_answer(int answer) :
```

```
            m_answer{std::make_unique<int>(answer)}
    { }

    ~the_answer()
    {
        if (m_answer) {
            std::cout << "The answer is: " << *m_answer << '\n';
        }
    }

public:

    the_answer(the_answer &&other) noexcept
    {
        *this = std::move(other);
    }

    the_answer &operator=(the_answer &&other) noexcept
    {
        m_answer = std::move(other.m_answer);
        return *this;
    }
};
```

The preceding class stores `std::unique_ptr` as a member variable and, on construction, instantiates the memory variable with an integer value. On destruction, the class checks to make sure `std::unique_ptr` is valid and if so, outputs the value to `stdout`.

At first glance, we might wonder why we must check for validity as `std::unique_ptr` is always constructed. The reason `std::unique_ptr` could become invalid is during a move. Since we are creating a move-only class (and not a non-copyable, non-movable class), we implement the move constructor and move assignment operator, which moves `std::unique_ptr`. `std::unique_ptr`, on moving, will transfer the contents of its internal pointer from one class to another, resulting in the class being moved from storing an invalid pointer (that is, `nullptr`). In other words, even though this class cannot be null-constructed, it can still store `nullptr` if it is moved, as in the following example:

```
int main(void)
{
    the_answer is_42{42};
    the_answer is = std::move(is_42);

    return 0;
}
```

As shown in the preceding example, only one class outputs to `stdout` as only one instance is valid. Like `std::unique_ptr`, a move-only class ensures that you always have a 1:1 relationship between the total number of resources being created and the total number of actual instantiations occurring.

It should be noted that since we are using `std::unique_ptr`, our class becomes a move-only class whether we like it or not. For example, attempting to add a copy constructor or copy assignment operator to enable the ability to copy will result in a compilation error:

```
the_answer(const the_answer &) = default;
the_answer &operator=(const the_answer &) = default;
```

In other words, every class that includes a move-only class as a member also becomes a move-only class itself. Although this might seem undesirable, you must first ask yourself: do you really need a class to be copyable? The likely answer is no. In fact, in most cases, even before C++11, most—if not all—of the classes that we work with should be move-only. The ability of a class to be copied when it should be moved can lead to wasted resources, corruption, and so on, which is one of the reasons move semantics were added to the specification. Move semantics allow us to define how we want the resources we allocate to be handled, and it provides us with a way to enforce the desired semantics at compile time.

You might wonder how the preceding example would be converted to allow for copying. The following example leverages a shared pointer to accomplish this:

```
#include <memory>
#include <iostream>

class the_answer
{
    std::shared_ptr<int> m_answer;

public:

    the_answer() = default;

    explicit the_answer(int answer) :
        m_answer{std::make_shared<int>(answer)}
    { }

    ~the_answer()
    {
        if (m_answer) {
            std::cout << "The answer is: " << *m_answer << '\n';
        }
    }
}
```

```
auto use_count()
{ return m_answer.use_count(); }
```

The preceding class uses `std::shared_ptr` instead of `std::unique_ptr`. Under the hood, `std::shared_ptr` keeps track of the number of copies that are made and only deletes the pointer it stored when the total number of copies is 0. In fact, you can query the total number of copies using the `use_count()` function.

Next, we define the move constructor, move assignment operator, copy constructor, and copy assignment operator, as follows:

```
public:

    the_answer(the_answer &&other) noexcept
    {
        *this = std::move(other);
    }

    the_answer &operator=(the_answer &&other) noexcept
    {
        m_answer = std::move(other.m_answer);
        return *this;
    }

    the_answer(const the_answer &other)
    {
        *this = other;
    }

    the_answer &operator=(const the_answer &other)
    {
        m_answer = other.m_answer;
        return *this;
    }
};
```

These definitions could have also been written using the = default syntax as these implementations are the same thing. Finally, we test this class using the following:

```
int main(void)
{
    {
        the_answer is_42{42};
        the_answer is = is_42;
        std::cout << "count: " << is.use_count() << '\n';
    }
```

```
    std::cout << '\n';

    {
        the_answer is_42{42};
        the_answer is = std::move(is_42);
        std::cout << "count: " << is.use_count() << '\n';
    }

    return 0;
}
```

If we execute the preceding code, we get the following:

In the preceding tests, we first create a copy of our class and output the total number of copies to see that two copies were in fact created. The second test performs `std::move()` instead of a copy, which results in only one copy being created as expected.

Implementing the noexcept move constructor

In this recipe, we will learn how to ensure a move constructor and a move assignment operator never throw an exception. The C++ specification doesn't prevent a move constructor from throwing (as it was determined that such a requirement would simply be too difficult to enforce, as too many legitimate examples exist even in the standard library). However, ensuring that exceptions are not thrown should be possible in most cases. Specifically, a move usually doesn't create resources but instead transfers resources and as a result, strong exception guarantees should be possible. A good example of a move that does create a resource is `std::list`, which must provide a valid `end()` iterator even on a move.

Getting ready

Before beginning, please ensure that all of the technical requirements are met, including installing Ubuntu 18.04 or higher and running the following in a Terminal window:

```
> sudo apt-get install build-essential git
```

This will ensure your operating system has the proper tools to compile and execute the examples in this recipe. Once this is complete, open a new Terminal. We will use this Terminal to download, compile, and run our examples.

How to do it...

You need to perform the following steps to try this recipe:

1. From a new Terminal, run the following to download the source code:

   ```
   > cd ~/
   > git clone
   https://github.com/PacktPublishing/Advanced-CPP-CookBook.git
   > cd Advanced-CPP-CookBook/chapter03
   ```

2. To compile the source code, run the following:

   ```
   > cmake .
   > make recipe04_examples
   ```

3. Once the source code is compiled, you can execute each example in this recipe by running the following commands:

   ```
   > ./recipe04_example01
   failed to move

   The answer is: 42
   ```

In the next section, we will step through each of these examples and explain what each example program does and how it relates to the lessons being taught in this recipe.

How it works...

As stated before, a move should not throw an exception to ensure strong exception guarantees (that is, the act of moving an object doesn't possibly corrupt the object), and in most cases, this is possible because a move (unlike a copy) doesn't create resources, it transfers them. The best way to ensure that your move constructors and move assignment operators do not throw is to only transfer member variables using `std::move()`, as in the following example:

```
m_answer = std::move(other.m_answer);
```

Assuming that the member variable you are moving doesn't throw, your class will not either. Using this simple technique will ensure that your move constructors and operators never throw. But what if this operation cannot be used? Let's explore this issue with the following example:

```cpp
#include <vector>
#include <iostream>

class the_answer
{
    std::vector<int> m_answer;

public:

    the_answer() = default;

    explicit the_answer(int answer) :
        m_answer{{answer}}
    { }

    ~the_answer()
    {
        if (!m_answer.empty()) {
            std::cout << "The answer is: " << m_answer.at(0) << '\n';
        }
    }
}
```

In the preceding example, we create a class with a vector as the member variable. The vector can either be initialized as empty by default, or it can be initialized with a single element. On destruction, if the vector has a value, we output the value to `stdout`. We implement the `move` constructor and operator as follows:

```cpp
public:

    the_answer(the_answer &&other) noexcept
```

```
    {
        *this = std::move(other);
    }

    the_answer &operator=(the_answer &&other) noexcept
    {
        if (&other == this) {
            return *this;
        }

        try {
            m_answer.emplace(m_answer.begin(), other.m_answer.at(0));
            other.m_answer.erase(other.m_answer.begin());
        }
        catch(...) {
            std::cout << "failed to move\n";
        }

        return *this;
    }
};
```

As shown, the move operator is transferring the single element from one instance to the other (not the best way to implement a move, but this implementation can demonstrate the point without being overly complicated). If the vector is empty, this operation will throw, as in the following example:

```
int main(void)
{
    {
        the_answer is_42{};
        the_answer is_what{};

        is_what = std::move(is_42);
    }

    std::cout << '\n';

    {
        the_answer is_42{42};
        the_answer is_what{};

        is_what = std::move(is_42);
    }

    return 0;
}
```

Finally, we attempt to move an instance of this class in two different tests. In the first test, both instances are default constructed, which results in empty classes, while the second test constructs the vector with a single element, which results in a valid move. In this case, we were able to prevent the move from throwing, but it should be noted that the resulting classes did not actually perform the move, resulting in both objects not containing the state that was desired. This is why move constructors should never throw. Even if we didn't catch the exception, it would be extremely difficult to assert the state of the program after the throw occurred. Did the move occur? What state is each instance in? In most cases, this type of error should lead to `std::terminate()` being called as the program enters a corrupt state.

A copy is different because the original class is left intact. The copy is invalid and the programmer can handle this case gracefully, as the original state of the instance being copied is unaffected (hence we mark it `const`).

Since, however, the instance being moved from is writable, both instances are in a corrupt state and there isn't a good way to know how to handle the program moving forward, as we don't know whether the original instance was left in a state that can be properly handled.

Learning to be wary of const&&

In this recipe, we will learn why a move constructor or operator should never be marked `const` (and why a copy constructor/operator is always marked as `const`). This is important because it gets to the heart of the difference between a move and a copy. Move semantics in C++ is one of its most powerful features and understanding why it is so important and what it is actually doing is critical to writing good C++ code.

Getting ready

Before beginning, please ensure that all of the technical requirements are met, including installing Ubuntu 18.04 or higher and running the following in a Terminal window:

```
> sudo apt-get install build-essential git
```

This will ensure your operating system has the proper tools to compile and execute the examples in this recipe. Once this is complete, open a new Terminal. We will use this Terminal to download, compile, and run our examples.

How to do it...

You need to perform the following steps to try this recipe:

1. From a new Terminal, run the following to download the source code:

```
> cd ~/
> git clone
https://github.com/PacktPublishing/Advanced-CPP-CookBook.git
> cd Advanced-CPP-CookBook/chapter03
```

2. To compile the source code, run the following:

```
> cmake .
> make recipe05_examples
```

3. Once the source code is compiled, you can execute each example in this recipe by running the following commands:

```
> ./recipe05_example01
copy
```

In the next section, we will step through each of these examples and explain what each example program does and how it relates to the lessons being taught in this recipe.

How it works...

In this recipe, we will learn why a const&& constructor or operator doesn't make sense and will result in unexpected behavior. A move transfers resources, which is why it is marked as non-const. This is because a transfer assumes that both instances are written to (one instance receives the resource while the other has the resource taken away). A copy creates resources, which is why they are not always marked as noexcept (creating resources absolutely could throw) and they are marked const (because the original instance is being copied, not modified). A const&& constructor is claiming to be a move that doesn't transfer, which must be a copy (if you are not writing to the original instance, you are not moving—you are copying), as in this example:

```cpp
#include <iostream>

class copy_or_move
{
public:

    copy_or_move() = default;
```

```
public:

    copy_or_move(copy_or_move &&other) noexcept
    {
        *this = std::move(other);
    }

    copy_or_move &operator=(copy_or_move &&other) noexcept
    {
        std::cout << "move\n";
        return *this;
    }

    copy_or_move(const copy_or_move &other)
    {
        *this = other;
    }

    copy_or_move &operator=(const copy_or_move &other)
    {
        std::cout << "copy\n";
        return *this;
    }
};

int main(void)
{
    const copy_or_move test1;
    copy_or_move test2;

    test2 = std::move(test1);
    return 0;
}
```

In the preceding example, we create a class that implements default move and copy constructors/operators. The only difference is that we add output to stdout to tell us whether a copy is being performed or a move is being performed.

We then create two instances of our class with the instance being moved from being marked as const. We then perform the move and what is output is a copy. This is because even though we asked for a move, the compiler used a copy. We could implement a const && move constructor/operator but there would be no way to write the move as a move, since we marked the object being moved from as const, so we cannot take its resources. Such a move would, in fact, be implemented as a copy, no different than what the compiler did for us automatically.

In the next recipe, we will learn how to add qualifiers to our member functions.

Referencing qualified member functions

In this recipe, we will learn about what a reference qualified member function is. Although this aspect of the C++ language is less used and understood, it is important because it provides the programmer with the ability to handle how resources are operated on, based on whether or not the class is in an l-value or r-value state when a function is called.

Getting ready

Before beginning, please ensure that all of the technical requirements are met, including installing Ubuntu 18.04 or higher and running the following in a Terminal window:

```
> sudo apt-get install build-essential git
```

This will ensure your operating system has the proper tools to compile and execute the examples in this recipe. Once this is complete, open a new Terminal. We will use this Terminal to download, compile, and run our examples.

How to do it...

You need to perform the following steps to try this recipe:

1. From a new Terminal, run the following to download the source code:

```
> cd ~/
> git clone
https://github.com/PacktPublishing/Advanced-CPP-CookBook.git
> cd Advanced-CPP-CookBook/chapter03
```

2. To compile the source code, run the following:

```
> cmake .
> make recipe06_examples
```

3. Once the source code is compiled, you can execute each example in this recipe by running the following commands:

```
> ./recipe06_example01
the answer is: 42
the answer is not: 0
the answer is not: 0
```

In the next section, we will step through each of these examples and explain what each example program does and how it relates to the lessons being taught in this recipe.

How it works...

In this example, we will look at what a reference qualified member function is. To explain what a reference-qualified member function is, let's look at the following example:

```cpp
#include <iostream>

class the_answer
{
public:

 ~the_answer() = default;

 void foo() &
 {
 std::cout << "the answer is: 42\n";
 }

 void foo() &&
 {
 std::cout << "the answer is not: 0\n";
 }

public:

 the_answer(the_answer &&other) noexcept = default;
 the_answer &operator=(the_answer &&other) noexcept = default;

 the_answer(const the_answer &other) = default;
 the_answer &operator=(const the_answer &other) = default;
};
```

In this example, we have implemented a `foo()` function, but we have two different versions. The first version has `&` at the end while the second has `&&` at the end. Which `foo()` function gets executed is dictated by whether or not the instance is an l-value or an r-value, as in the following example:

```
int main(void)
{
    the_answer is;

    is.foo();
    std::move(is).foo();
    the_answer{}.foo();
}
```

This results in the following when executed:

As shown in the preceding example, the first execution of `foo()` is an l-value, as the l-value version of `foo()` is executed (that is, the function with `&` at the end). The last two executions of `foo()` are r-values as the r-value versions of `foo()` are executed.

Reference-qualified member functions can be used to ensure that the function is only called in the right context. Another reason to use these types of functions is to ensure that the function is only called when an l-value or r-value reference exists.

For example, you might not want to allow `foo()` to be called as an r-value as this type of invocation doesn't ensure that an instance of the class actually has a lifetime outside of the call itself, as demonstrated in the preceding example.

In the next recipe, we will learn how to make a class that can neither be moved nor copied, and explain why you might do such a thing.

Exploring objects that cannot be moved or copied

In this recipe, we will learn about how to create an object that we cannot move or copy and why you might want to create such a class. Copying a class requires the ability to copy the contents of a class, which in some cases, could be impossible (for example, making a copy of a memory pool is not simple). Moving a class assumes that the class is allowed to exist in a potentially invalid state (for example, `std::unique_ptr`, when moved, takes on a `nullptr` value, which is invalid). Such cases may also be undesirable (you now have to check for validity). A non-movable class that we cannot copy can overcome these types of issues.

Getting ready

Before beginning, please ensure that all of the technical requirements are met, including installing Ubuntu 18.04 or higher and running the following in a Terminal window:

```
> sudo apt-get install build-essential git
```

This will ensure your operating system has the proper tools to compile and execute the examples in this recipe. Once this is complete, open a new Terminal. We will use this Terminal to download, compile, and run our examples.

How to do it...

You need to perform the following steps to try this recipe:

1. From a new Terminal, run the following to download the source code:

   ```
   > cd ~/
   > git clone
   https://github.com/PacktPublishing/Advanced-CPP-CookBook.git
   > cd Advanced-CPP-CookBook/chapter03
   ```

2. To compile the source code, run the following:

   ```
   > cmake .
   > make recipe07_examples
   ```

3. Once the source code is compiled, you can execute each example in this recipe by running the following commands:

```
> ./recipe07_example01
The answer is: 42
Segmentation fault (core dumped)
```

In the next section, we will step through each of these examples and explain what each example program does and how it relates to the lessons being taught in this recipe.

How it works...

Move-only classes prevent a class from being copied, which in some cases, can be a performance improvement. Move-only classes also ensure a 1:1 relationship between resources that are created versus the resources that are allocated, as copies cannot exist. Moving a class, however, can result in a class becoming invalid, as in this example:

```cpp
#include <iostream>

class the_answer
{
    std::unique_ptr<int> m_answer;

public:

    explicit the_answer(int answer) :
        m_answer{std::make_unique<int>(answer)}
    { }

    ~the_answer()
    {
        std::cout << "The answer is: " << *m_answer << '\n';
    }

public:

    the_answer(the_answer &&other) noexcept = default;
    the_answer &operator=(the_answer &&other) noexcept = default;
};

int main(void)
{
    the_answer is_42{42};
    the_answer is_what{42};

    is_what = std::move(is_42);
```

```
        return 0;
    }
```

If we run the preceding code, we get the following:

In the preceding example, we create a class that can be moved, which stores `std::unique_ptr`. In the destructor of the class, we dereference the class and output its value. We don't check the validity of `std::unique_ptr` because we wrote a constructor that forces a valid `std::unique_ptr`, forgetting that a move can undo this explicit validity. The result is that, when a move is performed, we get a segmentation fault.

To overcome this, we need a reminder that we made this assumption, as follows:

```
class the_answer
{
  std::unique_ptr<int> m_answer;

public:

  explicit the_answer(int answer) :
  m_answer{std::make_unique<int>(answer)}
  { }

  ~the_answer()
  {
  std::cout << "The answer is: " << *m_answer << '\n';
  }

public:

  the_answer(the_answer &&other) noexcept = delete;
  the_answer &operator=(the_answer &&other) noexcept = delete;

  the_answer(const the_answer &other) = delete;
  the_answer &operator=(const the_answer &other) = delete;
};
```

The preceding class explicitly deletes both the copy and move operations, and this is our desired intent. Now, if we accidentally move this class, we get the following:

```
/home/user/book/chapter03/recipe07.cpp: In function 'int main()':
/home/user/book/chapter03/recipe07.cpp:106:30: error: use of deleted
function 'the_answer& the_answer::operator=(the_answer&&)'
is_what = std::move(is_42);
          ^

/home/user/book/chapter03/recipe07.cpp:95:17: note: declared here
the_answer &operator=(the_answer &&other) noexcept = delete;
           ^~~~~~~~
```

This error tells us that it is assumed that the class is valid and therefore does not support moving. We either need to properly support moving (which means we must maintain support for invalid `std::unique_ptr`) or we need to remove the `move` operation. As shown, a class that cannot be moved or copied can ensure that our code works as intended, providing the compiler with a mechanism to warn us when we are doing something with our class that we didn't intend.

Using Templates for Generic Programming

4

In this chapter, we will learn advanced template programming techniques. These techniques include the ability to change the implementation of a template class based on the type that is provided, how to work different types of arguments including how to properly forward them, how to optimize your code both at runtime and compile time, and how to use some new features added to C++17. This is important because it provides a better understanding of how template programming works as well as how to ensure your templates are performing the way you expect.

Too often, we write template code assuming it is executing one way when, in fact, it is executing in another, either generating unreliable code, code with unexpected performance penalties, or both. This chapter will explain how to avoid these issues and provide the foundation for writing proper generic programs.

The recipes in this chapter are as follows:

- Implementing SFINAE
- Learning perfect forwarding
- Using `if constexpr`
- Using tuples to work with parameter packs
- Using traits to vary the behavior of template implementations
- Learning how to implement `template<auto>`
- Working with explicit template declarations

Technical requirements

To compile and run the examples in this chapter, you must have administrative access to a computer running Ubuntu 18.04 with a functional internet connection. Prior to running these examples, install the following:

```
> sudo apt-get install build-essential git cmake
```

If this is installed on any operating system other than Ubuntu 18.04, then GCC 7.4 or higher and CMake 3.6 or higher will be required.

Implementing SFINAE

In this recipe, we will learn how to use **Substitution Failure Is Not An Error (SFINAE)**. This recipe is important because, often, we create templates without ensuring the types passed to a template are what we expect. This can lead to unexpected behavior, suboptimal performance, and even buggy, unreliable code.

SFINAE allows us to be explicit about what types we are expecting in our template. It also provides us with a means to change the behavior of our templates based on the types we are provided. The problem with SFINAE for some is that this concept is difficult to understand. Our goal in this recipe is to demystify SFINAE and show how you can use this in your own code.

Getting ready

Before beginning, please ensure that all of the technical requirements are met, including installing Ubuntu 18.04 or higher and running the following in a Terminal window:

```
> sudo apt-get install build-essential git cmake
```

This will ensure your operating system has the proper tools to compile and execute the examples in this recipe. Once this is complete, open a new Terminal. We will use this Terminal to download, compile, and run our examples.

How to do it...

You need to perform the following steps to try this recipe:

1. From a new Terminal, run the following to download the source code:

```
> cd ~/
> git clone
https://github.com/PacktPublishing/Advanced-CPP-CookBook.git
> cd Advanced-CPP-CookBook/chapter04
```

2. To compile the source code, run the following:

```
> cmake .
> make recipe01_examples
```

3. Once the source code is compiled, you can execute each example in this recipe by running the following commands:

```
> ./recipe01_example01
The answer is: 23
The answer is: 42

> ./recipe01_example02
The answer is: 42

> ./recipe01_example03
The answer is: 42

> ./recipe01_example04
The answer is: 42

> ./recipe01_example05
The answer is: 42
The answer is: 42
The answer is: 42.12345678
```

In the next section, we will step through each of these examples and explain what each example program does and how it relates to the lessons being taught in this recipe.

How it works...

In this recipe, you will learn how to incorporate SFINAE in your own code. To start, we must first understand what SFINAE is and how the standard library uses it to implement type traits. Without knowing how type traits are implemented, it can be difficult to understand how to use them.

To start, the most important thing to understand with SFINAE is what its name says, which is that a *substitution failure is not an error*. What this means is that when a template type is being substituted, if a failure occurs, the compiler will *not* generate an error as a result. For example, we can write the following:

```cpp
#include <iostream>

struct the_answer
{
    using type = unsigned;
};

template<typename T>
void foo(typename T::type t)
{
    std::cout << "The answer is not: " << t << '\n';
}

template<typename T>
void foo(T t)
{
    std::cout << "The answer is: " << t << '\n';
}

int main(void)
{
    foo<the_answer>(23);
    foo<int>(42);

    return 0;
}
```

The output for each of these are depicted here:

```
The answer is: 23
The answer is: 42
```

In this example, we have created two versions of the `foo()` function. This first version takes a `T` type that has a `type` alias that we use to create the function's parameter. The second version just takes the `T` type itself. We then use both versions of the `foo()` function, one with an integer and the other with a struct that defines the `type` alias.

The takeaway from the preceding example is that when we call the `foo<int>()` version of the `foo()` function, the compiler doesn't generate an error when it attempts to match the `int` type with the version of the `foo()` function that takes a type with the `type` alias. This is what SFINAE is. All it says is that when the compiler attempts to take a given type and match it to a template, if a failure occurs, the compiler will not generate an error. The only time an error would occur is if the compiler cannot find a suitable substitution. For example, what happens if we comment out the second version of `foo()`? Let's see:

```
[~/book/chapter04/build]: make
[  6%] Built target recipe07_example02
[ 11%] Built target recipe07_example01
[ 15%] Built target recipe06_example03
[ 20%] Built target recipe06_example01
Scanning dependencies of target recipe01_example01
[ 22%] Building CXX object CMakeFiles/recipe01_example01.dir/recipe01.cpp.o
/home/user/book/chapter04/recipe01.cpp: In function 'int main()':
/home/user/book/chapter04/recipe01.cpp:47:16: error: no matching function for call to 'foo<int>(int)'
   47 |     foo<int>(42);
/home/user/book/chapter04/recipe01.cpp:33:6: note: candidate: 'template<class T> void foo(typename T::type)'
   33 | void foo(typename T::type t)
      |      ^~~
/home/user/book/chapter04/recipe01.cpp:33:6: note:   template argument deduction/substitution failed:
/home/user/book/chapter04/recipe01.cpp: In substitution of 'template<class T> void foo(typename T::type) [with T = int]':
/home/user/book/chapter04/recipe01.cpp:47:16:   required from here
/home/user/book/chapter04/recipe01.cpp:33:6: error: 'int' is not a class, struct, or union type
make[2]: *** [CMakeFiles/recipe01_example01.dir/build.make:63: CMakeFiles/recipe01_example01.dir/recipe01.cpp.o] Error 1
make[1]: *** [CMakeFiles/Makefile2:221: CMakeFiles/recipe01_example01.dir/all] Error 2
make: *** [Makefile:84: all] Error 2
[~/book/chapter04/build]:
```

As you can see from the preceding error output, the compiler is even saying that the error is a substitution error. The template that we provide is not a valid candidate based on the type that was provided.

The other important takeaway from this example is that the compiler was able to pick between the two different versions of our `foo()` function based on the type that was provided. We can use this to our advantage. Specifically, this gives us the power to do different things based on the type that is provided. All we need is a means to write our `foo()` function so that we can enable/disable different versions of our templates based on the types that we are provided.

This is where `std::enable_if` comes into play. `std::enable_if` takes the idea of SFINAE to the next step, allowing us to define a type if its parameter is true. Otherwise, it will generate a substitution error, purposely forcing the compiler to pick a different version of the template. `std::enable_if` is defined as follows:

```
template<bool B, class T = void>
struct enable_if {};

template<class T>
struct enable_if<true, T> { typedef T type; };
```

This first defines a struct that takes `bool B` and a `T` type that defaults to `void`. It then defines a specialization of this `struct` type when `bool` is true. Specifically, when the `bool` value is `true`, the type that is provided is returned, which, as we stated before, defaults to `void`. To see how this is used, let's look at an example:

```
#include <iostream>
#include <type_traits>

template<typename T>
constexpr auto is_int()
{
    return false;
}

template<>
constexpr auto is_int<int>()
{
    return true;
}

template<
    typename T,
    std::enable_if_t<is_int<T>(), int> = 0
    >
void the_answer(T is)
{
    std::cout << "The answer is: " << is << '\n';
}

int main(void)
{
    the_answer(42);
    return 0;
}
```

The output is as follows:

In this example, we create a function called `is_int()` that always returns `false`. We then create a template specialization of this function for `int` that returns `true`. Next, we create a function that takes any type, but we add `std::enable_if_t` (the added `_t` part is a shorthand that was added to C++17 for `::type`) to the template definition that uses our `is_int()` function. If the `T` type that is provided is `int`, our `is_int()` function will return `true`.

`std::enable_if` does nothing by default. If it is `true`, however, it returns a `type` alias, which, in the preceding example, is the `int` type that we are passing as the second parameter of `std::enable_if`. What this is saying is that if `std::enable_if` is `true`, it will return an `int` type. We then set this `int` type to `0`, which is a valid thing to do. This doesn't generate a failure; our template function becomes a valid substitution and, therefore, is used. In summary, if `T` is an `int` type, `std::enable_if` turns into an `int` type itself that we then set to `0`, which compiles without an issue. If our `T` type is not `int`, `std::enable_if` turns into nothing. Attempting to set nothing to `0` results in a compilation error, but since this is SFINAE, the compiler error becomes nothing more than a substitution error.

Let's look at the error case. If we set `42` to `42.0`, which is a `double`, not `int`, we get the following:

As you can see from the preceding error, the compiler is saying that there is no type named `type` in `enable_if`. If you look at the definition of `std::enable_if`, this is expected because `std::enable_if` doesn't do anything if it is false. It only creates a type named `type` if it is true.

To better understand how this works, let's look at another example:

```
#include <iostream>
#include <type_traits>

template<
    typename T,
    std::enable_if_t<std::is_integral_v<T>>* = nullptr
    >
void the_answer(T is)
{
    std::cout << "The answer is: " << is << '\n';
}

int main(void)
{
    the_answer(42);
    return 0;
}
```

The output is as follows:

In the preceding example, we use `std::is_integral_v`, which does the same thing as our `is_int()` function, with the difference being that it is provided by the standard library and can handle CV types. In fact, the standard library has a massive list of different versions of these functions including different types, inheritance properties, CV properties, and so on. If you need to check for a `type` property of any kind, chances are that the standard library has an `std:is_xxx` function that you can use.

The preceding example is nearly identical to our previous one with the difference being that we do not return `int` in our `std::enable_if` method. Instead, we use `* = nullptr`. This works because `std::enable_if` returns `void` by default. The `*` character turns this void into a void pointer, which we then set to `nullptr`.

In the next example, we show another twist on this:

```cpp
#include <iostream>
#include <type_traits>

template<typename T>
std::enable_if_t<std::is_integral_v<T>>
the_answer(T is)
{
    std::cout << "The answer is: " << is << '\n';
}

int main(void)
{
    the_answer(42);
    return 0;
}
```

The output is as follows:

```
user@localhost:~/book/chapter04/build
[~/book/chapter04/build]: ./recipe01_example04
The answer is: 42
[~/book/chapter04/build]:
```

In this example, void for our function is created by std::enable_if. If T is not an integer, void is not returned and we see this error (instead of the code compiling and allowing us to execute it in the first place):

```
user@localhost:~/book/chapter04/build
Scanning dependencies of target recipe01_example04
[ 40%] Building CXX object CMakeFiles/recipe01_example04.dir/recipe01.cpp.o
/home/user/book/chapter04/recipe01.cpp: In function 'int main()':
/home/user/book/chapter04/recipe01.cpp:130:20: error: no matching function for call to 'the_answer(double)'
  130 |     the_answer(42.0);
      |                    ^
/home/user/book/chapter04/recipe01.cpp:123:1: note: candidate: 'template<class T> std::enable_if_t<is_integral_v<T> > the_answer(T)'
  123 | the_answer(T is)
      | ^~~~~~~~~~
/home/user/book/chapter04/recipe01.cpp:123:1: note:   template argument deduction/substitution failed:
In file included from /usr/include/c++/9/bits/move.h:55,
                 from /usr/include/c++/9/bits/nested_exception.h:40,
                 from /usr/include/c++/9/exception:144,
                 from /usr/include/c++/9/ios:39,
                 from /usr/include/c++/9/ostream:38,
                 from /usr/include/c++/9/iostream:39,
                 from /home/user/book/chapter04/recipe01.cpp:118:
/usr/include/c++/9/type_traits: In substitution of 'template<bool _Cond, class _Tp> using enable_if_t = typename std::en
able_if::type [with bool _Cond = std::is_integral_v<double>; _Tp = void]':
/home/user/book/chapter04/recipe01.cpp:123:1:   required by substitution of 'template<class T> std::enable_if_t<is_integ
ral_v<T> > the_answer(T) [with T = double]'
/home/user/book/chapter04/recipe01.cpp:130:20:   required from here
/usr/include/c++/9/type_traits:2384:11: error: no type named 'type' in 'struct std::enable_if<false, void>'
 2384 |     using enable_if_t = typename enable_if<_Cond, _Tp>::type;
      |           ^~~~~~~~~~~
make[2]: *** [CMakeFiles/recipe01_example04.dir/build.make:63: CMakeFiles/recipe01_example04.dir/recipe01.cpp.o] Error 1
make[1]: *** [CMakeFiles/Makefile2:508: CMakeFiles/recipe01_example04.dir/all] Error 2
make: *** [Makefile:84: all] Error 2
[~/book/chapter04/build]:
```

In summary, `std::enable_if` will create a type named `type`, which is based on the type that you provide it. By default, this is `void` but you can pass in any type that you want. Not only can this functionality be used to enforce a type for our templates, but it can also be used to define different functions based on the type that we are provided, as shown in this example:

```cpp
#include <iostream>
#include <type_traits>
#include <iomanip>

template<
    typename T,
    std::enable_if_t<std::is_integral_v<T>>* = nullptr
    >
void the_answer(T is)
{
    std::cout << "The answer is: " << is << '\n';
}

template<
    typename T,
    std::enable_if_t<std::is_floating_point_v<T>>* = nullptr
    >
void the_answer(T is)
{
    std::cout << std::setprecision(10);
    std::cout << "The answer is: " << is << '\n';
}

int main(void)
{
    the_answer(42);
    the_answer(42U);
    the_answer(42.12345678);

    return 0;
}
```

The output for the preceding code is as follows:

Like our first example in this recipe, we have created two different versions of the same function. SFINAE allows the compiler to pick the most suitable version based on the type that was provided.

Learning perfect forwarding

In this recipe, we will learn how to use perfect forwarding. This recipe is important because, often, when writing templates, we pass template parameters to other functions. If we do not use perfect forwarding, we can inadvertently convert r-value references into l-value references, resulting in a potential copy taking place instead of a move, which, in some cases, could be suboptimal. Perfect forwarding also provides the compiler with hints that could be leveraged to improve function inlining and unwrapping.

Getting ready

Before beginning, please ensure that all of the technical requirements are met, including installing Ubuntu 18.04 or higher and running the following in a Terminal window:

```
> sudo apt-get install build-essential git cmake
```

This will ensure your operating system has the proper tools to compile and execute the examples in this recipe. Once this is complete, open a new Terminal. We will use this Terminal to download, compile, and run our examples.

How to do it...

You need to perform the following steps to try this recipe:

1. From a new Terminal, run the following to download the source code:

```
> cd ~/
> git clone
https://github.com/PacktPublishing/Advanced-CPP-CookBook.git
> cd Advanced-CPP-CookBook/chapter04
```

2. To compile the source code, run the following:

```
> cmake .
> make recipe02_examples
```

3. Once the source code is compiled, you can execute each example in this recipe by running the following commands:

```
> ./recipe02_example01
l-value
l-value

> ./recipe02_example02
l-value
r-value

> ./recipe02_example03
l-value: 42
r-value: 42
```

In the next section, we will step through each of these examples and explain what each example program does and how it relates to the lessons being taught in this recipe.

How it works...

In this recipe, we will learn how to use perfect forwarding to ensure that, when we pass parameters in our templates (that is, forward our parameters), we do so in a way that doesn't erase r-valueness. To better understand the issue, let's look at the following example:

```cpp
#include <iostream>

struct the_answer
{ };

void foo2(const the_answer &is)
{
    std::cout << "l-value\n";
}

void foo2(the_answer &&is)
{
    std::cout << "r-value\n";
}

template<typename T>
void foo1(T &&t)
{
    foo2(t);
}
```

```
int main(void)
{
    the_answer is;
    foo1(is);
    foo1(the_answer());

    return 0;
}
```

The output is as follows:

In the preceding example, we have two different versions of a `foo()` function: one that takes an l-value reference and one that takes an r-value reference. We then call `foo()` from a template function. This template function takes a forwarding reference (also called a universal reference), which is an r-value reference paired with either `auto` or a template function. Finally, from our main function, we call our template to see which `foo()` function is called. The first time we call our template, we pass in an l-value. Since we are given an l-value, the universal reference becomes an l-value, and the l-value version of our `foo()` function is called. The problem is, the second time we call our template function, we give it an r-value, but it calls the l-value version of our `foo()` function, even though it was given an r-value.

The common mistake here is that even though the template function takes a universal reference and we have a version of the `foo()` function that also takes an r-value, we assume this `foo()` function would be called. Scott Meyers does a great job explaining this in many of his lectures on universal references. The problem is that the moment you use a universal reference, it becomes an l-value. The very act of passing the `names` parameter, which means it must be an l-value. It forces the compiler to convert to an l-value because it sees you using it, even though all you are doing is passing the parameter. It should be noted that our example doesn't compile with optimizations as the compiler is free to optimize the l-value out if it can safely determine that the variable is not used.

To prevent this issue, we need to tell the compiler that we wish to forward the parameter. Normally, we would use `std::move()` for this. The problem is, if we were originally given an l-value, we cannot use `std::move()` as that would convert an l-value into an r-value. This is why the standard library has `std::forward()`, which is implemented using the following:

```
static_cast<T&&>(t)
```

All `std::forward()` does is cast the parameter back to its original reference type. This tells the compiler explicitly to treat the parameter as an r-value if it was originally an r-value, as in the following example:

```
#include <iostream>

struct the_answer
{ };

void foo2(const the_answer &is)
{
    std::cout << "l-value\n";
}

void foo2(the_answer &&is)
{
    std::cout << "r-value\n";
}

template<typename T>
void foo1(T &&t)
{
    foo2(std::forward<T>(t));
}

int main(void)
{
    the_answer is;
    foo1(is);
    foo1(the_answer());

    return 0;
}
```

The output is as follows:

The preceding example is identical to the first example with the only difference being that we pass the parameter in our template function using `std::forward()`. This time, when we call our template function with an r-value, it calls the r-value version of our `foo()` function. This is called **perfect forwarding**. It ensures that we maintain CV properties and l-/r-value properties when passing parameters. It should be noted that perfect forwarding only works when using template functions or `auto`. What this means is that perfect forwarding is usually only useful when writing wrappers. A good example of a standard library wrapper is `std::make_unique()`.

One issue with a wrapper such as `std::make_unique()` is that you might not know how many parameters need to be passed. That is, you might end up needing variadic template arguments in your wrapper. Perfect forwarding supports this by doing the following:

```cpp
#include <iostream>

struct the_answer
{ };

void foo2(const the_answer &is, int i)
{
    std::cout << "l-value: " << i << '\n';
}

void foo2(the_answer &&is, int i)
{
    std::cout << "r-value: " << i << '\n';
}

template<typename... Args>
void foo1(Args &&...args)
{
    foo2(std::forward<Args>(args)...);
}

int main(void)
{
    the_answer is;
```

```
        foo1(is, 42);
        foo1(the_answer(), 42);

        return 0;
    }
```

The output is as follows:

```
user@localhost:~/book/chapter04/build                    □    ×
[~/book/chapter04/build]: ./recipe02_example03 ∧
l-value: 42
r-value: 42
[~/book/chapter04/build]:
```

The preceding example works because the variadic template arguments being passed to our `foo()` function are replaced by a comma-separated list of perfect forwards.

Using if constexpr

In this recipe, we will learn how to use a new feature in C++17 called `constexpr if`. This recipe is important because it will teach you how to create `if` statements that are evaluated at runtime. Specifically, what this means is that the branch logic is picked at compile time and not at runtime. This allows you to change the behavior of a function at compile time without sacrificing performance, something that, in the past, could only be done with macros, which is not useful in template programming, as we will show.

Getting ready

Before beginning, please ensure that all of the technical requirements are met, including installing Ubuntu 18.04 or higher and running the following in a Terminal window:

```
> sudo apt-get install build-essential git
```

This will ensure your operating system has the proper tools to compile and execute the examples in this recipe. Once this is complete, open a new Terminal. We will use this Terminal to download, compile, and run our examples.

How to do it...

You need to perform the following steps to try this recipe:

1. From a new Terminal, run the following to download the source code:

```
> cd ~/
> git clone
https://github.com/PacktPublishing/Advanced-CPP-CookBook.git
> cd Advanced-CPP-CookBook/chapter04
```

2. To compile the source code, run the following:

```
> cmake .
> make recipe03_examples
```

3. Once the source code is compiled, you can execute each example in this recipe by running the following commands:

```
> ./recipe03_example01
The answer is: 42

> ./recipe03_example02
The answer is: 42
The answer is: 42.12345678
```

In the next section, we will step through each of these examples and explain what each example program does and how it relates to the lessons being taught in this recipe.

How it works...

Sometimes, we wish to change the behavior of our programs but the code that we are creating is always constant, meaning the compiler is capable of determining the value of the branch itself, as shown in this example:

```
if (!NDEBUG) {}
```

This is a common `if` statement used in a lot of code, including the standard library. If debugging is enabled, this code evaluates to `true`. We use this by adding debug statements to our code, which can be turned off. The compiler is smart enough to see that `NDEBUG` is `true` or `false` and will either add the code or remove the code completely. In other words, the compiler can make a simple optimization and reduce the size of the code as well as remove an unneeded branch as it knows the value of this `if` statement will never change at runtime. The problem is, this trick relies on the fact that the compiler is smart. The removal of the logic is implicitly trusted, which often leads to assumptions about what the compiler is doing. C++17 added a `constexpr if` statement that allows us to be explicit instead. It allows us to tell the compiler: that the statement I am providing should be evaluated at compile time, not at runtime. What makes this truly powerful is that we get compile-time errors when this assumption is not true, meaning the optimizations we were implicitly trusting the compiler to perform, we can now verify at compile time, and if the assumptions are false, we are told so that we can fix the issue, as shown in this example:

```
#include <iostream>

constexpr auto answer = 42;

int main(void)
{
    if constexpr (answer == 42) {
        std::cout << "The answer is: " << answer << '\n';
    }
    else {
        std::cout << "The answer is not: " << answer << '\n';
    }

    return 0;
}
```

The output is as follows:

In the preceding example, we create `constexpr` and evaluate it at compile time instead of runtime. If we change `constexpr` to an actual variable, `constexpr if` will result in the following error:

We can then use this in our template functions to change the behavior of our template functions based on the type that we are given, as shown in this example:

```cpp
#include <iostream>
#include <iomanip>

template<typename T>
constexpr void foo(T &&t)
{
    if constexpr (std::is_floating_point_v<T>) {
        std::cout << std::setprecision(10);
    }

    std::cout << "The answer is: " << std::forward<T>(t) << '\n';
}

int main(void)
{
    foo(42);
    foo(42.12345678);
    return 0;
}
```

In the preceding example, we use the `std::is_floating_point_v` type trait to determine whether the type that we were provided is a floating point or not. If the type is not a floating point, this will return `constexpr false`, which the compiler can optimize out. Since we are using `constexpr if`, we can ensure that our `if` statement is actually `constexpr` and not a runtime conditional.

Using tuples to work with parameter packs

In this recipe, we will learn how to work with variadic parameter lists using `std::tuple`. This is important because a variadic parameter list is meant to be used in wrapper functions where the wrapper doesn't know anything about the arguments being passed to it but instead will forward these arguments to something that does. There are, however, use cases where you will care about the arguments being passed, and you must have a way of working with these arguments. This recipe will demonstrate how to do that including how to deal with any number of arguments.

Getting ready

Before beginning, please ensure that all of the technical requirements are met, including installing Ubuntu 18.04 or higher and running the following in a Terminal window:

```
> sudo apt-get install build-essential git cmake
```

This will ensure your operating system has the proper tools to compile and execute the examples in this recipe. Once this is complete, open a new Terminal. We will use this Terminal to download, compile, and run our examples.

How to do it...

You need to perform the following steps to try this recipe:

1. From a new Terminal, run the following to download the source code:

   ```
   > cd ~/
   > git clone
   https://github.com/PacktPublishing/Advanced-CPP-CookBook.git
   > cd Advanced-CPP-CookBook/chapter04
   ```

2. To compile the source code, run the following:

   ```
   > cmake .
   > make recipe04_examples
   ```

3. Once the source code is compiled, you can execute each example in this recipe by running the following commands:

   ```
   > ./recipe04_example01
   ```

   ```
   > ./recipe04_example02
   ```

```
the answer is: 42

> ./recipe04_example03
The answer is: 42

> ./recipe04_example04
2
2

> ./recipe04_example05
The answer is: 42
```

In the next section, we will step through each of these examples and explain what each example program does and how it relates to the lessons being taught in this recipe.

How it works...

Variadic templates provide the programmer with the ability to define a template function without needing to define all of the arguments. These are used heavily in wrapper functions as they prevent the wrapper from having to have any knowledge of the function's arguments, as shown in this example:

```cpp
#include <iostream>

template<typename... Args>
void foo(Args &&...args)
{ }

int main(void)
{
    foo("The answer is: ", 42);
    return 0;
}
```

As shown in the preceding example, we have created a `foo` function that can take any number of arguments. In this example, we use the universal reference notation, `Args &&...args`, which ensures the CV qualifiers and l-/r-valueness is preserved, meaning we can then use `std::forward()` to pass the variable arguments list to any other function with as little loss in performance as possible. Functions such as `std::make_unique()` make heavy use of variadic parameters.

Sometimes, however, you might want to access one of the arguments in the list that is provided. To do this, we can use `std::tuple`. This is a data structure that takes a variable number of arguments and provides an `std::get()` function to get any data from `std::tuple`, as shown in this example:

```
#include <tuple>
#include <iostream>

int main(void)
{
    std::tuple t("the answer is: ", 42);
    std::cout << std::get<0>(t) << std::get<1>(t) << '\n';
    return 0;
}
```

The output is as follows:

In the preceding example, we create `std::tuple` and then we output the contents of `std::tuple` to `stdout` using the `std:get()` function. If you attempt to access data that is out of range, the compiler will know at compile time, and give you an error that looks something like this:

Using `std::tuple`, we can access the data from a variadic parameter list as follows:

```
#include <tuple>
#include <iostream>

template<typename... Args>
void foo(Args &&...args)
{
    std::tuple t(std::forward<Args>(args)...);
    std::cout << std::get<0>(t) << std::get<1>(t) << '\n';
}

int main(void)
{
    foo("The answer is: ", 42);
    return 0;
}
```

The output is as follows:

In the preceding example, we create a function with a variadic parameter list. We then pass this list using `std::forward()` to preserve the l-/r-valueness to `std::tuple`. Finally, we use `std::tuple` to access the arguments. If we didn't use `std::forward()`, we would end up with l-value versions of the data passed to `std::tuple`.

The obvious problem with the preceding examples is that we have hardcoded the 0 and 1 indexes into `std::tuple`. Variadic parameters are not a runtime, dynamic array of parameters. Instead, they are a way of saying *I don't care about the parameters I have been given*, which is why they are normally used by wrappers. A wrapper is wrapping something that does care about the parameters. In the case of `std::make_unique()`, the function is creating `std::unique_ptr`. To do this, `std::make_unique()` will allocate `std::unique_ptr` for you, using the variadic parameter list to initialize the newly allocated type and then provide the pointer to this type to `std::unique_ptr` for you, as shown in this example:

```
template<
    typename T,
    typename... Args
    >
void make_unique(Args &&...args)
```

```
{
    return unique_ptr<T>(new T(std::forward<Args>(args)...));
}
```

The wrapper doesn't care about the arguments being passed. The constructor for T does. If you attempt to access the variadic arguments, you are saying *I do care about the arguments*, in which case, if you care, you must have some idea of the layout of the parameters being passed.

There are some tricks that allow you to work with an unknown number of arguments, however. The biggest problem with attempting to do this is the library facilities for working with variadic parameters are best used during runtime, which doesn't help in most cases, as shown in this example:

```
#include <tuple>
#include <iostream>

template<typename... Args>
void foo(Args &&...args)
{
    std::cout << sizeof...(Args) << '\n';
    std::cout << std::tuple_size_v<std::tuple<Args...>> << '\n';
}

int main(void)
{
    foo("The answer is: ", 42);
    return 0;
}
```

The output is as follows:

In the preceding example, we attempt to get the total size of the number of arguments in the variadic parameter list. We can do this either using the variadic version of the sizeof() function or we can use the std::tuple_size trait. The problem is this doesn't help us during compile time as we cannot loop through the parameters using this size information (as there is no for loop for compile-time logic).

To overcome this, one trick that we can use is something called compile-time recursion. This trick uses templates to create a recursive template function that will loop through all of the arguments in a variadic parameter list. Check out this example:

```
#include <tuple>
#include <iostream>

template<
    std::size_t I = 0,
    typename ... Args,
    typename FUNCTION
    >
constexpr void
for_each(const std::tuple<Args...> &t, FUNCTION &&func)
{
    if constexpr (I < sizeof...(Args)) {
        func(std::get<I>(t));
        for_each<I + 1>(t, std::forward<FUNCTION>(func));
    }
}
```

We start with a template function that performs all of the magic. This first template parameter is I, which is an integer that starts as 0. The next is a variadic template parameter and the last is a function type. Our template function takes std::tuple, which we wish to iterate over (in this case, we show a constant version, but we could overload this to provide a non-constant version as well), and a function that we wish to call for each element in std::tuple. In other words, this function will loop over each element in std::tuple and call the provided function with each element iterated over, just like for_each(), which we are used to using at runtime in other languages or C++ libraries.

Inside this function, we check to see whether we have reached the total size of the tuple. If we have not, we get the element in the tuple for the current value of I, pass it to the provided function, and then call our for_each() function again with I++. To use this for_each() function, we can do the following:

```
template<typename... Args>
void foo(Args &&...args)
{
    std::tuple t(std::forward<Args>(args)...);
    for_each(t, [](const auto &arg) {
        std::cout << arg;
    });
}
```

Here, we have been given a variadic parameter list and we wish to iterate over this list and output each argument to `stdout`. To do this, we create `std::tuple` as we have previously, but this time, we pass `std::tuple` to our `for_each()` function:

```
int main(void)
{
    foo("The answer is: ", 42);
    std::cout << '\n';

    return 0;
}
```

The output is as follows:

```
[~/book/chapter04/build]: ./recipe04_example05
The answer is: 42
[~/book/chapter04/build]:
```

Just like we did in the previous examples, we call our `foo` function with some text that we wish to output to `stdout`, hence demonstrating how to work with variadic function parameters using `std:tuple`, even if we don't know the total number of arguments we will be given.

Using type traits to overload functions and objects

One issue that C++ had to deal with when C++11 was created was how to handle resizing `std::vector`, which is capable of taking any type, including types that can throw from `std::move()`. When resizing, new memory is created and the elements from the old vector are moved to the new vector. This works great because, if `std::move()` cannot throw, the resize can safely be performed as once the resizing function starts to move elements from one array to the other, no errors can occur.

If `std::move()` can throw, however, it is possible that part of the way through the loop, an error could occur. The `resize()` function, however, would have no way to put the old memory back to normal as attempting to move to the old memory could also throw an exception. In this case, `resize()` performs a copy instead of a move. A copy ensures that the old memory has a valid copy of each object; so, if an exception is thrown, the original array is left intact and the exception can be thrown as needed.

In this recipe, we will explore how this is done by changing the behavior of a template class using traits.

Getting ready

Before beginning, please ensure that all of the technical requirements are met, including installing Ubuntu 18.04 or higher and running the following in a Terminal window:

```
> sudo apt-get install build-essential git cmake
```

This will ensure your operating system has the proper tools to compile and execute the examples in this recipe. Once this is complete, open a new Terminal. We will use this Terminal to download, compile, and run our examples.

How to do it...

You need to perform the following steps to try this recipe:

1. From a new Terminal, run the following to download the source code:

```
> cd ~/
> git clone
https://github.com/PacktPublishing/Advanced-CPP-CookBook.git
> cd Advanced-CPP-CookBook/chapter04
```

2. To compile the source code, run the following:

```
> cmake .
> make recipe05_examples
```

3. Once the source code is compiled, you can execute each example in this recipe by running the following commands:

```
> ./recipe05_example01
noexcept: r-value
can throw: l-value

> ./recipe05_example02
move
move
move
move
move
--------------
```

```
copy
copy
copy
copy
copy
```

In the next section, we will step through each of these examples and explain what each example program does and how it relates to the lessons being taught in this recipe.

How it works...

C++ added a function called `std::move_if_noexcept()`. This function will cast as an r-value if the move constructor/assignment operator cannot throw, and will cast as an l-value otherwise. For example, take a look at the following code:

```cpp
#include <iostream>

struct the_answer_noexcept
{
    the_answer_noexcept() = default;

    the_answer_noexcept(const the_answer_noexcept &is) noexcept
    {
        std::cout << "l-value\n";
    }

    the_answer_noexcept(the_answer_noexcept &&is) noexcept
    {
        std::cout << "r-value\n";
    }
};
```

To try this, we will perform the following steps:

1. First, we will create a class that has a move/copy constructor that cannot throw:

```cpp
struct the_answer_can_throw
{
    the_answer_can_throw() = default;

    the_answer_can_throw(const the_answer_can_throw &is)
    {
        std::cout << "l-value\n";
    }

    the_answer_can_throw(the_answer_can_throw &&is)
```

```
        {
            std::cout << "r-value\n";
        }
    };
```

2. Next, we will provide a class that has a move/copy constructor that can throw. Finally, let's use `std::move_if_noexcept()` to see whether a move or a copy occurs when attempting to move an instance of each of these preceding classes:

```
int main(void)
{
    the_answer_noexcept is1;
    the_answer_can_throw is2;

    std::cout << "noexcept: ";
    auto is3 = std::move_if_noexcept(is1);

    std::cout << "can throw: ";
    auto is4 = std::move_if_noexcept(is2);

    return 0;
}
```

The output for the preceding code is as follows:

As shown in the preceding example, in one case, the move constructor is called and in the other case, the copy constructor is called based on whether or not the type can throw an exception when performing a move.

3. Now, let's create a simple mock vector with a resize function to demonstrate how we can change the behavior of our `template` class using traits:

```
#include <memory>
#include <iostream>
#include <stdexcept>

template<typename T>
class mock_vector
{
public:
    using size_type = std::size_t;
```

```
                mock_vector(size_type s)  :
                    m_size{s},
                    m_buffer{std::make_unique<T[]>(m_size)}
                { }

                void resize(size_type size)
                    noexcept(std::is_nothrow_move_constructible_v<T>)
                {
                    auto tmp = std::make_unique<T[]>(size);

                    for (size_type i = 0; i < m_size; i++) {
                        tmp[i] = std::move_if_noexcept(m_buffer[i]);
                    }

                    m_size = size;
                    m_buffer = std::move(tmp);
                }

            private:
                size_type m_size{};
                std::unique_ptr<T[]> m_buffer{};
        };
```

Our mock vector has an internal buffer and a size. When the vector is created, we allocate the internal buffer using the given size. We then provide a `resize()` function that can be used to resize the internal buffer given a new size. The first thing we do is create our new internal buffer, and then we loop through each element and the element from one buffer to the other. If `T` cannot throw, no exception will fire during the execution of the loop, in which case, the new buffer will be valid. If `T` can throw, a copy will occur instead. If an exception fires, the old buffer has not yet been replaced with the new one. Instead, the new buffer is deleted along with all of the elements that were copied.

To use this, let's create a class that can throw in the move constructor/assignment operator:

```
    struct suboptimal
    {
        suboptimal() = default;

        suboptimal(suboptimal &&other)
        {
            *this = std::move(other);
        }

        suboptimal &operator=(suboptimal &&)
        {
            std::cout << "move\n";
            return *this;
```

```
    }

    suboptimal(const suboptimal &other)
    {
        *this = other;
    }

    suboptimal &operator=(const suboptimal &)
    {
        std::cout << "copy\n";
        return *this;
    }
};
```

Let's also add a class that cannot throw from the move constructor/assignment operator:

```
struct optimal
{
    optimal() = default;

    optimal(optimal &&other) noexcept
    {
        *this = std::move(other);
    }

    optimal &operator=(optimal &&) noexcept
    {
        std::cout << "move\n";
        return *this;
    }

    optimal(const optimal &other)
    {
        *this = other;
    }

    optimal &operator=(const optimal &)
    {
        std::cout << "copy\n";
        return *this;
    }
};
```

Finally, we will create a vector using both of these classes and attempt to resize it:

```
int main(void)
{
    mock_vector<optimal> d1(5);
    mock_vector<suboptimal> d2(5);

    d1.resize(10);
    std::cout << "--------------\n";
    d2.resize(10);

    return 0;
}
```

The output for the preceding code is as follows:

```
user@localhost:~/book/chapter04/build                      —      □      ×
[~/book/chapter04/build]: ./recipe05_example02
move
move
move
move
move
--------------
copy
copy
copy
copy
copy
[~/book/chapter04/build]:
```

As shown in the preceding example, when we attempt to resize the class, a move is performed when a move cannot throw, and a copy is performed otherwise. In other words, the behavior of the class changes depending on the traits of the T type.

Learning how to implement template<auto>

C++ has had the ability to create templates for a long time, which allows the programmer to create generic implementations of classes and functions, given a type. You can also, however, provide non-type parameters.

In C++17, you can now use auto to provide for generic, non-type template arguments. In this recipe, we will explore how to use this feature. This is important because it allows you to create more generic templates in your code.

Getting ready

Before beginning, please ensure that all of the technical requirements are met, including installing Ubuntu 18.04 or higher and running the following in a Terminal window:

```
> sudo apt-get install build-essential git cmake
```

This will ensure your operating system has the proper tools to compile and execute the examples in this recipe. Once this is complete, open a new Terminal. We will use this Terminal to download, compile, and run our examples.

How to do it...

You need to perform the following steps to try this recipe:

1. From a new Terminal, run the following to download the source code:

```
> cd ~/
> git clone
https://github.com/PacktPublishing/Advanced-CPP-CookBook.git
> cd Advanced-CPP-CookBook/chapter04
```

2. To compile the source code, run the following:

```
> cmake .
> make recipe06_examples
```

3. Once the source code is compiled, you can execute each example in this recipe by running the following commands:

```
> ./recipe06_example01
The answer is: 42
> ./recipe06_example02
The answer is: 42
The answer is: 42
> ./recipe06_example03
The answer is: 42
```

In the next section, we will step through each of these examples and explain what each example program does and how it relates to the lessons being taught in this recipe.

How it works...

Before C++17, you could provide non-type template arguments in a template, but you had to state the variable type in the definition, as shown in this example:

```
#include <iostream>

template<int answer>
void foo()
{
    std::cout << "The answer is: " << answer << '\n';
}

int main(void)
{
    foo<42>();
    return 0;
}
```

The output is as follows:

```
[~/book/chapter04/build]: ./recipe06_example01
The answer is: 42
[~/book/chapter04/build]:
```

In the preceding example, we create a template argument variable of the int type and output the value of this variable to stdout. In C++17, we can now do the following:

```
#include <iostream>

template<auto answer>
void foo()
{
    std::cout << "The answer is: " << answer << '\n';
}

int main(void)
{
    foo<42>();
    return 0;
}
```

The output is as follows:

As shown in the preceding, instead of having to state `int`, we can now state `auto`. This allows us to create a single function that can take more than one non-type template parameter. We can also use type traits to establish which non-type parameters are allowed, as shown in this example:

```cpp
#include <iostream>
#include <type_traits>

template<
    auto answer,
 std::enable_if_t<std::is_integral_v<decltype(answer)>, int> = 0
 >
void foo()
{
    std::cout << "The answer is: " << answer << '\n';
}

int main(void)
{
    foo<42>();
    return 0;
}
```

The output is as follows:

In the preceding example, our template non-type parameter can only be an integer type.

Working with explicit template declarations

In this recipe, we will explore how to speed up the compilation of your template classes by creating an explicit template declaration. This is important because templates require the compiler to create instances of your classes as needed. In certain cases, explicit template declaration might provide the programmer with a means to speed up compilation by caching the template types that are most likely to be used, preventing the need to include the entire definition of a template.

Getting ready

Before beginning, please ensure that all of the technical requirements are met, including installing Ubuntu 18.04 or higher and running the following in a Terminal window:

```
> sudo apt-get install build-essential git cmake
```

This will ensure your operating system has the proper tools to compile and execute the examples in this recipe. Once this is complete, open a new Terminal. We will use this Terminal to download, compile, and run our examples.

How to do it...

You need to perform the following steps to try this recipe:

1. From a new Terminal, run the following to download the source code:

   ```
   > cd ~/
   > git clone
   https://github.com/PacktPublishing/Advanced-CPP-CookBook.git
   > cd Advanced-CPP-CookBook/chapter04
   ```

2. To compile the source code, run the following:

   ```
   > cmake .
   > make recipe07_examples
   ```

3. Once the source code is compiled, you can execute each example in this recipe by running the following commands:

   ```
   > ./recipe07_example01
   The answer is: 42
   The answer is: 42
   The answer is: 42.1
   ```

```
> ./recipe07_example02
The answer is: 4
```

In the next section, we will step through each of these examples and explain what each example program does and how it relates to the lessons being taught in this recipe.

How it works...

Each time the compiler sees the use of a template class with a given type, it creates a version of that type implicitly. This, however, can happen multiple times, reducing the speed of the compiler. If, however, the types that are expected to be used are known upfront, this issue can be solved using explicit template specialization. Take a look at this example:

```cpp
#include <iostream>

template<typename T>
class the_answer
{
public:
    the_answer(T t)
    {
        std::cout << "The answer is: " << t << '\n';
    }
};
```

Earlier, we created a simple structure that outputs to stdout during construction. Normally, this class would be created by the compiler once the first specialization of the class is seen. We can, however, perform the following:

```cpp
template class the_answer<int>;
template class the_answer<unsigned>;
template class the_answer<double>;
```

This is similar to a class prototype, and it explicitly creates the specializations that we expect to use. These must be stated before they are used in code (which means they are usually stated after the definition of the template); however, once they are stated, they can be used as follows:

```cpp
int main(void)
{
    the_answer{42};
    the_answer{42U};
    the_answer{42.1};
```

```
        return 0;
    }
```

The output for the code is as follows:

```
[~/book/chapter04/build]: ./recipe07_example01
The answer is: 42
The answer is: 42
The answer is: 42.1
[~/book/chapter04/build]:
```

As shown in the preceding example, we can create instances of our template as normal, but, in this case, we can speed up the compiler in scenarios where this class is used a lot. This is because, in the source code, we do not need to include the implementation of the template. To demonstrate this, let's look at another, more complicated example. In a header file (called `recipe07.h`), we will create our template using the following:

```
template<typename T>
struct the_answer
{
    T m_answer;

    the_answer(T t);
    void print();
};
```

As you can see, we have a `template` class with no implementation for the provided functions. We will then provide the implementation of this template using the following in its own source file:

```
#include <iostream>
#include "recipe07.h"

template<typename T>
the_answer<T>::the_answer(T t) :
    m_answer{t}
{ }

template<typename T>
void the_answer<T>::print()
{
    std::cout << "The answer is: " << m_answer << '\n';
}

template class the_answer<int>;
```

As you can see in the preceding example, we added an explicit template declaration. This ensures that we generate the implementations for the class that we expect. The compiler will create the instances for the class that we expect explicitly, just like any other source that we would normally write. The difference is, we can explicitly define this class for whatever types we want. Finally, we will call this code as follows:

```
#include "recipe07.h"

int main(void)
{
    the_answer is{42};
    is.print();

    return 0;
}
```

The output is as follows:

As you can see, we can call our class the same way we would if the class were defined with explicit types instead of a template class using a normal header file that is small and doesn't have the full implementation, allowing the compiler to speed up.

5
Concurrency and Synchronization

In this chapter, we will learn how to properly handle concurrency, synchronization, and parallelism in C++. Here, it is essential that you have a general knowledge of C++ and C++ threads. This chapter is important because working with C++ typically requires the use of shared resources, which can easily become corrupt if thread-safety is not implemented properly. We will start with an extensive overview of `std::mutexes`, which provides a means to synchronizing C++ threads. We will then look at atomic data types, which provide another mechanism for handling parallelism safely.

This chapter has recipes that demonstrate how to handle different scenarios while working with C++ threads, including handling `const &`, thread-safety wrapping, blocking versus asynchronous programming, and C++ promises and futures. This is important, as this knowledge is critical when working with multiple threads of execution.

The following recipes are covered in this chapter:

- Working with mutexes
- Using atomic data types
- Understanding what `const &` mutable mean in the context of multiple threads
- Making a class thread-safe
- Synchronization wrappers and how to implement them
- Blocking operations versus asynchronous programming
- Working with promises and futures

Technical requirements

To compile and run the examples in this chapter, you must have administrative access to a computer running Ubuntu 18.04 with a functional internet connection. Prior to running these examples, you must install the following:

```
> sudo apt-get install build-essential git cmake
```

If this is installed on any operating system other than Ubuntu 18.04, then GCC 7.4 or higher and CMake 3.6 or higher will be required.

Working with mutexes

In this recipe, we will learn why and how to use a mutex in C++. When working with multiple threads in C++, it is common to establish resources that are shared between threads. As we will demonstrate in this recipe, attempting to use these shared resources simultaneously leads to race conditions that are capable of corrupting the resource.

A mutex (in C++, this is written as `std::mutex`) is an object that is used to guard a shared resource, ensuring that more than one thread can access a shared resource in a controlled manner. This prevents it from becoming corrupt.

Getting ready

Before we begin, please ensure that all of the technical requirements are met, including installing Ubuntu 18.04 or higher and running the following in a terminal window:

```
> sudo apt-get install build-essential git
```

This will ensure your operating system has the proper tools to compile and execute the examples in this recipe. Once this is complete, open a new terminal. We will use this terminal to download, compile, and run our examples.

How to do it...

You need to perform the following steps to try this recipe:

1. From a new terminal, run the following to download the source code:

```
> cd ~/
> git clone
https://github.com/PacktPublishing/Advanced-CPP-CookBook.git
> cd Advanced-CPP-CookBook/chapter05
```

2. To compile the source code, run the following:

```
> cmake .
> make recipe01_examples
```

3. Once the source code is compiled, you can execute each example in this recipe by running the following commands:

```
> ./recipe01_example01
The answer is: 42
The answer is: 42
The answer is: 42
The
 answer is: 42
The answer is: 42
...

> ./recipe01_example02
The answer is: 42
The answer is: 42
The answer is: 42
The answer is: 42
The answer is: 42
...

> ./recipe01_example03
...

> ./recipe01_example04
The answer is: 42

> ./recipe01_example05
The answer is: 42
The answer is: 42
The answer is: 42
The answer is: 42
The answer is: 42
```

```
. . .

> ./recipe01_example06
The answer is: 42
The answer is: 42

> ./recipe01_example07

> ./recipe01_example08
lock acquired
lock failed
```

In the next section, we will step through each of these examples and explain what each example program does and how it relates to the lessons being taught in this recipe.

How it works...

In this recipe, we will learn how to use `std::mutex` to protect a shared resource from becoming corrupt. To start, let's first review how a resource could become corrupt when more than one thread is accessing it at the same time:

```cpp
#include <thread>
#include <string>
#include <iostream>

void foo()
{
    static std::string msg{"The answer is: 42\n"};
    while(true) {
        for (const auto &c : msg) {
            std::clog << c;
        }
    }
}

int main(void)
{
    std::thread t1{foo};
    std::thread t2{foo};

    t1.join();
    t2.join();

    // Never reached
    return 0;
}
```

When executed, we get the following output:

In the preceding example, we create a function that outputs to stdout in an endless loop. We then create two threads, with each thread executing the previously defined function. As you can see, when both threads execute, the resulting output becomes corrupt. This is because while one thread is in the middle of outputting its text to stdout, the other thread outputs to stdout at the same time, resulting in the output from one thread being mixed with the output of the other thread.

To deal with this issue, we must ensure that, once one of the threads attempts to output its text to stdout, it should be allowed to finish its output before the other thread is able to output. In other words, each thread must take turns outputting to stdout. While one thread is outputting, the other thread must wait its turn. To do this, we will leverage an std::mutex object.

std::mutex

A mutex is an object that is used to guard a shared resource to ensure the use of the shared resource does not result in corruption. To accomplish this, std::mutex has a lock() function and an unlock() function. The lock function *acquires* access to a shared resource (sometimes referred to as a critical section). unlock() *releases* this previously acquired access. Any attempt to execute the lock() function after another thread has already executed lock() will result in the thread having to wait until the unlock() function is executed.

How std::mutex is implemented depends on the CPU's architecture and the operating system; however, in general, a mutex can be implemented with a simple integer. If the integer is 0, the lock() function will set the integer to 1 and return, which tells the mutex that it is acquired. If the integer is 1, meaning the mutex is already acquired, the lock() function will wait (that is, block) until the integer becomes 0, and then it will set the integer to 1 and return. How this wait is implemented depends on the operating system. For example, the wait() function can loop forever until the integer becomes 0, which is called a **spinlock**, or it can execute a sleep() function and wait for a period of time, allowing other threads and processes to execute while the mutex is locked. The release function always sets the integer to 0, meaning the mutex is no longer acquired. The trick to ensuring the mutex works properly is to ensure the integer is read/written using atomic operations. If non-atomic operations are used, the integer itself would suffer the same shared resource corruption the mutex is trying to prevent.

For example, consider the following:

```
#include <mutex>
#include <thread>
#include <string>
#include <iostream>

std::mutex m{};

void foo()
{
    static std::string msg{"The answer is: 42\n"};
    while(true) {
        m.lock();
        for (const auto &c : msg) {
            std::clog << c;
        }
        m.unlock();
    }
}
```

```
int main(void)
{
    std::thread t1{foo};
    std::thread t2{foo};

    t1.join();
    t2.join();

    // Never reached
    return 0;
}
```

This example, when run, outputs the following:

In the preceding example, we create the same function that outputs to `stdout`. The difference is, before we output to `stdout`, we acquire `std::mutex` by executing the `lock()` function. Once we are done outputting to `stdout`, we release the mutex by executing the `unlock()` function. The code in between the `lock()` and `unlock()` functions is called the **critical region**. Any code in the critical region can only be executed by one thread at any given time, ensuring our use of `stdout` does not become corrupt.

Ensuring shared resources do not become corrupt by controlling access to the shared resource (for example, using a mutex) is called **synchronization**. Although the majority of scenarios where thread synchronization is needed are not complicated, some scenarios can result in thread synchronization schemes that require an entire college course to cover. For this reason, thread synchronization is considered an extremely difficult paradigm in computer science to program correctly.

In this recipe, we will cover some of these scenarios. To start, let's discuss something called a **deadlock**. A deadlock occurs when a thread enters an endless wait state when calling the lock() function. A deadlock is often extremely difficult to debug and is the result of several reasons, including the following:

- A thread never calling unlock() due to programmer error or the thread that acquired the mutex crashing
- The same thread calling the lock() function more than once before it calls unlock()
- Each thread locking more than one mutex in a different order

To demonstrate this, let's look at the following example:

```cpp
#include <mutex>
#include <thread>

std::mutex m{};

void foo()
{
    m.lock();
}

int main(void)
{
    std::thread t1{foo};
    std::thread t2{foo};

    t1.join();
    t2.join();

    // Never reached
    return 0;
}
```

In the preceding example, we create two threads, both of which attempt to lock the mutex but never call `unlock()`. As a result, the first thread acquires the mutex and then returns without releasing it. When the second thread attempts to acquire the mutex, it is forced to wait for the first thread to execute `unlock()`, which it never does, resulting in a deadlock (that is, the program never returns).

Deadlock, in this example, is simple to identify and correct; however, in real-world scenarios, identifying deadlock is a lot more complicated. Let's look at the following example:

```
#include <array>
#include <mutex>
#include <thread>
#include <string>
#include <iostream>

std::mutex m{};
std::array<int,6> numbers{4,8,15,16,23,42};

int foo(int index)
{
    m.lock();
    auto element = numbers.at(index);
    m.unlock();

    return element;
}

int main(void)
{
    std::cout << "The answer is: " << foo(5) << '\n';
    return 0;
}
```

In the preceding example, we wrote a function that returns an element in an array, given an index. In addition, we acquire a mutex that guards the array and releases the mutex just before returning. The challenge here is that we have to `unlock()` the mutex where the function can return, which includes not only every possible branch that returns from the function, but all possible scenarios where an exception could be thrown. In the preceding example, if the index that is provided is larger than the array, the `std::array` object will throw an exception, resulting in the function returning before the function has a chance to call `unlock()`, which would result in deadlock if another thread is sharing this array.

std::lock_guard

Instead of littering your code with `try/catch` blocks to prevent deadlock, which assumes the programmer is even capable of determining every possible scenario where this could occur without making a mistake, C++ provides an `std::lock_guard` object to simplify the use of the `std::mutex` object.

For example, consider the following code:

```cpp
#include <mutex>
#include <thread>
#include <iostream>

std::mutex m{};

void foo()
{
    static std::string msg{"The answer is: 42\n"};

    while(true) {
        std::lock_guard lock(m);
        for (const auto &c : msg) {
            std::clog << c;
        }
    }
}

int main(void)
{
    std::thread t1{foo};
    std::thread t2{foo};

    t1.join();
    t2.join();

    // Never reached
    return 0;
}
```

When executed, we see the following:

As shown in the preceding example, `std::lock_guard` is used when we would normally call `lock()` on the mutex. `std::lock_guard` calls the `lock()` function on the mutex when it is created and then calls `unlock()` on the mutex when it is destroyed (an idiom called **Resource Acquisition Is Initialization** or **RAII**). No matter how the function returns (either from a normal return or an exception), the mutex will always be released, ensuring deadlock is not possible, preventing the programmer from having to accurately determine every possible scenario where the function could return.

Although `std::lock_guard` is capable of preventing deadlock in cases where `unlock()` is never called, it is not capable of preventing deadlock from occurring in cases where `lock()` is called by the same thread more than once prior to `unlock()` being called. To handle this scenario, C++ provides `std::recursive_mutex`.

std::recursive_mutex

A recursive mutex increments the integer stored inside the mutex each time the same thread calls the `lock()` function without causing the `lock()` function to wait. For example, if the mutex is released (that is, the integer in the mutex is 0), when thread #1 calls the `lock()` function, the integer in the mutex is set to 1. Normally, if thread #1 calls the `lock()` function again, the `lock()` function would see that the integer is 1 and enter a wait state until the integer is set to 0. Instead, a recursive mutex will determine which thread is calling the `lock()` function, and, if the thread that acquired the mutex is the same thread calling the `lock()` function, the integer in the mutex is incremented again (now resulting in 2) using an atomic operation. For the mutex to be released, the thread must call `unlock()`, which decrements the integer using an atomic operation, until the integer in the mutex is 0.

The recursive mutex allows the same thread to call the `lock()` function as many times as it wants, preventing multiple calls to the `lock()` function and resulting in deadlock at the expense that the `lock()` and `unlock()` functions must include an added function call to get the thread's `id()` instance, so that the mutex can determine which thread is calling `lock()` and `unlock()`.

For example, consider the following code snippet:

```cpp
#include <mutex>
#include <thread>
#include <string>
#include <iostream>

std::recursive_mutex m{};

void foo()
{
    m.lock();
    m.lock();

    std::cout << "The answer is: 42\n";

    m.unlock();
    m.unlock();
}

int main(void)
{
    std::thread t1{foo};
    std::thread t2{foo};

    t1.join();
```

```
    t2.join();

    return 0;
}
```

The preceding example results in the following:

In the preceding example, we define a function that calls the `lock()` function for a recursive mutex twice, outputs to `stdout`, and then calls the `unlock()` function twice. We then create two threads that execute this function, resulting in no corruption to `stdout` and no deadlock.

std::shared_mutex

Up until this point, our synchronization primitives have serialized access to our shared resource. That is, each thread must execute one at a time when accessing the critical region. Although this ensures corruption is not possible, it is inefficient for certain types of scenarios. To better understand this, we must examine what causes corruption in the first place.

Let's consider an integer variable that is incremented by two threads simultaneously. The process for incrementing an integer variable is as follows: $i = i + 1$.

Let's write this as follows:

```
int i = 0;

auto tmp = i;
tmp++;
i = tmp; // i == 1
```

To prevent corruption, we use a mutex to ensure that if two threads increment the integer, they do so synchronously:

```
auto tmp_thread1 = i;
tmp_thread1++;
i = tmp_thread1; // i == 1
```

```
auto tmp_thread2 = i;
tmp_thread2++;
i = tmp_thread2; // i == 2
```

Corruption occurs when these operations mix (that is, when both operations execute simultaneously in different threads). For example, consider this code:

```
auto tmp_thread1 = i; // 0
auto tmp_thread2 = i; // 0
tmp_thread1++; // 1
tmp_thread2++; // 1
i = tmp_thread1; // i == 1
i = tmp_thread2; // i == 1
```

Instead of the integer being 2, it is 1, because the integer is read before the first increment is allowed to finish. This scenario is possible because both threads are attempting to write to the same shared resource. We call these types of threads **producers**.

What if, however, we create a million threads that read the shared resource simultaneously. Since the integer never changes, no matter what order the threads execute in, they will all read the same value, and therefore corruption is not possible. We call these threads **consumers**. If we only ever have consumers, we do not need thread synchronization as corruption is not possible.

Finally, what happens if we have the same 1 million consumers, but we add a single producer to the mix? Now, we must use thread synchronization because it is possible that while the producer is in the middle of attempting to write a value to the integer that a consumer attempts to read, it will result in a corrupt result. To prevent this, we must use a mutex to guard the integer. If we use std::mutex, however, all 1 million consumers would have to wait on each other, even though the consumers themselves can safely execute simultaneously without the fear of corruption. It is only when the producer attempts to execute that we must be worried.

To handle this obvious performance problem, C++ provides the std::shared_mutex object. For example, consider this code:

```
#include <mutex>
#include <shared_mutex>
#include <thread>
#include <iostream>

int count_rw{};
const auto &count_ro = count_rw;

std::shared_mutex m{};
```

```
void reader()
{
    while(true) {
        std::shared_lock lock(m);
        if (count_ro >= 42) {
            return;
        }
    }
}

void writer()
{
    while(true) {
        std::unique_lock lock(m);
        if (++count_rw == 100) {
            return;
        }
    }
}

int main(void)
{
    std::thread t1{reader};
    std::thread t2{reader};
    std::thread t3{reader};
    std::thread t4{reader};
    std::thread t5{writer};

    t1.join();
    t2.join();
    t3.join();
    t4.join();
    t5.join();

    return 0;
}
```

In the preceding example, we create a producer function (called the `reader` function) and a consumer function (called the `writer` function). The producer locks the mutex using `std::unique_lock()`, while the consumer locks the mutex using `std::shared_lock()`. Whenever the mutex is locked using `std::unique_lock()`, all other threads must wait (producer and consumer alike). If, however, the mutex is locked using `std::shared_lock()`, additional attempts to lock the mutex using `std::shared_lock()` do not result in the thread waiting.

It's only when `std::unique_lock()` is called that a wait must occur. This allows the consumers to execute without waiting on each other. It's only when the producer attempts to execute that the consumers must wait, preventing the consumers from serializing each other, ultimately resulting in better performance (especially if the number of consumers is 1 million).

It should be noted that we use the `const` keyword to ensure that a consumer is not a producer. This simple trick ensures that the programmer doesn't accidentally think they have programmed a consumer when, in fact, they have created a producer, as the compiler would warn the programmer if this occurred.

std::timed_mutex

Finally, we have not dealt with the scenario where a thread that acquired a mutex crashed. In this scenario, any thread that attempts to acquire the same mutex would enter a deadlock state as the thread that crashed never gets a chance to call `unlock()`. One way to prevent this issue is to use `std::timed_mutex`.

For example, consider the following code:

```cpp
#include <mutex>
#include <thread>
#include <iostream>

std::timed_mutex m{};

void foo()
{
    using namespace std::chrono;

    if (m.try_lock_for(seconds(1))) {
        std::cout << "lock acquired\n";
    }
    else {
        std::cout << "lock failed\n";
    }
}

int main(void)
{
    std::thread t1{foo};
    std::thread t2{foo};

    t1.join();
    t2.join();
```

```
    return 0;
}
```

When this is executed, we get the following:

In the preceding example, we tell C++ that the thread is only allowed to wait for 1 second. If the mutex is already acquired and it is not released after 1 second, the `try_lock_for()` function will exit and return false, allowing the thread to gracefully exit and handle the error without entering a deadlock.

Using atomic data types

In this recipe, we will learn how to use atomic data types in C++. Atomic data types provide the ability to read and write simple data types (that is, a Boolean or integer) without the need for thread synchronization (that is, the use of `std::mutex` and friends). To accomplish this, atomic data types are implemented using special CPU instructions that ensure when an operation is executed, it is done so as a single, atomic operation.

For example, incrementing an integer can be written as follows:

```
int i = 0;

auto tmp = i;
tmp++;
i = tmp; // i == 1
```

An atomic data type ensures that this increment is executed such that no other attempts to increment the integer simultaneously can interleave, and therefore result in corruption. How this is done by the CPU is out of the scope of this book. That's because this is extremely complicated in modern, super-scalar, pipelined CPUs that support the execution of instructions in parallel, out-of-order, and speculatively on multiple cores and sockets.

Getting ready

Before we begin, please ensure that all of the technical requirements are met, including installing Ubuntu 18.04 or higher and running the following in a terminal window:

```
> sudo apt-get install build-essential git
```

This will ensure your operating system has the proper tools to compile and execute the examples in this recipe. Once this is complete, open a new terminal. We will use this terminal to download, compile, and run our examples.

How to do it...

You need to perform the following steps to try this recipe:

1. From a new terminal, run the following to download the source code:

   ```
   > cd ~/
   > git clone
   https://github.com/PacktPublishing/Advanced-CPP-CookBook.git
   > cd Advanced-CPP-CookBook/chapter05
   ```

2. To compile the source code, run the following:

   ```
   > cmake .
   > make recipe02_examples
   ```

3. Once the source code is compiled, you can execute each example in this recipe by running the following commands:

   ```
   > ./recipe02_example01
   count: 711
   atomic count: 1000
   ```

In the next section, we will step through each of these examples and explain what each example program does and how it relates to the lessons being taught in this recipe.

How it works...

In this recipe, we will learn how to use C++'s atomic data types. Atomic data types are limited to simple data types such as integers, and since these data types are extremely complicated to implement, the only operations that are supported are simple operations such as add, subtract, increment, and decrement.

Let's take a look at a simple example that not only demonstrates how to use an atomic data type in C++, but also demonstrates why atomic data types are so important:

```cpp
#include <atomic>
#include <thread>
#include <iostream>

int count{};
std::atomic<int> atomic_count{};

void foo()
{
    do {
        count++;
        atomic_count++;
    }
    while (atomic_count < 99999);
}

int main(void)
{
    std::thread t1{foo};
    std::thread t2{foo};

    t1.join();
    t2.join();

    std::cout << "count: " << count << '\n';
    std::cout << "atomic count: " << atomic_count << '\n';

    return 0;
}
```

When this code is executed, we get the following:

```
[~/book/chapter05/build]: ./recipe02_example01
count: 31789
atomic count: 100000
[~/book/chapter05/build]:
```

In the preceding example, we have two integers. The first integer is a normal C/C++ integer type, while the second is an atomic data type (of type integer). We then define a function that loops until the atomic data type is `1000`. Finally, we execute this function from two threads, which means our global integers are incremented by two threads simultaneously.

As you can see, the output of this simple test shows that the simple C/C++ integer data type is not the same value as the atomic data type, yet both are incremented the same number of times. The reason for this can be seen in the assembly of this function (on an Intel CPU), as follows:

```
user@localhost:~/book/chapter05/build                                         —   □   ✕
[~/book/chapter05/build]: objdump -d recipe02_example01 | grep "<_Z3foov>" -A 18
0000000000401206 <_Z3foov>:
  401206:     55                    push    %rbp
  401207:     48 89 e5              mov     %rsp,%rbp
  40120a:     8b 05 a4 2f 00 00     mov     0x2fa4(%rip),%eax        # 4041b4 <count>
  401210:     83 c0 01              add     $0x1,%eax
  401213:     89 05 9b 2f 00 00     mov     %eax,0x2f9b(%rip)        # 4041b4 <count>
  401219:     be 00 00 00 00        mov     $0x0,%esi
  40121e:     bf b8 41 40 00        mov     $0x4041b8,%edi
  401223:     e8 00 02 00 00        callq   401428 <_ZNSt13__atomic_baseIiEppEi>
  401228:     bf b8 41 40 00        mov     $0x4041b8,%edi
  40122d:     e8 26 02 00 00        callq   401458 <_ZNKSt13__atomic_baseIiEcviEv>
  401232:     3d 9e 86 01 00        cmp     $0x1869e,%eax
  401237:     0f 9e c0              setle   %al
  40123a:     84 c0                 test    %al,%al
  40123c:     74 02                 je      401240 <_Z3foov+0x3a>
  40123e:     eb ca                 jmp     40120a <_Z3foov+0x4>
  401240:     90                    nop
  401241:     5d                    pop     %rbp
  401242:     c3                    retq
[~/book/chapter05/build]:
```

To increment an integer (without optimizations enabled), the compiler must move the contents of memory into a register, add 1 to the register, and then write the results of the register back to memory. Since this code is executing simultaneously in two different threads, this code interleaves, resulting in corruption. The atomic data type does not suffer this same problem. This is because the process of incrementing the atomic data type occurs in a single, special instruction that the CPU ensures to execute, without interleaving its internal state with the same internal state of other instructions, on other CPUs.

Atomic data types are typically used to implement synchronization primitives such as std::mutex (although, in practice, std::mutex is implemented using test and set instructions, which use a similar principle but oftentimes execute faster than atomic instructions). These data types can also be used to implement special data structures called lock-free data structures, which are capable of operating in multithreaded environments without the need for std::mutex. The benefit of lockless data structures is that there are no wait states when dealing with thread synchronization at the expense of more complicated CPU hardware and other types of performance penalties (most CPU optimizations provided by the hardware have to be temporarily disabled when the CPU encounters an atomic instruction). So, like anything in computer science, they have their time and place.

Understanding what const & mutable mean in the context of multiple threads

In this recipe, we will learn how to deal with objects that are labeled `const`, but contain `std::mutex` that must be used to ensure thread synchronization. This recipe is important because it is useful to store `std::mutex` as a private member of a class, but, as soon as you do this, passing an instance of this object as a constant reference (that is, `const &`) will result in a compiler error. In this recipe, we will demonstrate why this occurs and how to overcome it.

Getting ready

Before we begin, please ensure that all of the technical requirements are met, including installing Ubuntu 18.04 or higher and running the following in a terminal window:

```
> sudo apt-get install build-essential git
```

This will ensure your operating system has the proper tools to compile and execute the examples in this recipe. Once this is complete, open a new terminal. We will use this terminal to download, compile, and run our examples.

How to do it...

You need to perform the following steps to try this recipe:

1. From a new terminal, run the following to download the source code:

```
> cd ~/
> git clone https://github.com/PacktPublishing/Advanced-CPP-CookBook.git
> cd Advanced-CPP-CookBook/chapter05
```

2. To compile the source code, run the following:

```
> cmake .
> make recipe03_examples
```

3. Once the source code is compiled, you can execute each example in this recipe by running the following commands:

```
> ./recipe03_example01
The answer is: 42

> ./recipe03_example03
The answer is: 42
```

In the next section, we will step through each of these examples and explain what each example program does and how it relates to the lessons being taught in this recipe.

How it works...

In this recipe, we will learn how to add `std::mutex` to a class's private members while still being able to handle `const` scenarios. Generally speaking, there are two ways to ensure an object is thread-safe. The first method is to place `std::mutex` at the global level. Doing this ensures an object can be passed as a constant reference or the object itself can have a function marked as `const`.

For this, consider the following code example:

```cpp
#include <mutex>
#include <thread>
#include <iostream>

std::mutex m{};

class the_answer
{
public:
    void print() const
    {
        std::lock_guard lock(m);
        std::cout << "The answer is: 42\n";
    }
};

int main(void)
{
    the_answer is;
    is.print();

    return 0;
}
```

In the preceding example, we create an object that outputs to `stdout` when the `print()` function is executed. The `print()` function is labeled as `const`, which tells the compiler that the `print()` function will not modify any class members (that is, the function is read-only). Since `std::mutex` is global, the const-qualifier of the object is maintained and the code compiles and executes without an issue.

The problem with a global `std::mutex` object is that every instance of the object must use the same `std::mutex` object. This is fine if the user intends this, but what if you want each instance of the object to have its own `std::mutex` object (for example, when the same instance of the object might be executed by more than one thread)?

For this, let's take a look at how that happens using the following example:

```cpp
#include <mutex>
#include <thread>
#include <iostream>

class the_answer
{
    std::mutex m{};

public:
    void print() const
    {
        std::lock_guard lock(m);
        std::cout << "The answer is: 42\n";
    }
};

int main(void)
{
    the_answer is;
    is.print();

    return 0;
}
```

If we attempt to compile this, we get the following:

In the preceding example, all we did was take the previous example and move `std::mutex` inside the class as a private member. As a result, when we attempt to compile the class, we get a compiler error. This is because the `print()` function is marked as `const`, which tells the compiler that the `print()` function will not modify any of the class's members. The problem is that when you attempt to lock `std::mutex`, you must modify it, resulting in a compiler error.

To overcome this, we must tell the compiler to ignore this error by marking `std::mutex` as mutable. Marking a member as mutable tells the compiler that the member is allowed to be modified, even when the object is passed as a constant reference or when the object defines a constant function.

For example, this is how the code appears on `const` marked as `mutable`:

```
#include <mutex>
#include <thread>
#include <iostream>

class the_answer
{
    mutable std::mutex m{};

public:
    void print() const
    {
        std::lock_guard lock(m);
        std::cout << "The answer is: 42\n";
```

```
    }
};

int main(void)
{
    the_answer is;
    is.print();

    return 0;
}
```

As you can see in the preceding example, once we mark `std::mutex` as mutable, the code compiles and executes as we would expect. It should be noted that `std::mutex` is one of the few examples for which the use of mutable is acceptable. The mutable keyword can easily be abused, resulting in code that doesn't compile or operate as expected.

Making a class thread-safe

In this recipe, we will learn how to make a class thread-safe (that is, how to ensure a class's public member functions can be called at any time, by any number of threads simultaneously). Most classes, especially those provided by the C++ standard library are not thread-safe and, instead, assume the user will add thread-synchronization primitives such as an `std::mutex` object as needed. The problem with this approach is that every object has two instances that must be tracked in code: the class itself and its `std::mutex`. The user must also wrap each of the object's functions with custom versions that protect the class using `std::mutex`, resulting in not only two objects that must be managed, but also a bunch of C-style wrapper functions.

This recipe is important because it will demonstrate how to address these issues in your code by making a thread-safe class, which combines everything into a single class.

Getting ready

Before we begin, please ensure that all of the technical requirements are met, including installing Ubuntu 18.04 or higher and running the following in a terminal window:

```
> sudo apt-get install build-essential git
```

This will ensure your operating system has the proper tools to compile and execute the examples in this recipe. Once this is complete, open a new terminal. We will use this terminal to download, compile, and run our examples.

How to do it...

You need to perform the following steps to try this recipe:

1. From a new terminal, run the following to download the source code:

```
> cd ~/
> git clone
https://github.com/PacktPublishing/Advanced-CPP-CookBook.git
> cd Advanced-CPP-CookBook/chapter05
```

2. To compile the source code, run the following:

```
> cmake .
> make recipe04_examples
```

3. Once the source code is compiled, you can execute each example in this recipe by running the following commands:

```
> ./recipe04_example01
```

In the next section, we will step through each of these examples and explain what each example program does and how it relates to the lessons being taught in this recipe.

How it works...

In this recipe, we will learn how to make a thread-safe class by implementing our own thread-safe stack. The C++ standard library does not provide thread-safe data structures, and, as a result, if you wish to use a data structure as a global resource across multiple threads, you add thread-safety manually. This can be done by implementing wrapper functions, or by creating a wrapper class.

The advantage of creating wrapper functions is that, for global objects, the amount of code that is needed is oftentimes smaller and easier to understand, while the advantage of a thread-safe class is that you can create multiple instances of the class, as std::mutex is self-contained.

This can be tried with the following code example:

```cpp
#include <mutex>
#include <stack>
#include <iostream>

template<typename T>
class my_stack
```

```
{
    std::stack<T> m_stack;
    mutable std::mutex m{};

public:

    template<typename ARG>
    void push(ARG &&arg)
    {
        std::lock_guard lock(m);
        m_stack.push(std::forward<ARG>(arg));
    }

  void pop()
    {
        std::lock_guard lock(m);
        m_stack.pop();
    }

    auto empty() const
    {
        std::lock_guard lock(m);
        return m_stack.empty();
    }
};
```

In the preceding example, we implement our own stack. This stack has `std::stack` and `std::mutex` as member variables. We then reimplement some of the functions the `std::stack` provides. Each of these functions first attempts to acquire `std::mutex` and then calls the associated function in `std::stack`. In the case of the `push()` function, we leverage `std::forward` to ensure the arguments passed to the `push()` function are preserved.

Finally, we can use our custom stack the same way we would use `std::stack`. For example, take a look at the following code:

```
int main(void)
{
    my_stack<int> s;

    s.push(4);
    s.push(8);
    s.push(15);
    s.push(16);
    s.push(23);
    s.push(42);
```

```
    while(s.empty()) {
        s.pop();
    }

    return 0;
}
```

As you can see, the only difference between `std::stack` and our custom stack is that our stack is thread-safe.

Synchronization wrappers and how to implement them

In this recipe, we will learn how to make thread-safe synchronization wrappers. By default, the C++ standard library is not thread-safe as not all applications will need this functionality. One mechanism to ensure the C++ standard library is thread-safe is to create a thread-safe class, which adds the data structure you wish to use as well as `std::mutex` to the class as private members, and then reimplements the data structure's functions to first acquire `std::mutex` and then forward the function call to the data structure. The problem with this approach is there is a lot of extra code that is added to your program if the data structure is a global resource, making the resulting code hard to read and maintain.

This recipe is important because it will demonstrate how to address these issues in your code by making thread-safe synchronization wrappers.

Getting ready

Before we begin, please ensure that all of the technical requirements are met, including installing Ubuntu 18.04 or higher and running the following in a terminal window:

```
> sudo apt-get install build-essential git
```

This will ensure your operating system has the proper tools to compile and execute the examples in this recipe. Once this is complete, open a new terminal. We will use this terminal to download, compile, and run our examples.

How to do it...

You need to perform the following steps to try this recipe:

1. From a new terminal, run the following to download the source code:

```
> cd ~/
> git clone
https://github.com/PacktPublishing/Advanced-CPP-CookBook.git
> cd Advanced-CPP-CookBook/chapter05
```

2. To compile the source code, run the following:

```
> cmake .
> make recipe05_examples
```

3. Once the source code is compiled, you can execute each example in this recipe by running the following command:

```
> ./recipe05_example01
```

In the next section, we will step through each of these examples and explain what each example program does and how it relates to the lessons being taught in this recipe.

How it works...

In this recipe, we will learn how to create thread-safe synchronization wrappers, which allow us to add thread-safety to the C++ standard library data structures, which, by default, are not thread-safe.

To do this, we will create wrapper functions for each function in the C++ standard library that we intend to use. These wrapper functions will first attempt to acquire std::mutex, before forwarding the same function call to the C++ standard library data structure.

To do this, consider the following code example:

```cpp
#include <mutex>
#include <stack>
#include <iostream>

std::mutex m{};

template<typename S, typename T>
void push(S &s, T &&t)
{
```

```
        std::lock_guard lock(m);
        s.push(std::forward<T>(t));
}

template<typename S>
void pop(S &s)
{
        std::lock_guard lock(m);
        s.pop();
}

template<typename S>
auto empty(S &s)
{
        std::lock_guard lock(m);
        return s.empty();
}
```

In the preceding example, we have created a wrapper function for the `push()`, `pop()`, and `empty()` functions. These functions attempt to acquire our global `std::mutex` object before calling the data structure, which, in this case, is a template. The use of a template creates what is called a concept. Our wrapper functions can be used by any data structure that implements `push()`, `pop()`, and `empty()`. Also, note that we use `std::forward` in our `push()` function to ensure the l-valueness and CV qualifiers of the argument being pushed remain unchanged.

Finally, we can use our wrappers the same way we would use the data structure's functions, with the slight difference being that the data structure is passed as the first argument. For example, take a look at the following code block:

```
int main(void)
{
        std::stack<int> mystack;

        push(mystack, 4);
        push(mystack, 8);
        push(mystack, 15);
        push(mystack, 16);
        push(mystack, 23);
        push(mystack, 42);

        while(empty(mystack)) {
                pop(mystack);
        }

        return 0;
}
```

As you can see in the preceding example, the use of our synchronization wrappers is simple, while ensuring the stack that we created is now thread-safe.

Blocking operations versus asynchronous programming

In this recipe, we will learn the difference between a blocking operation and an asynchronous operation. This recipe is important because blocking operations serialize the execution of each operation on a single CPU. This is typically fine if the execution of each operation must be executed in serial order; however, if these operations can be executed in parallel, asynchronous programming can be a useful optimization, ensuring that, while an operation is waiting, others can still execute on the same CPU.

Getting ready

Before we begin, please ensure that all of the technical requirements are met, including installing Ubuntu 18.04 or higher and running the following in a terminal window:

```
> sudo apt-get install build-essential git
```

This will ensure that your operating system has the proper tools to compile and execute the examples in this recipe. Once this is complete, open a new terminal. We will use this terminal to download, compile, and run our examples.

How to do it...

You need to perform the following steps to try this recipe:

1. From a new terminal, run the following to download the source code:

```
> cd ~/
> git clone
https://github.com/PacktPublishing/Advanced-CPP-CookBook.git
> cd Advanced-CPP-CookBook/chapter05
```

2. To compile the source code, run the following:

```
> cmake .
> make recipe06_examples
```

3. Once the source code is compiled, you can execute each example in this recipe by running the following commands:

```
> time ./recipe06_example01
999999
999999
999999
999999

real 0m1.477s
. . .

> time ./recipe06_example02
999999
999999
999999
999999

real 0m1.058s
. . .

> time ./recipe06_example03
999999
999999
999998
999999

real 0m1.140s
. . .
```

In the next section, we will step through each of these examples and explain what each example program does and how it relates to the lessons being taught in this recipe.

How it works...

A blocking operation is an operation that must be completed before the next operation can take place. Most programs are written serially, meaning each instruction must execute before the next instruction. The problem, however, is that some operations can be executed in parallel (that is, either concurrently or asynchronously). Serializing these operations can, in the best case, lead to poor performance and, in some cases, can actually lead to deadlock (the program entering an endless wait state) if the operation that is blocking is waiting on another operation that is never given a chance to execute.

To demonstrate a blocking operation, let's examine the following:

```
#include <vector>
#include <iostream>
#include <algorithm>

constexpr auto size = 1000000;

int main(void)
{
    std::vector<int> numbers1(size);
    std::vector<int> numbers2(size);
    std::vector<int> numbers3(size);
    std::vector<int> numbers4(size);
```

The preceding code creates a main function with four `std::vector` objects of the `int` type. In the following steps, we will use these vectors to demonstrate a blocking operation:

1. First, we create four vectors that we can store integers in:

    ```
    std::generate(numbers1.begin(), numbers1.end(), []() {
      return rand() % size;
    });
    std::generate(numbers2.begin(), numbers2.end(), []() {
      return rand() % size;
    });
    std::generate(numbers3.begin(), numbers3.end(), []() {
      return rand() % size;
    });
    std::generate(numbers4.begin(), numbers4.end(), []() {
      return rand() % size;
    });
    ```

2. Next, we fill each array with random numbers using `std::generate`, which results in an array with numbers and a random order:

    ```
    std::sort(numbers1.begin(), numbers1.end());
    std::sort(numbers2.begin(), numbers2.end());
    std::sort(numbers3.begin(), numbers3.end());
    std::sort(numbers4.begin(), numbers4.end());
    ```

3. Next, we sort the array of integers, which is the main goal of this example, as this operation takes a while to execute:

    ```
    std::cout << numbers1.back() << '\n';
    std::cout << numbers2.back() << '\n';
    std::cout << numbers3.back() << '\n';
    std::cout << numbers4.back() << '\n';
    ```

```
        return 0;
    }
```

4. Finally, we output the last entry in each array, which will usually be `999999` (but doesn't have to be since the numbers were generated using a random number generator).

The problem with the preceding example is that the operations could be executed in parallel because each array is independent. To address this, we can execute these operations asynchronously, meaning the arrays will be created, filled, sorted, and outputted in parallel. For example, consider the following code:

```cpp
#include <future>
#include <thread>
#include <vector>
#include <iostream>
#include <algorithm>

constexpr auto size = 1000000;

int foo()
{
    std::vector<int> numbers(size);
    std::generate(numbers.begin(), numbers.end(), []() {
      return rand() % size;
    });

    std::sort(numbers.begin(), numbers.end());
    return numbers.back();
}
```

The first thing we do is implement a function called `foo()` that creates our vector, fills it with random numbers, sorts the list, and returns the last entry in the array (which is identical to the preceding example with the exception that we only work with one array at a time and not 4):

```cpp
int main(void)
{
    auto a1 = std::async(std::launch::async, foo);
    auto a2 = std::async(std::launch::async, foo);
    auto a3 = std::async(std::launch::async, foo);
    auto a4 = std::async(std::launch::async, foo);

    std::cout << a1.get() << '\n';
    std::cout << a2.get() << '\n';
    std::cout << a3.get() << '\n';
    std::cout << a4.get() << '\n';
```

```
        return 0;
    }
```

We then use `std::async` to execute this `foo()` function four times, resulting in the same four arrays, just like our previous example. The `std::async()` function in this example does the same thing as executing four threads manually. The result of `std::aync()` is a `std::future` object, which stores the result of the function once it has finished executing. The last thing we do in this example is use the `get()` function to return the value of the function once it is ready.

If we time the results of these functions, we can see that the asynchronous version is faster than the blocking version. The following code shows this (the `real` time is the time to look for):

```
user@localhost:~/book/chapter05/build                          —    □   ✕
[~/book/chapter05/build]: time ./recipe06_example02
999999
999999
999997
999999

real      0m0.608s
user      0m2.153s
sys       0m0.156s
[~/book/chapter05/build]:
```

The `std::async()` function can also be used to execute our array function asynchronously in the same thread. For example, consider the following code:

```
int main(void)
{
    auto a1 = std::async(std::launch::deferred, foo);
    auto a2 = std::async(std::launch::deferred, foo);
    auto a3 = std::async(std::launch::deferred, foo);
    auto a4 = std::async(std::launch::deferred, foo);

    std::cout << a1.get() << '\n';
    std::cout << a2.get() << '\n';
    std::cout << a3.get() << '\n';
    std::cout << a4.get() << '\n';

    return 0;
}
```

As you can see in the preceding example, we changed the operation from `std::launch::async` to `std::launch::deferred`, which results in each function executing once the result of the function is needed (that is, when the `get()` function is called). This is useful if you are not sure whether the function needs to execute in the first place (that is, only execute the function when needed), with the downside being that the execution of the program is slower, as threads are not typically used as an optimization method.

Working with promises and futures

In this recipe, we will learn how to use C++ promises and futures. C++ `promise` is an argument to a C++ thread, while C++ `future` is the return value of the thread, and can be used to manually implement the same functionality of an `std::async` call. This recipe is important because a call to `std::aync` requires that each thread stops execution to get its result, while manually implementing a C++ `promise` and `future` allows the user to get the return value of a thread while the thread is still executing.

Getting ready

Before we begin, please ensure that all of the technical requirements are met, including installing Ubuntu 18.04 or higher and running the following in a terminal window:

```
> sudo apt-get install build-essential git
```

This will ensure your operating system has the proper tools to compile and execute the examples in this recipe. Once this is complete, open a new terminal. We will use this terminal to download, compile, and run our examples.

How to do it...

You need to perform the following steps to try this recipe:

1. From a new terminal, run the following to download the source code:

```
> cd ~/
> git clone
https://github.com/PacktPublishing/Advanced-CPP-CookBook.git
> cd Advanced-CPP-CookBook/chapter05
```

2. To compile the source code, run the following:

```
> cmake .
> make recipe07_examples
```

3. Once the source code is compiled, you can execute each example in this recipe by running the following commands:

```
> ./recipe07_example01
The answer is: 42

> ./recipe07_example02
The answer is: 42
```

In the next section, we will step through each of these examples and explain what each example program does and how it relates to the lessons being taught in this recipe.

How it works...

In this recipe, we will learn how to manually use a C++ promise and future to provide a function that is executed in parallel with an argument, as well as get the function's return value. To start, let's demonstrate how this is done in its most simplistic form, with the following code:

```cpp
#include <thread>
#include <iostream>
#include <future>

void foo(std::promise<int> promise)
{
    promise.set_value(42);
}

int main(void)
{
    std::promise<int> promise;
    auto future = promise.get_future();

    std::thread t{foo, std::move(promise)};
    t.join();

    std::cout << "The answer is: " << future.get() << '\n';

    return 0;
}
```

The preceding example results in the following when executed:

As you can see in the preceding code, the C++ `promise` is an argument to the function that is threaded. The thread returns its value by setting the `promise` argument, which, in turn, sets a C++ `future` that the user can get from the `promise` argument it provides to the thread. It should be noted that we use `std::move()` to prevent the `promise` argument from being copied (which the compiler will prohibit as the C++ `promise` is a move-only class). Finally, we use the `get()` function to get the result of the thread, the same way you would get the result of a thread executed using `std::async`.

One of the benefits of using `promise` and `future` manually is that you can get the result of the thread before it completes, allowing the thread to continue to do work. For example, take a look at the following:

```cpp
#include <thread>
#include <iostream>
#include <future>

void foo(std::promise<int> promise)
{
    promise.set_value(42);
    while (true);
}

int main(void)
{
    std::promise<int> promise;
    auto future = promise.get_future();

    std::thread t{foo, std::move(promise)};

    future.wait();
    std::cout << "The answer is: " << future.get() << '\n';

    t.join();

    // Never reached
    return 0;
}
```

This results in the following when executed:

In the preceding example, we created the same thread, but we looped forever in the thread, meaning the thread will never return. We then created the thread the same way, but outputted the result of the C++ `future` as soon as it was ready, which we can determine using the `wait()` function.

6
Optimizing Your Code for Performance

Optimizing your code for performance ensures your code is getting the most out of what C++ can offer. Unlike other high-level languages, C++ is capable of providing high-level syntactical freedom without sacrificing performance, although admittedly at the expense of a higher learning curve.

This chapter is important because it will demonstrate more advanced methods for optimizing your code, including how to benchmark your software at the unit level, how to examine the resulting assembly code your compiler produces for potential optimizations, how to reduce the number of memory resources your application is using, and why compiler hints such as `noexcept` are important. After reading this chapter, you will have the skills to write more efficient C++.

In this chapter, we will cover the following recipes:

- Benchmarking your code
- Looking at assembly code
- Reducing the number of memory allocations
- Declaring noexcept

Technical requirements

To compile and run the examples in this chapter, you must have administrative access to a computer running Ubuntu 18.04 with a functional internet connection. Prior to running these examples, you must install the following:

```
> sudo apt-get install build-essential git cmake valgrind
```

If this is installed on any operating system other than Ubuntu 18.04, then GCC 7.4 or higher and CMake 3.6 or higher will be required.

Benchmarking your code

In this recipe, you will learn how to benchmark and optimize your source code. Optimizing source code will result in more efficient C++, which increases battery life, improves performance, and so on. This recipe is important as the process of optimizing source code starts with determining which resource you plan to optimize, which could include speed, memory, and even power. Without benchmarking tools, it is extremely difficult to compare different approaches to the same problem.

There are countless benchmarking tools (anything that measures a single property of your program) available to C++ programmers, including C++ APIs such as Boost, Folly, and Abseil, and CPU-specific tools such as Intel's vTune. There are also several profiling tools (anything the helps you understand the behavior of your program) such as valgrind and gprof. In this recipe, we will focus on two of these: Hayai and Valgrind. Hayai provides a simple example of a micro-benchmarking, while Valgrind provides an example of a more complete, though more complicated, dynamic analysis/profiling tool.

Getting ready

Before beginning, please ensure that all of the technical requirements have been met, including installing Ubuntu 18.04 or higher and running the following in a Terminal window:

```
> sudo apt-get install build-essential git valgrind cmake
```

This will ensure your operating system has the proper tools to compile and execute the examples in this recipe. Once you've done this, open a new Terminal. We will use this Terminal to download, compile, and run our examples.

How to do it...

Perform the following steps to complete this recipe:

1. From a new Terminal, run the following to download the source code:

```
> cd ~/
> git clone
https://github.com/PacktPublishing/Advanced-CPP-CookBook.git
> cd Advanced-CPP-CookBook/chapter06
```

2. To compile the source code, run the following command:

```
> cmake -DCMAKE_BUILD_TYPE=Debug .
> make recipe01_examples
```

3. Once the source code has been compiled, you can execute each example in this recipe by running the following commands:

```
> ./recipe01_example01
[==========] Running 2 benchmarks.
[ RUN ] vector.push_back (10 runs, 100 iterations per run)
[ DONE ] vector.push_back (0.200741 ms)
. . .
[ RUN ] vector.emplace_back (10 runs, 100 iterations per run)
[ DONE ] vector.emplace_back (0.166699 ms)
. . .

> ./recipe01_example02
```

In the next section, we will step through each of these examples and explain what each example program does and how it relates to the lessons being taught in this recipe.

How it works...

The most common optimization that's applied to C++ is the speed of execution. To optimize C++ for speed, we must start by developing different approaches to the same problem and then benchmark each solution to determine which solution executes the fastest. Benchmarking tools such as Hayai, a C++ based benchmarking library on GitHub, aid in making this determination. To explain this, let's look at a simple example:

```
#include <string>
#include <vector>
#include <hayai.hpp>
```

```cpp
std::vector<std::string> data;

BENCHMARK(vector, push_back, 10, 100)
{
    data.push_back("The answer is: 42");
}

BENCHMARK(vector, emplace_back, 10, 100)
{
    data.emplace_back("The answer is: 42");
}
```

When we execute the preceding code, we get the following output:

In the preceding example, we use the Hayai library to benchmark the performance difference between adding a string to a vector using push_back() versus emplace_back(). The difference between push_back() and emplace_back() is that push_back() creates the object and then copies or moves it into the vector, while emplace_back() creates the object in the vector itself without the need for the temporary object and subsequent copy/move. That is to say, if you use push_back(), an object must be constructed and then either copied or moved into the vector. If you use emplace_back(), the object is simply constructed. As expected, emplace_back() outperforms push_back(), which is why tools such as Clang-Tidy recommend the use of emplace_back() over push_back() whenever possible.

Benchmark libraries such as Hayai are simple to use and extremely effective at aiding the programmer with optimizing source code and are capable of not only benchmarking speed but also resource usage as well. The problem with these libraries is they are better leveraged at the *unit* level and not at the *integration* and *system* level; that is, to test an entire executable, these libraries are not well suited to aid the programmer as they do not scale well as the size of the test increases. To analyze an entire executable and not a single function, tools such as Valgrind exist, which help you profile which functions need the most attention with respect to optimizations. From there, a benchmarking tool can be used to analyze the functions that need the most attention.

Valgrind is a dynamic analysis tool that's capable of detecting memory leaks and tracing the execution of a program. To see this in action, let's look at the following example:

```
volatile int data = 0;

void foo()
{
    data++;
}

int main(void)
{
    for (auto i = 0; i < 100000; i++) {
        foo();
    }
}
```

In the preceding example, we increment a global variable (marked volatile to ensure the compiler does not optimize away the variable) from a function named foo() and then execute this function 100,000 times. To analyze this example, run the following (which uses callgrind to output how many times each function is called in your program):

```
> valgrind --tool=callgrind ./recipe01_example02
> callgrind_annotate callgrind.out.*
```

This results in the following output:

```
user@localhost:~/book/chapter06/build
Thresholds:        99
Include dirs:
User annotated:
Auto-annotation:  off
--------------------------------------------------------------------
Ir
--------------------------------------------------------------------
3,639,158  PROGRAM TOTALS
--------------------------------------------------------------------
Ir          file:function
--------------------------------------------------------------------
928,796   ???:_dl_lookup_symbol_x [/usr/lib64/ld-2.30.so]
800,000   ???:foo() [/home/user/book/chapter06/build/recipe01_example02]
687,907   ???:do_lookup_x [/usr/lib64/ld-2.30.so]
500,009   ???:main [/home/user/book/chapter06/build/recipe01_example02]
367,484   ???:_dl_relocate_object [/usr/lib64/ld-2.30.so]
118,759   ???:check_match [/usr/lib64/ld-2.30.so]
 92,113   ???:strcmp [/usr/lib64/libc-2.30.so]
 66,761   ???:_dl_addr [/usr/lib64/libc-2.30.so]
 12,781   ???:__GI___tunables_init [/usr/lib64/ld-2.30.so]
  8,936   ???:_dl_check_map_versions [/usr/lib64/ld-2.30.so]
  7,136   ???:_dl_map_object_from_fd [/usr/lib64/ld-2.30.so]
  4,521   ???:_dl_name_match_p [/usr/lib64/ld-2.30.so]
  4,131   ???:_dl_cache_libcmp [/usr/lib64/ld-2.30.so]
  3,168   ???:_dl_map_object [/usr/lib64/ld-2.30.so]
  2,720   ???:_dl_map_object_deps [/usr/lib64/ld-2.30.so]
[~/book/chapter06/build]:
```

As we can see, the `foo()` function is listed near the top of the preceding output (with the dynamic linker's `_dl_lookup_symbol_x()` function called the most, which is used to link the program prior to execution). It should be noted that the program lists (on the left-hand side) the total number of instructions for the `foo()` function as 800,000. This is due to the `foo()` function being 8 assembly instructions long and being executed 100,000 times. For example, let's look at the assembly of the `foo()` function using `objdump` (a tool capable of outputting the compiled assembly of an executable), as follows:

```
user@localhost:~/book/chapter06/build
[~/book/chapter06/build]: objdump -d recipe01_example02 | grep "<_Z3foov>:" -A9
0000000000401106 <_Z3foov>:
  401106:    55                     push   %rbp
  401107:    48 89 e5               mov    %rsp,%rbp
  40110a:    8b 05 10 2f 00 00      mov    0x2f10(%rip),%eax    # 404020 <__TMC_END__>
  401110:    83 c0 01               add    $0x1,%eax
  401113:    89 05 07 2f 00 00      mov    %eax,0x2f07(%rip)    # 404020 <__TMC_END__>
  401119:    90                     nop
  40111a:    5d                     pop    %rbp
  40111b:    c3                     retq
[~/book/chapter06/build]:
```

Using Valgrind, it is possible to profile an executable to determine which functions take the longest to execute. For example, let's look at `ls`:

```
> valgrind --tool=callgrind ls
> callgrind_annotate callgrind.out.*
```

This results in the following output:

As we can see, the `strcmp` function is called a lot. This information can be combined with benchmarking APIs at the *unit* level to determine whether a faster version of `strcmp` can be written (for example, using handwritten assembly and special CPU instructions). Using tools such as Hayai and Valgrind, it is possible to isolate which functions in your program are consuming the most CPU, memory, and even power, and rewrite them to provide better performance while focusing your efforts on the optimizations that will provide the best return of investment.

Looking at assembly code

In this recipe, we will take a look at the resulting assembly from two different optimizations: loop unrolling and pass-by-reference parameters. This recipe is important because it will teach you how to dive deeper into how the compiler converts C++ into executable code. This information will shed light on why C++ specifications such as the C++ Core Guidelines make the recommendations it does with respect to optimizations and performance. This is often critical when you're attempting to write better C++ code, especially when you want to optimize it.

Getting ready

Before beginning, please ensure that all of the technical requirements have been met, including installing Ubuntu 18.04 or higher and running the following in a Terminal window:

```
> sudo apt-get install build-essential git cmake
```

This will ensure your operating system has the proper tools to compile and execute the examples in this recipe. Once you've done this, open a new Terminal. We will use this Terminal to download, compile, and run our examples.

How to do it...

Perform the following steps to complete this recipe:

1. From a new Terminal, run the following to download the source code:

```
> cd ~/
> git clone
https://github.com/PacktPublishing/Advanced-CPP-CookBook.git
> cd Advanced-CPP-CookBook/chapter06
```

2. To compile the source code, run the following command:

```
> cmake -DCMAKE_BUILD_TYPE=Debug .
> make recipe02_examples
```

3. Once the source code has been compiled, you can execute each example in this recipe by running the following commands:

```
> ./recipe02_example01
```

```
> ./recipe02_example02
```

```
> ./recipe02_example03
```

```
> ./recipe02_example04
```

```
> ./recipe02_example05
```

In the next section, we will step through each of these examples and explain what each example program does and how it relates to the lessons being taught in this recipe.

How it works...

One of the best ways to learn how to optimize your C++ code is to learn how to analyze the resulting assembly code that the compiler generates after compilation. In this recipe, we will learn how this analysis is done by looking at two different examples: loop unrolling and pass-by-reference parameters.

Before we look at these examples, let's look at a simple example:

```
int main(void)
{ }
```

In the preceding example, we have nothing more than a main() function. We haven't included any C or C++ libraries and the main() function itself is empty. If we compile this example, we will see that the resulting binary is still pretty large:

In this case, the example is 22kb in size. To show the resulting assembly that the compiler generated for this code, we can do the following:

```
> objdump -d recipe02_example01
```

The resulting output of the preceding command should be surprising as there is a lot of code for an application that does absolutely nothing.

To get a better feel for how much code there really is, we can refine the output by using `grep`, a tool that lets us filter text from any command. Let's look at all of the functions in the code:

```
[~/book/chapter06/build]: objdump -d ./recipe02_example01 | grep ">:"
0000000000401000 <_init>:
0000000000401020 <_start>:
000000000040104f <.annobin_init.c>:
0000000000401050 <_dl_relocate_static_pie>:
0000000000401055 <.annobin__dl_relocate_static_pie.end>:
0000000000401060 <deregister_tm_clones>:
0000000000401090 <register_tm_clones>:
00000000004010d0 <__do_global_dtors_aux>:
0000000000401100 <frame_dummy>:
0000000000401106 <main>:
0000000000401120 <__libc_csu_init>:
0000000000401190 <__libc_csu_fini>:
0000000000401198 <_fini>:
[~/book/chapter06/build]:
```

As we can see, there are several functions the compiler automatically adds to the code for you. This includes the `_init()`, `_fini()`, and `_start()` functions. We can also look at a specific function, such as our main function, as follows:

```
[~/book/chapter06/build]: objdump -d ./recipe02_example01 | awk '/main>:/,/retq/'
0000000000401106 <main>:
  401106:    55                      push   %rbp
  401107:    48 89 e5                mov    %rsp,%rbp
  40110a:    b8 00 00 00 00          mov    $0x0,%eax
  40110f:    5d                      pop    %rbp
  401110:    c3                      retq
[~/book/chapter06/build]:
```

In the preceding example, we search the output of `objdump` for `main>:` and RETQ. All the function names end with `>:` and the last instruction (typically) for each function is RETQ on an Intel 64-bit system.

The following is the resulting assembly:

```
401106: push %rbp
401107: mov %rsp,%rbp
```

First, it stores the current stack frame pointer (`rbp`) to the stack and loads the stack frame pointer with the current address of the stack (`rsp`) for the `main()` function.

This can be seen in every function and is called the function's prolog. The only code that `main()` executes is `return 0`, which was added to the code automatically by the compiler:

```
40110a: mov $0x0,%eax
```

Finally, the last assembly in this function contains the function's epilog, which restores the stack frame pointer and returns:

```
40110f: pop %rbp
401110: retq
```

Now that we have a better understanding of how to get and read the resulting assembly for compiled C++, let's look at an example of loop unrolling, which is the process of replacing a loop of instructions with its equivalent version of the instructions without a loop. To do this, ensure that the examples are compiled in release mode (that is, with compiler optimizations enabled) by configuring them using the following command:

```
> cmake -DCMAKE_BUILD_TYPE=Release .
> make
```

To understand loop unrolling, let's look at the following code:

```
volatile int data[1000];

int main(void)
{
    for (auto i = 0U; i < 1000; i++) {
        data[i] = 42;
    }
}
```

When the compiler encounters a loop, the resulting assembly it generates contains the following code:

```
[~/book/chapter06/build]: objdump -d ./recipe02_example02 | awk '/main>:/,/ret/'
0000000000401020 <main>:
  401020:    31 c0                      xor    %eax,%eax
  401022:    66 0f 1f 44 00 00          nopw   0x0(%rax,%rax,1)
  401028:    89 c2                      mov    %eax,%edx
  40102a:    83 c0 01                   add    $0x1,%eax
  40102d:    c7 04 95 40 40 40 00       movl   $0x2a,0x404040(,%rdx,4)
  401034:    2a 00 00 00
  401038:    3d e8 03 00 00             cmp    $0x3e8,%eax
  40103d:    75 e9                      jne    401028 <main+0x8>
  40103f:    31 c0                      xor    %eax,%eax
  401041:    c3                         retq
[~/book/chapter06/build]:
```

Let's break this down:

```
401020: xor %eax,%eax
401022: nopw 0x0(%rax,%rax,1)
```

The first two instructions belong to the for (auto i = 0U; portion of the code. In this case, the i variable is stored in the EAX register and is set to 0 using the XOR instruction (the XOR instruction is faster on Intel for setting a register to 0 than a MOV instruction). The NOPW instruction can be safely ignored.

The next couple of instructions are interleaved, as follows:

```
401028: mov %eax,%edx
40102a: add $0x1,%eax
40102d: movl $0x2a,0x404040(,%rdx,4)
```

These instructions represent the i++; and data[i] = 42; code. The first instruction stores the current value of the i variable and then increments it by one before storing 42 into the memory address indexed by i. Conveniently, this resulting assembly demonstrates a possible opportunity for optimization as the compiler could have achieved the same functionality using the following:

```
movl $0x2a,0x404040(,%rax,4)
add $0x1,%eax
```

The preceding code stores the value 42 before executing i++, thus removing the need for the following:

```
mov %eax,%edx
```

A number of methods exist to realize this potential optimization, including using a different compiler or handwriting the assembly. The next set of instructions execute the i < 1000; portion of our for loop:

```
401038: cmp $0x3e8,%eax
40103d: jne 401028 <main+0x8>
```

The CMP instruction checks to see if the i variable is 1000 and, if not, uses the JNE instruction to jump to the top of the function to continue the loop. Otherwise, the remaining code executes:

```
40103f: xor %eax,%eax
401041: retq
```

To see how loop unrolling works, let's change the number of iterations the loop takes from `1000` to `4`, as follows:

```
volatile int data[4];

int main(void)
{
    for (auto i = 0U; i < 4; i++) {
        data[i] = 42;
    }
}
```

As we can see, the code is identical except for the number of iterations the loop takes. The resulting assembly is as follows:

As we can see, the `CMP` and `JNE` instructions are missing. Now, the following code is compiled (*but there's more!*):

```
    for (auto i = 0U; i < 4; i++) {
        data[i] = 42;
    }
```

The compiled code is converted into the following code:

```
        data[0] = 42;
        data[1] = 42;
        data[2] = 42;
        data[3] = 42;
```

`return 0;` shows up in the assembly in-between the assignments. This is allowed because the return value of the function is independent of the assignment (since the assignment instructions never touch `RAX`), which provides the CPU with an additional optimization (as it can execute `return 0;` in parallel, though this is a topic that is out of the scope of this book). It should be noted that loop unrolling doesn't require a small number of loop iterations to be used. Some compilers will partially unroll a loop to achieve optimizations (for example, executing the loop in groups of `4` instead of `1` at a time).

Our last example will look at pass-by-reference instead of pass-by-value. To start, recompile the code in debug mode:

```
> cmake -DCMAKE_BUILD_TYPE=Debug .
> make
```

Let's look at the following example:

```
struct mydata {
    int data[100];
};

void foo(mydata d)
{
    (void) d;
}

int main(void)
{
    mydata d;
    foo(d);
}
```

In this example, we've created a large structure and passed it by-value to a function named foo() in our main function. The resulting assembly for the main function is as follows:

```
user@localhost ~/book/chapter06/build                                       —  □  X
[~/book/chapter06/build]: objdump -d ./recipe02_example04 | awk '/main>:/,/ret/'
000000000040110d <main>:
    40110d:     55                      push    %rbp
    40110e:     48 89 e5                mov     %rsp,%rbp
    401111:     48 81 ec 90 01 00 00    sub     $0x190,%rsp
    401118:     48 81 ec 90 01 00 00    sub     $0x190,%rsp
    40111f:     48 89 e0                mov     %rsp,%rax
    401122:     48 89 c7                mov     %rax,%rdi
    401125:     48 8d 85 70 fe ff ff    lea     -0x190(%rbp),%rax
    40112c:     ba 32 00 00 00          mov     $0x32,%edx
    401131:     48 89 c6                mov     %rax,%rsi
    401134:     48 89 d1                mov     %rdx,%rcx
    401137:     f3 48 a5                rep movsq %ds:(%rsi),%es:(%rdi)
    40113a:     e8 c7 ff ff ff          callq   401106 <_Z3foo6mydata>
    40113f:     48 81 c4 90 01 00 00    add     $0x190,%rsp
    401146:     b8 00 00 00 00          mov     $0x0,%eax
    40114b:     c9                      leaveq
    40114c:     c3                      retq
[~/book/chapter06/build]:
```

The important instructions from the preceding example are as follows:

```
401137:  rep movsq %ds:(%rsi),%es:(%rdi)
40113a:  callq 401106 <_Z3foo6mydata>
```

The preceding instructions copy the large structure to the stack and then call our `foo()` function. The copy occurs because the structure is passed by value, which means the compiler must perform a copy. As a side note, if you would like to see the output in a readable format and not a mangled format, add a `c` to the options, as follows:

```
[~/book/chapter06/build]: objdump -dc ./recipe02_example04 | awk '/main>:/,/ret/'
000000000040110d <main>:
  40110d:    55                      push   %rbp
  40110e:    48 89 e5                mov    %rsp,%rbp
  401111:    48 81 ec 90 01 00 00    sub    $0x190,%rsp
  401118:    48 81 ec 90 01 00 00    sub    $0x190,%rsp
  40111f:    48 89 e0                mov    %rsp,%rax
  401122:    48 89 c7                mov    %rax,%rdi
  401125:    48 8d 85 70 fe ff ff    lea    -0x190(%rbp),%rax
  40112c:    ba 32 00 00 00          mov    $0x32,%edx
  401131:    48 89 c6                mov    %rax,%rsi
  401134:    48 89 d1                mov    %rdx,%rcx
  401137:    f3 48 a5                rep movsq %ds:(%rsi),%es:(%rdi)
  40113a:    e8 c7 ff ff ff          callq  401106 <foo(mydata)>
  40113f:    48 81 c4 90 01 00 00    add    $0x190,%rsp
  401146:    b8 00 00 00 00          mov    $0x0,%eax
  40114b:    c9                      leaveq
  40114c:    c3                      retq
[~/book/chapter06/build]:
```

Finally, let's pass-by-reference to see the resulting improvement:

```
struct mydata {
    int data[100];
};

void foo(mydata &d)
{
    (void) d;
}

int main(void)
{
    mydata d;
    foo(d);
}
```

As we can see, we pass the structure by-reference instead of by-value. The resulting assembly is as follows:

```
user@localhost:~/book/chapter06/build
[~/book/chapter06/build]: objdump -d ./recipe02_example05 | awk '/main>:/,/ret/'
0000000000401111 <main>:
  401111:       55                      push   %rbp
  401112:       48 89 e5                mov    %rsp,%rbp
  401115:       48 81 ec 90 01 00 00    sub    $0x190,%rsp
  40111c:       48 8d 85 70 fe ff ff    lea    -0x190(%rbp),%rax
  401123:       48 89 c7                mov    %rax,%rdi
  401126:       e8 db ff ff ff          callq  401106 <_Z3fooR6mydata>
  40112b:       b8 00 00 00 00          mov    $0x0,%eax
  401130:       c9                      leaveq
  401131:       c3                      retq
[~/book/chapter06/build]:
```

Here, there is far less code, resulting in a faster executable. As we have learned, examining what the compiler produces can be effective if we wish to understand what the compiler is producing as this provides more information about potential changes you can make to write more efficient C++ code.

Reducing the number of memory allocations

Hidden memory allocations are produced by C++ all the time when an application runs. This recipe will teach you how to determine when memory is allocated by C++ and how to remove these allocations when possible. Understanding how to remove memory allocations is important because functions such as new(), delete(), malloc(), and free() are not only slow, but the memory they provide is also finite. Removing unneeded allocations not only improves the overall performance of your application, but it also helps to reduce its overall memory requirements.

Getting ready

Before beginning, please ensure that all of the technical requirements have been met, including installing Ubuntu 18.04 or higher and running the following in a Terminal window:

```
> sudo apt-get install build-essential git valgrind cmake
```

This will ensure your operating system has the proper tools to compile and execute the examples in this recipe. Once you've done this, open a new Terminal. We will use this Terminal to download, compile, and run our examples.

How to do it...

Perform the following steps to complete this recipe:

1. From a new Terminal, run the following to download the source code:

```
> cd ~/
> git clone
https://github.com/PacktPublishing/Advanced-CPP-CookBook.git
> cd Advanced-CPP-CookBook/chapter06
```

2. To compile the source code, run the following command:

```
> cmake .
> make recipe03_examples
```

3. Once the source code has been compiled, you can execute each example in this recipe by running the following commands:

```
> ./recipe03_example01
```

```
> ./recipe03_example02
```

```
> ./recipe03_example03
```

```
> ./recipe03_example04
```

```
> ./recipe03_example05
```

```
> ./recipe03_example06
```

```
> ./recipe03_example07
```

In the next section, we will step through each of these examples and explain what each example program does and how it relates to the lessons being taught in this recipe.

How it works...

In this recipe, we will learn how to monitor how much memory an application is consuming, as well as the different ways that C++ can allocate memory behind the scenes. To start, let's look at a simple application that does nothing:

```
int main(void)
{
}
```

As we can see, this application does nothing. To see how much memory the application has used, we will use Valgrind, a dynamic analysis tool, as follows:

```
user@localhost:~/book/chapter06/build
[~/book/chapter06/build]: valgrind ./recipe03_example01
==256788== Memcheck, a memory error detector
==256788== Copyright (C) 2002-2017, and GNU GPL'd, by Julian Seward et al.
==256788== Using Valgrind-3.15.0 and LibVEX; rerun with -h for copyright info
==256788== Command: ./recipe03_example01
==256788==
==256788==
==256788== HEAP SUMMARY:
==256788==     in use at exit: 0 bytes in 0 blocks
==256788==   total heap usage: 1 allocs, 1 frees, 72,704 bytes allocated
==256788==
==256788== All heap blocks were freed -- no leaks are possible
==256788==
==256788== For lists of detected and suppressed errors, rerun with: -s
==256788== ERROR SUMMARY: 0 errors from 0 contexts (suppressed: 0 from 0)
[~/book/chapter06/build]:
```

As shown in the preceding example, our application has allocated heap memory (that is, memory allocated using `new()`/`delete()` or `malloc()`/`free()`). To determine where this allocation occurred, let's use Valgrind again, but this time, we will enable a tool called **Massif**, which will trace where the memory allocation came from:

```
user@localhost:~/book/chapter06/build
[~/book/chapter06/build]: valgrind --tool=massif ./recipe03_example01
==256817== Massif, a heap profiler
==256817== Copyright (C) 2003-2017, and GNU GPL'd, by Nicholas Nethercote
==256817== Using Valgrind-3.15.0 and LibVEX; rerun with -h for copyright info
==256817== Command: ./recipe03_example01
==256817==
==256817==
[~/book/chapter06/build]:
```

To see the output of the preceding example, we must output a file that was created for us automatically:

```
> cat massif.out.*
```

This results in us retrieving the following output:

```
user@localhost:~/book/chapter06/build
#-----------
snapshot=1
#-----------
time=2372448
mem_heap_B=72704
mem_heap_extra_B=8
mem_stacks_B=0
heap_tree=empty
#-----------
snapshot=2
#-----------
time=2384591
mem_heap_B=72704
mem_heap_extra_B=8
mem_stacks_B=0
heap_tree=peak
n1: 72704 (heap allocation functions) malloc/new/new[], --alloc-fns, etc.
 n1: 72704 0x49150A9: ??? (in /usr/lib64/libstdc++.so.6.0.27)
  n1: 72704 0x400FD59: call_init.part.0 (in /usr/lib64/ld-2.30.so)
   n1: 72704 0x400FE60: _dl_init (in /usr/lib64/ld-2.30.so)
    n0: 72704 0x4001149: ??? (in /usr/lib64/ld-2.30.so)
#-----------
snapshot=3
#-----------
time=2384591
mem_heap_B=0
mem_heap_extra_B=0
mem_stacks_B=0
heap_tree=empty
[~/book/chapter06/build]:
```

As we can see, the dynamic linker's `init()` function is performing the allocation, which is 72,704 bytes in size. To further demonstrate how to use Valgrind, let's take a look at this simple example, where we perform our own allocation:

```
int main(void)
{
    auto ptr = new int;
    delete ptr;
}
```

To see the memory allocation of the preceding source, we need to run Valgrind again:

```
user@localhost:~/book/chapter06/build
[~/book/chapter06/build]: valgrind ./recipe03_example02
==256915== Memcheck, a memory error detector
==256915== Copyright (C) 2002-2017, and GNU GPL'd, by Julian Seward et al.
==256915== Using Valgrind-3.15.0 and LibVEX; rerun with -h for copyright info
==256915== Command: ./recipe03_example02
==256915==
==256915==
==256915== HEAP SUMMARY:
==256915==     in use at exit: 0 bytes in 0 blocks
==256915==   total heap usage: 2 allocs, 2 frees, 72,708 bytes allocated
==256915==
==256915== All heap blocks were freed -- no leaks are possible
==256915==
==256915== For lists of detected and suppressed errors, rerun with: -s
==256915== ERROR SUMMARY: 0 errors from 0 contexts (suppressed: 0 from 0)
[~/book/chapter06/build]:
```

As we can see, we have allocated $72,708$ bytes. Since we know that the application will allocate $72,704$ bytes for us automatically, we can see that Valgrind has successfully detected the 4 bytes we allocated (the size of an integer on Intel 64-bit systems running Linux). To see where this allocation occurred, let's use Massif again:

```
user@localhost:~/book/chapter06/build
[~/book/chapter06/build]: valgrind --tool=massif --threshold=0.1 ./recipe03_example02
==256939== Massif, a heap profiler
==256939== Copyright (C) 2003-2017, and GNU GPL'd, by Nicholas Nethercote
==256939== Using Valgrind-3.15.0 and LibVEX; rerun with -h for copyright info
==256939== Command: ./recipe03_example02
==256939==
==256939==
[~/book/chapter06/build]:
```

As we can see, we've added the `--threshold=0.1` to the command-line options as this tells Valgrind that any allocation that makes up .1% of the allocations should be logged. Let's `cat` the results (the `cat` program simply echoes the contents of a file to the console):

```
> cat massif.out.*
```

By doing this, we get the following output:

```
user@localhost:~/book/chapter06/build                        —   □   X
snapshot=3
#-----------
time=2376770
mem_heap_B=72708
mem_heap_extra_B=28
mem_stacks_B=0
heap_tree=peak
n2: 72708 (heap allocation functions) malloc/new/new[], --alloc-fns, etc.
 n1: 72704 0x49150A9: ??? (in /usr/lib64/libstdc++.so.6.0.27)
  n1: 72704 0x400FD59: call_init.part.0 (in /usr/lib64/ld-2.30.so)
   n1: 72704 0x400FE60: _dl_init (in /usr/lib64/ld-2.30.so)
    n0: 72704 0x4001149: ??? (in /usr/lib64/ld-2.30.so)
 n0: 4 in 1 place, below massif's threshold (0.10%)
#-----------
snapshot=4
#-----------
time=2376770
mem_heap_B=72704
mem_heap_extra_B=8
mem_stacks_B=0
heap_tree=empty
#-----------
snapshot=5
#-----------
time=2387637
mem_heap_B=0
mem_heap_extra_B=0
mem_stacks_B=0
heap_tree=empty
[~/book/chapter06/build]:
```

As we can see, Valgrind has detected the memory allocations from the `init()` function, as well as from our `main()` function.

Now that we know how to analyze the memory allocations our application makes, let's look at some different C++ APIs to see what types of memory allocations they make behind the scenes. To start, let's look at an `std::vector`, as follows:

```
#include <vector>
std::vector<int> data;

int main(void)
{
    for (auto i = 0; i < 10000; i++) {
        data.push_back(i);
    }
}
```

Here, we've created a global vector of integers and then added 10,000 integers to the vector. Using Valgrind, we get the following output:

```
[~/book/chapter06/build]: valgrind ./recipe03_example03
==257040== Memcheck, a memory error detector
==257040== Copyright (C) 2002-2017, and GNU GPL'd, by Julian Seward et al.
==257040== Using Valgrind-3.15.0 and LibVEX; rerun with -h for copyright info
==257040== Command: ./recipe03_example03
==257040==
==257040==
==257040== HEAP SUMMARY:
==257040==     in use at exit: 0 bytes in 0 blocks
==257040==   total heap usage: 16 allocs, 16 frees, 203,772 bytes allocated
==257040==
==257040== All heap blocks were freed -- no leaks are possible
==257040==
==257040== For lists of detected and suppressed errors, rerun with: -s
==257040== ERROR SUMMARY: 0 errors from 0 contexts (suppressed: 0 from 0)
[~/book/chapter06/build]:
```

Here, we can see 16 allocations, with a total of 203,772 bytes. We know that the application will allocate 72,704 bytes for us, so we must remove this from our total, leaving us with 131,068 bytes of memory. We also know that we allocated 10,000 integers, which is 40,000 bytes in total. So, the question is, where did the other 91,068 bytes come from?

The answer is in how `std::vector` works under the hood. `std::vector` must ensure a continuous view of memory at all times, which means that when an insertion occurs and the `std::vector` is out of space, it must allocate a new, larger buffer and then copy the contents of the old buffer into the new buffer. The problem is that `std::vector` doesn't know what the total size of the buffer will be when all of the insertions are complete, so when the first insertion is performed, it creates a small buffer to ensure memory is not wasted and then proceeds to increase the size of the `std::vector` in small increments as the vector grows, resulting in several memory allocations and memory copies.

To prevent such allocation from happening, C++ provides the `reserve()` function, which provides the user of a `std::vector` to estimate how much memory the user thinks they will need. For example, consider the following code:

```cpp
#include <vector>
std::vector<int> data;

int main(void)
{
    data.reserve(10000);  // <--- added optimization
```

```
        for (auto i = 0; i < 10000; i++) {
            data.push_back(i);
        }
    }
```

The code in the preceding example is the same as it is in the previous example, with the difference being that we added a call to the `reserve()` function, which tells the `std::vector` how large we think the vector will be. Valgrind's output is as follows:

As we can see, the application allocated `112,704` bytes. If we remove our `72,704` bytes that the application creates by default, we are left with `40,000` bytes, which is the exact size we expected (since we are adding `10,000` integers to the vector, with each integer being `4` bytes in size).

Data structures are not the only type of C++ Standard Library API that performs hidden allocations. Let's look at an `std::any`, as follows:

```
#include <any>
#include <string>

std::any data;

int main(void)
{
    data = 42;
    data = std::string{"The answer is: 42"};
}
```

In this example, we created an `std::any` and assigned it an integer and an `std::string`. Let's look at the output of Valgrind:

```
user@localhost:~/book/chapter06/build
[~/book/chapter06/build]: valgrind ./recipe03_example05
==257123== Memcheck, a memory error detector
==257123== Copyright (C) 2002-2017, and GNU GPL'd, by Julian Seward et al.
==257123== Using Valgrind-3.15.0 and LibVEX; rerun with -h for copyright info
==257123== Command: ./recipe03_example05
==257123==
==257123==
==257123== HEAP SUMMARY:
==257123==     in use at exit: 0 bytes in 0 blocks
==257123==   total heap usage: 3 allocs, 3 frees, 72,754 bytes allocated
==257123==
==257123== All heap blocks were freed -- no leaks are possible
==257123==
==257123== For lists of detected and suppressed errors, rerun with: -s
==257123== ERROR SUMMARY: 0 errors from 0 contexts (suppressed: 0 from 0)
[~/book/chapter06/build]:
```

As we can see, 3 allocations occurred. The first allocation occurs by default, while the second allocation is produced by the `std::string`. The last allocation is produced by the `std::any`. This occurs because `std::any` has to adjust its internal storage to account for any new random data type that it sees. In other words, to handle a *generic* data type, C++ has to perform an allocation. This is made worse if we keep changing the data type. For example, consider the following code:

```cpp
#include <any>
#include <string>

std::any data;

int main(void)
{
    data = 42;
    data = std::string{"The answer is: 42"};
    data = 42;                                 // <--- keep swapping
    data = std::string{"The answer is: 42"};   // <--- keep swapping
    data = 42;                                 // <--- keep swapping
    data = std::string{"The answer is: 42"};   // ...
    data = 42;
    data = std::string{"The answer is: 42"};
}
```

The preceding code is identical to the previous example, with the only difference being that we swap between data types. Valgrind produces the following output:

```
user@localhost: ~/book/chapter06/build                               —    □    ✕
[~/book/chapter06/build]: valgrind ./recipe03_example06
==257149== Memcheck, a memory error detector
==257149== Copyright (C) 2002-2017, and GNU GPL'd, by Julian Seward et al.
==257149== Using Valgrind-3.15.0 and LibVEX; rerun with -h for copyright info
==257149== Command: ./recipe03_example06
==257149==
==257149==
==257149== HEAP SUMMARY:
==257149==     in use at exit: 0 bytes in 0 blocks
==257149==   total heap usage: 9 allocs, 9 frees, 72,904 bytes allocated
==257149==
==257149== All heap blocks were freed -- no leaks are possible
==257149==
==257149== For lists of detected and suppressed errors, rerun with: -s
==257149== ERROR SUMMARY: 0 errors from 0 contexts (suppressed: 0 from 0)
[~/book/chapter06/build]:
```

As we can see, 9 allocations occurred instead of 3. To solve this problem, we need to use an `std::variant` instead of `std::any`, as follows:

```cpp
#include <variant>
#include <string>

std::variant<int, std::string> data;

int main(void)
{
    data = 42;
    data = std::string{"The answer is: 42"};
}
```

The difference between `std::any` and `std::variant` is that `std::variant` requires that the user states which types the variant must support, removing the need for dynamic memory allocation on assignment. Valgrind's output is as follows:

```
user@localhost:~/book/chapter06/build                                —    □    ✕
[~/book/chapter06/build]: valgrind ./recipe03_example07
==257176== Memcheck, a memory error detector
==257176== Copyright (C) 2002-2017, and GNU GPL'd, by Julian Seward et al.
==257176== Using Valgrind-3.15.0 and LibVEX; rerun with -h for copyright info
==257176== Command: ./recipe03_example07
==257176==
==257176==
==257176== HEAP SUMMARY:
==257176==     in use at exit: 0 bytes in 0 blocks
==257176==   total heap usage: 2 allocs, 2 frees, 72,722 bytes allocated
==257176==
==257176== All heap blocks were freed -- no leaks are possible
==257176==
==257176== For lists of detected and suppressed errors, rerun with: -s
==257176== ERROR SUMMARY: 0 errors from 0 contexts (suppressed: 0 from 0)
[~/book/chapter06/build]:
```

Now, we only have 2 allocations, as expected (the default allocation and the allocation from `std::string`). As shown in this recipe, libraries, including the C++ Standard Library, can hide memory allocations, potentially slowing down your code and using more memory resources than you intended. Tools such as Valgrind can be used to identify these types of problems, allowing you to create more efficient C++ code.

Declaring noexcept

C++11 introduced the `noexcept` keyword, which, besides simplifying how exceptions were used in general, also included a better implementation of C++ exceptions that removed some of their performance hits. However, this doesn't mean that exceptions do not include *overhead* (that is, performance penalties). In this recipe, we will explore how exceptions add overhead to an application and how the `noexcept` keyword can help reduce these penalties (depending on the compiler).

This recipe is important because it will demonstrate that if a function doesn't throw an exception, then it should be marked as such to prevent the additional overhead regarding the total size of the application, resulting in an application that loads faster.

Getting ready

Before beginning, please ensure that all of the technical requirements have been met, including installing Ubuntu 18.04 or higher and running the following in a Terminal window:

```
> sudo apt-get install build-essential git cmake
```

This will ensure your operating system has the proper tools to compile and execute the examples in this recipe. Once you've done this, open a new Terminal. We will use this Terminal to download, compile, and run our examples.

How to do it...

Perform the following steps to complete this recipe:

1. From a new Terminal, run the following to download the source code:

```
> cd ~/
> git clone
https://github.com/PacktPublishing/Advanced-CPP-CookBook.git
> cd Advanced-CPP-CookBook/chapter06
```

2. To compile the source code, run the following command:

```
> cmake .
> make recipe04_examples
```

3. Once the source code has been compiled, you can execute each example in this recipe by running the following commands:

```
> ./recipe04_example01
```

```
> ./recipe04_example02
```

In the next section, we will step through each of these examples and explain what each example program does and how it relates to the lessons being taught in this recipe.

How it works...

In this recipe, we will learn why it is so important to mark a function as noexcept if it shouldn't throw an exception. This is because it removes the added overhead to the application for exception support, which can improve execution time, application size, and even load time (this depends on the compiler, which Standard Library you are using, and so on). To show this, let's create a simple example:

```
class myclass
{
    int answer;

public:
    ~myclass()
    {
        answer = 42;
    }
};
```

The first thing we need to do is create a class that sets a `private` member variable when it is destructed, as follows:

```cpp
void foo()
{
    throw 42;
}

int main(void)
{
    myclass c;

    try {
        foo();
    }
    catch (...) {
    }
}
```

Now, we can create two functions. The first function throws an exception, while the second function is our main function. This function creates an instance of our class and calls the `foo()` function inside a `try/catch` block. In other words, at no time will the `main()` function throw an exception. If we look at the assembly for the main function, we'll see the following:

```
user@localhost ~/book/chapter06/build
[~/book/chapter06/build]: objdump -d ./recipe04_example01 | awk '/main>:/,/ret/'
000000000040119c <main>:
  40119c:       55                      push   %rbp
  40119d:       48 89 e5                mov    %rsp,%rbp
  4011a0:       53                      push   %rbx
  4011a1:       48 83 ec 18             sub    $0x18,%rsp
  4011a5:       e8 cc ff ff ff          callq  401176 <_Z3foov>
  4011aa:       48 8d 45 ec             lea    -0x14(%rbp),%rax
  4011ae:       48 89 c7                mov    %rax,%rdi
  4011b1:       e8 38 00 00 00          callq  4011ee <_ZN7myclassD1Ev>
  4011b6:       b8 00 00 00 00          mov    $0x0,%eax
  4011bb:       eb 29                   jmp    4011e6 <main+0x4a>
  4011bd:       48 89 c7                mov    %rax,%rdi
  4011c0:       e8 6b fe ff ff          callq  401030 <__cxa_begin_catch@plt>
  4011c5:       e8 86 fe ff ff          callq  401050 <__cxa_end_catch@plt>
  4011ca:       eb de                   jmp    4011aa <main+0xe>
  4011cc:       48 89 c3                mov    %rax,%rbx
  4011cf:       48 8d 45 ec             lea    -0x14(%rbp),%rax
  4011d3:       48 89 c7                mov    %rax,%rdi
  4011d6:       e8 13 00 00 00          callq  4011ee <_ZN7myclassD1Ev>
  4011db:       48 89 d8                mov    %rbx,%rax
  4011de:       48 89 c7                mov    %rax,%rdi
  4011e1:       e8 9a fe ff ff          callq  401080 <_Unwind_Resume@plt>
  4011e6:       48 83 c4 18             add    $0x18,%rsp
  4011ea:       5b                      pop    %rbx
  4011eb:       5d                      pop    %rbp
  4011ec:       c3                      retq
[~/book/chapter06/build]:
```

As we can see, our main function makes a call to _Unwind_Resume, which is used by the exception unwinder. This extra logic is due to the fact that C++ has to add additional exception logic to the end of the function. To remove this extra logic, tell the compiler that the main() function isn't thrown:

```cpp
int main(void) noexcept
{
    myclass c;

    try {
        foo();
    }
    catch (...) {
    }
}
```

Adding noexcept tells the compiler that an exception cannot be thrown. As a result, the function no longer contains the extra logic for handling an exception, as follows:

```
user@localhost:~/book/chapter06/build
[~/book/chapter06/build]: objdump -d ./recipe04_example02 | awk '/main>:/,/ret/'
000000000040118c <main>:
  40118c:    55                      push   %rbp
  40118d:    48 89 e5                mov    %rsp,%rbp
  401190:    48 83 ec 10             sub    $0x10,%rsp
  401194:    e8 cd ff ff ff          callq  401166 <_Z3foov>
  401199:    48 8d 45 fc             lea    -0x4(%rbp),%rax
  40119d:    48 89 c7                mov    %rax,%rdi
  4011a0:    e8 19 00 00 00          callq  4011be <_ZN7myclassD1Ev>
  4011a5:    b8 00 00 00 00          mov    $0x0,%eax
  4011aa:    eb 0f                   jmp    4011bb <main+0x2f>
  4011ac:    48 89 c7                mov    %rax,%rdi
  4011af:    e8 7c fe ff ff          callq  401030 <__cxa_begin_catch@plt>
  4011b4:    e8 97 fe ff ff          callq  401050 <__cxa_end_catch@plt>
  4011b9:    eb de                   jmp    401199 <main+0xd>
  4011bb:    c9                      leaveq
  4011bc:    c3                      retq
[~/book/chapter06/build]:
```

As we can see, the unwind function is no longer present. It should be noted that there are calls to catch functions, which are due to the try/catch block and not the overhead of an exception.

Debugging and Testing 7

In this chapter, you will learn how to properly test and debug your C++ applications. This is important because without good testing and debugging, it is highly likely that your C++ applications will contain hard-to-detect bugs that will reduce their overall reliability, stability, and security.

This chapter will start with a comprehensive overview of unit testing, which is the act of testing code at the unit level, and will also look at how to leverage existing libraries to speed up the process of writing tests. Next, it will demonstrate how to use the ASAN and UBSAN dynamic analysis tools to check for memory corruption and undefined behavior. Lastly, the chapter will conclude with a quick look at how to leverage the NDEBUG macro in your own code for adding debug logic when attempting to resolve issues.

This chapter contains the following recipes:

- Getting to grips with unit testing
- Working with ASAN, the address sanitizer
- Working with UBSAN, the undefined behavior sanitizer
- Using #ifndef NDEBUG to conditionally execute additional checks

Technical requirements

To compile and run the examples in this chapter, you must have administrative access to a computer running Ubuntu 18.04 with a functional internet connection. Prior to running these examples, you must have installed the following:

```
> sudo apt-get install build-essential git cmake
```

If this is installed on any operating system other than Ubuntu 18.04, then GCC 7.4 or higher and CMake 3.6 or higher will be required.

Code files for the chapter can be found at `https://github.com/PacktPublishing/Advanced-CPP-CookBook/tree/master/chapter07`.

Getting to grips with unit testing

In this recipe, we will learn how to unit test our C++ code. There are several different ways to ensure that your C++ code executes with reliability, stability, security, and to specification.

Unit testing, which is the act of testing your code at the fundamental unit level, is a key component of any testing strategy. This recipe is important not only because it will teach you how to unit test your code, but because it will also explain why unit testing is so critical, as well as how to speed up the process of unit testing your C++ using existing libraries.

Getting ready

Before beginning, please ensure that all of the technical requirements are met, including the installation of Ubuntu 18.04 or higher and running the following in a Terminal window:

```
> sudo apt-get install build-essential git cmake
```

This will ensure that your operating system has the proper tools to compile and execute the examples in this recipe. Once this is complete, open a new Terminal. We will use this Terminal to download, compile, and run our examples.

How to do it...

Go through the following steps to work through the recipe:

1. From a new Terminal, run the following to download the source code:

```
> cd ~/
> git clone
https://github.com/PacktPublishing/Advanced-CPP-CookBook.git
> cd Advanced-CPP-CookBook/chapter07
```

2. To compile the source code, run the following:

```
> cmake .
> make recipe01_examples
```

3. Once the source code is compiled, you can execute each example in this recipe by running the following commands:

```
> ./recipe01_example01
===============================================================
========
All tests passed (1 assertion in 1 test case)

> ./recipe01_example02
===============================================================
========
All tests passed (6 assertions in 1 test case)

> ./recipe01_example03
===============================================================
========
All tests passed (8 assertions in 1 test case)

> ./recipe01_example04
===============================================================
========
All tests passed (1 assertion in 1 test case)

> ./recipe01_example05
. . .
===============================================================
========
test cases: 1 | 1 passed
assertions: - none -

> ./recipe01_example06
. . .
===============================================================
========
test cases: 5 | 3 passed | 2 failed
assertions: 8 | 6 passed | 2 failed

> ./recipe01_example07
===============================================================
========
test cases: 1 | 1 passed
assertions: - none -
```

```
> ./recipe01_example08
================================================================
========
All tests passed (3 assertions in 1 test case)
```

In the next section, we will step through each of these examples and explain what each example program does and how it relates to the lessons being taught in this recipe.

How it works...

Simply writing your C++ application and hoping it works as expected without any testing is guaranteed to result in reliability-, stability-, and security-related bugs. This recipe is important because testing your applications prior to release ensures that your applications execute as expected, ultimately saving you time and money in the future.

There are several different ways to test your code, including system-level, integration, long-term stability, and static and dynamic analysis, among others. In this recipe, we will focus on **unit testing**. Unit testing breaks an application up into functional **units** and tests each unit to ensure that it executes as expected. Typically, in practice, each function and object (that is, class) is a unit that should be tested independently.

There are several different theories as to how unit testing should be performed, with entire books written on the subject. Some believe that every line of code within a function or object should be tested, leveraging coverage tools to ensure compliance, while others believe that unit testing should be requirement-driven, using a black-box approach. A common development process called **test-driven development** states that all tests, including unit tests, should be written before any source code is written, whereas **behavioral-driven development** takes test-driven development a step further with a specific, story-driven approach to unit testing.

Every testing model has its pros and cons, and which method you choose will be based on the type of application you are writing, the type of software development process you adhere to, and any policies you may or may not be required to follow. Regardless of this choice, unit testing will likely be a part of your testing scheme, and this recipe will provide the foundation for how to unit test your C++ applications.

Although unit testing can be done with standard C++ (for example, this is how `libc++` is unit tested), unit-test libraries help to simplify this process. In this recipe, we will leverage the `Catch2` unit-test library, which can be found at
https://github.com/catchorg/Catch2.git.

Although we will be reviewing Catch2, the principles that are being discussed apply to most of the unit-test libraries that are available, or even standard C++, if you choose not to use a helper library. To leverage Catch2, simply execute the following:

```
> git clone https://github.com/catchorg/Catch2.git catch
> cd catch
> mkdir build
> cd build
> cmake ..
> make
> sudo make install
```

You can also use CMake's ExternalProject_Add, as we did in our examples on GitHub to leverage a local copy of the library.

To find out how to use Catch2, let's look at the following simple example:

```
#define CATCH_CONFIG_MAIN
#include <catch.hpp>

TEST_CASE("the answer")
{
    CHECK(true);
}
```

When this is run, we see the following output:

In the preceding example, we start by defining CATCH_CONFIG_MAIN. This tells the Catch2 library that we want it to create the main() function for us. This must be defined before we include the Catch2 include statement, which we did in the preceding code.

The next step is to define a test case. Each unit is broken up into test cases that test the unit in question. The granularity of each test case is up to you: some choose to have a single test case for each unit being tested, while others, for example, choose to have a test case for each function being tested. The TEST_CASE() takes a string that allows you to provide a description of the test case, which is helpful when a test fails as Catch2 will output this string to help you identify where in your test code the failure occurred. The last step in our simple example is to use the CHECK() macro. This macro performs a specific test. Each TEST_CASE() will likely have several CHECK() macros designed to provide the unit with a specific input and then validate the resulting output.

Once compiled and executed, the unit-test library will provide some output text describing how to execute tests. In this case, the library states that all of the tests passed, which is the desired outcome.

To better understand how to leverage unit testing in your own code, let's look at the following, more complicated example:

```cpp
#define CATCH_CONFIG_MAIN
#include <catch.hpp>

#include <vector>
#include <iostream>
#include <algorithm>

TEST_CASE("sort a vector")
{
    std::vector<int> v{4, 8, 15, 16, 23, 42};
    REQUIRE(v.size() == 6);

    SECTION("sort descending order") {
        std::sort(v.begin(), v.end(), std::greater<int>());

        CHECK(v.front() == 42);
        CHECK(v.back()  == 4);
    }

    SECTION("sort ascending order") {
        std::sort(v.begin(), v.end(), std::less<int>());

        CHECK(v.front() == 4);
        CHECK(v.back()  == 42);
    }
}
```

Like the previous example, we include Catch2 with the CATCH_CONFIG_MAIN macro and then define a single test case with a description. In this example, we are testing the ability to sort a vector, so this is the description we provide. The first thing we do in our test is to create a vector of integers with a predefined list of integers.

The next thing we do is use the REQUIRE() macro to test, making sure that the vector has 6 elements in the vector. The REQUIRE() macro is similar to the CHECK() as both check to make sure that the statement inside the macro is true. The difference is that the CHECK() macro will report an error and then continue execution while the REQUIRE() macro will stop the execution, halting the unit test. This is useful to ensure that the unit test is properly constructed based on any assumptions that the test might be making. The use of REQUIRE() is important as unit tests mature over time, and other programmers add to and modify the unit tests, ensuring that bugs are not introduced into the unit tests over time, as there is nothing worse than having to test and debug your unit tests.

The SECTION() macro is used to further break up our tests with better descriptions and provide the ability to add common setup code for each test. In the preceding example, we are testing the sort() function for a vector. The sort() function can sort in different directions, which this unit test must validate. Without the SECTION() macro, if a test failed, it would be difficult to know whether the failure was from sorting in ascending or descending order. Furthermore, the SECTION() macro ensures that each test doesn't affect the results of other tests.

Finally, we use the CHECK() macro to ensure that the sort() function worked as expected. Unit tests should check for exceptions as well. In the following example, we will ensure that exceptions are thrown properly:

```
#define CATCH_CONFIG_MAIN
#include <catch.hpp>

#include <vector>
#include <iostream>
#include <algorithm>

void foo(int val)
{
    if (val != 42) {
        throw std::invalid_argument("The answer is: 42");
    }
}

TEST_CASE("the answer")
{
    CHECK_NOTHROW(foo(42));
```

```
    REQUIRE_NOTHROW(foo(42));

    CHECK_THROWS(foo(0));
    CHECK_THROWS_AS(foo(0), std::invalid_argument);
    CHECK_THROWS_WITH(foo(0), "The answer is: 42");

    REQUIRE_THROWS(foo(0));
    REQUIRE_THROWS_AS(foo(0), std::invalid_argument);
    REQUIRE_THROWS_WITH(foo(0), "The answer is: 42");
}
```

As with the previous example, we define the CATCH_CONFIG_MAIN macro, add the includes that we require, and define a single TEST_CASE(). We also define a foo() function that is thrown if the input to the foo() function is invalid.

In our test case, we first test the foo() function with a valid input. Since the foo() function doesn't have an output (that is, the function returns void), we check to ensure that the function has executed properly by ensuring that no exception has been thrown using the CHECK_NOTHROW() macro. It should be noted that, like the CHECK() macro, the CHECK_NOTHROW() macro has the equivalent REQUIRE_NOTHROW(), which will halt the execution if the check fails.

Finally, we ensure that the foo() function throws an exception when its input is invalid. There are several different ways to do this. The CHECK_THROWS() macro simply ensures that an exception has been thrown. The CHECK_THROWS_AS() macro ensures that not only has an exception been thrown, but that the exception is of the std::runtime_error type. Both must be true for the test to pass. Finally, the CHECK_THROWS_WITH() macro ensures that an exception has thrown and that the what() string returned what we expect from the exception matches. As with the other version of CHECK() macros, there are also REQUIRE() versions of each of these macros.

Although the Catch2 library provides macros that let you dive into the specific details of each exception type, it should be noted that the generic CHECK_THROWS() macro should be used unless the exception type and string are specifically defined in your API requirements—for example, the at() function is defined by the specification to always return an std::out_of_range exception when the index is invalid. In this case, the CHECK_THROWS_AS() macro should be used to ensure that the at() function matches the specification. The string that this exception returns is not specified as part of the specification, and therefore, the CHECK_THROWS_WITH() should be avoided. This is important, as a common mistake when writing unit tests is to write unit tests that are over-specified. Over-specified unit tests must often be updated when the code under test is updated, which is not only costly, but prone to error.

Unit tests should be detailed enough to ensure that the unit executes as expected but generic enough to ensure that modifications to the source code do not require updates to the unit tests themselves, unless the API's requirements change, resulting in a set of unit tests that age well while still providing the necessary tests for ensuring reliability, stability, security, and even compliance.

Once you have a set of unit tests to validate that each unit executes as expected, the next step is to ensure that the unit tests are executed whenever the code is modified. This can be done manually or it can be done automatically by a **continuous integration** (**CI**) server, such as TravisCI; however, when you decide to do this, ensure that the unit test returns the proper error code. In the previous examples, the unit test itself exited with EXIT_SUCCESS when the unit tests passed and printed a simple string stating that all of the tests passed. For most CIs, this is enough, but in some cases it might be useful to have Catch2 output the results in a format that can be easily parsed.

For example, consider the following code:

```
#define CATCH_CONFIG_MAIN
#include <catch.hpp>

TEST_CASE("the answer")
{
    CHECK(true);
}
```

Let's run this with the following:

```
> ./recipe01_example01 -r xml
```

If we do this, then we get the following:

In the preceding example, we created a simple test case (the same as our first example in this recipe), and instructed Catch2 to output the results of the test to XML using the -r xml option. Catch2 has several different output formats, including XML and JSON.

In addition to output formats, Catch2 can also be used to benchmark our code. For example, consider the following code snippet:

```
#define CATCH_CONFIG_MAIN
#define CATCH_CONFIG_ENABLE_BENCHMARKING
#include <catch.hpp>

#include <vector>
#include <iostream>

TEST_CASE("the answer")
{
    std::vector<int> v{4, 8, 15, 16, 23, 42};

    BENCHMARK("sort vector") {
        std::sort(v.begin(), v.end());
    };
}
```

In the preceding example, we create a simple test case that sorts a vector with predefined vector numbers. We then sort this list inside a BENCHMARK() macro, which results in the following output when executed:

As shown in the preceding screenshot, Catch2 executed the function several times, taking on average `197` nanoseconds to sort the vector. The `BENCHMARK()` macro is useful to ensure that the code not only executes as expected with the proper outputs given specific inputs, but also that the code executes given a specific amount of time. Paired with a more detailed output format, such as XML or JSON, this type of information can be used to ensure that as the source code is modified, the resulting code executes in the same amount of time or faster.

To better understand how unit testing can truly improve your C++, we will conclude this recipe with two additional examples designed to provide more realistic scenarios.

In the first example, we will create a **vector**. Unlike an `std::vector`, which in C++ is a dynamic, C-style array, a vector in mathematics is a point in *n*-dimensional space (in our example, we limit this to 2D space), with a magnitude that is the distance between the point and the origin (that is, 0,0). We implement this vector in our example as follows:

```
#define CATCH_CONFIG_MAIN
#include <catch.hpp>

#include <cmath>
#include <climits>

class vector
{
    int m_x{};
    int m_y{};
```

The first thing we do (besides the usual macros and includes) is to define a class with `x` and `y` coordinates:

```
public:

    vector() = default;

    vector(int x, int y) :
        m_x{x},
        m_y{y}
    { }

    auto x() const
    { return m_x; }

    auto y() const
    { return m_y; }

    void translate(const vector &p)
```

```
      {
          m_x += p.m_x;
          m_y += p.m_y;
      }

      auto magnitude()
      {
          auto a2 = m_x * m_x;
          auto b2 = m_y * m_y;

          return sqrt(a2 + b2);
      }
};
```

Next, we add some helper functions and constructors. The default constructor makes a vector with no direction or magnitude as *x* and *y* are set to the origin. In order to create vectors that have a direction and magnitude, we also provide another constructor that allows you to provide the vector's initial *x* and *y* coordinates. To get the vector's direction, we provide getters that return the vector's *x* and *y* values. Finally, we provide two helper functions. The first helper function **translates** the vector, which in mathematics is another term for changing a vector's *x* and *y* coordinates given another vector. The final helper function returns the vector's magnitude, which is the length of the vector's hypotenuse if the vector's *x* and *y* values were used to construct a triangle (that is, we must use Pythagoras's theorem to calculate a vector's magnitude). Next, we move on to adding operators, which we do as follows:

```
bool operator== (const vector &p1, const vector &p2)
{ return p1.x() == p2.x() && p1.y() == p2.y(); }

bool operator!= (const vector &p1, const vector &p2)
{ return !(p1 == p2); }

constexpr const vector origin;
```

We add some equivalence operators, which can be used to check whether two vectors are equal. We also define a vector that represents the origin, which is a vector whose *x* and *y* values are 0.

To test this vector, we add the following tests:

```
TEST_CASE("default constructor")
{
    vector p;

    CHECK(p.x() == 0);
    CHECK(p.y() == 0);
```

```
    }

TEST_CASE("origin")
{
    CHECK(vector{0, 0} == origin);
    CHECK(vector{1, 1} != origin);
}

TEST_CASE("translate")
{
    vector p{-4, -8};
    p.translate({46, 50});

    CHECK(p.x() == 42);
    CHECK(p.y() == 42);
}

TEST_CASE("magnitude")
{
    vector p(1, 1);
    CHECK(Approx(p.magnitude()).epsilon(0.1) == 1.4);
}

TEST_CASE("magnitude overflow")
{
    vector p(INT_MAX, INT_MAX);
    CHECK(p.magnitude() == 65536);
}
```

The first test ensures that a default constructed vector is in fact the origin. Our next test ensures that our global **origin** vector is the origin. This is important because we should not assume that the origin is constructed by default—that is, it is possible for someone in the future to accidentally change the origin to something other than 0, 0. This test case ensures that the origin is in fact 0, 0, so that in the future, if someone accidentally changes this, this test will fail. Since the origin must result in *x* and *y* both being 0, this test is not over-specified.

Next, we test both the translate and magnitude functions. In the magnitude test case, we use the Approx() macro. This is needed because the magnitude that is returned is a floating point, whose size and precision depend on the hardware, and is irrelevant to our test. The Approx() macro allows us to state the level of precision to which we want to validate the result of the magnitude() function, which uses the epsilon() modifier to actually state the precision. In this case, we only wish to validate to one decimal point.

The last test case is used to demonstrate how all inputs to these functions should be tested. If a function takes an integer, then valid, invalid, and extreme inputs should all be tested. In this case, we are passing INT_MAX for both x and y. The resulting magnitude() function does not provide a valid result. This is because the process of calculating the magnitude overflows the integer type. This type of error should either be accounted for in the code (that is, you should check for possible overflows and throw an exception) or the API's specification should call out these types of issues (that is, the C++ specification would likely state that the result of this type of input is undefined). Either way, if a function takes an integer, then all possible integer values should be tested, and this process should be repeated for all input types.

The results of this test are as follows:

```
user@localhost:~/book/chapter07/build                          —    □    X
~~~~~~~~~~~~~~~~~~~~~~~~~~~~~~~~~~~~~~~~~~~~~~~~~~~~~~~~~~~~~~~~~~~~~~
recipe01_example06 is a Catch v2.10.2 host application.
Run with -? for options

-------------------------------------------------------------------
origin
-------------------------------------------------------------------
/home/user/book/chapter07/recipe01.cpp:235
...................................................................

/home/user/book/chapter07/recipe01.cpp:241: FAILED:
  REQUIRE( v2 != origin )
with expansion:
  {?} != {?}

-------------------------------------------------------------------
magnitude overflow
-------------------------------------------------------------------
/home/user/book/chapter07/recipe01.cpp:265
...................................................................

/home/user/book/chapter07/recipe01.cpp:268: FAILED:
  CHECK( p.magnitude() == 65536 )
with expansion:
  1.4142135624 == 65536 (0x10000)

===================================================================
test cases: 5 | 3 passed | 2 failed
assertions: 8 | 6 passed | 2 failed
```

As shown in the preceding screenshot, the unit fails the last test. As stated previously, to fix this issue, the magnitude function should be changed to either throw when an overflow occurs, find a way to prevent the overflow, or remove the test and state that such input is undefined.

In our final example, we will demonstrate how to handle functions that do not return a value, but instead, manipulate an input.

Let's start this example by creating a class that writes to a file and another class that uses the first class to write a string to said file, as follows:

```cpp
#define CATCH_CONFIG_MAIN
#include <catch.hpp>

#include <string>
#include <fstream>

class file
{
    std::fstream m_file{"test.txt", std::fstream::out};

public:

    void write(const std::string &str)
    {
        m_file.write(str.c_str(), str.length());
    }
};

class the_answer
{
public:

    the_answer(file &f)
    {
        f.write("The answer is: 42\n");
    }
};
```

As shown in the preceding code, the first class writes to a file called `test.txt`, while the second class takes the first class as an input and uses it to write a string to the file.

We test the second class as follows:

```cpp
TEST_CASE("the answer")
{
    file f;
    the_answer{f};
}
```

The problem with the preceding test is that we do not have any CHECK() macros. This is because, other than CHECK_NOTHROW(), we have nothing to check. In this test, we are testing to make sure that the the_answer{} class calls file{} classes and the write() function properly. We could open the test.txt file and check to make sure that it was written with the right string, but this is a lot of work. This type of check would also be over-specifying as we are not testing the file{} class—we are only testing the the_answer{} class. If in the future we decide that the file{} class should write to a network file and not a file on disk, the unit test would have to change.

To overcome this issue, we can leverage a concept called **mocking**. A Mock class is a class that pretends to be the class that is inputted, providing the unit test with **seams** that allow the unit test to verify the result of a test. This is different from a Stub, which provides fake input. Sadly, C++ does not have good support for mocking when compared to other languages. Helper libraries, such as GoogleMock, attempt to fix this issue at the expense of requiring all of your mockable classes to contain a vTable (that is, inheriting pure virtual base classes) and define each mockable class twice (once in your code and a second time in your test, using a set of APIs defined by Google). This is far from optimal. Libraries such as Hippomocks attempt to address these issues at the expense of some vTable black magic that only works in certain environments and is nearly impossible to debug when things go wrong. Although Hippomocks is likely one of the best options (that is, until C++ enables native mocking), the following example is another method for mocking using standard C++, with its only downside being verbosity:

```
#define CATCH_CONFIG_MAIN
#include <catch.hpp>

#include <string>
#include <fstream>

class file
{
    std::fstream m_file{"test.txt", std::fstream::out};

public:
    VIRTUAL ~file() = default;

    VIRTUAL void write(const std::string &str)
    {
        m_file.write(str.c_str(), str.length());
    }
};

class the_answer
{
```

```
public:
    the_answer(file &f)
    {
        f.write("The answer is: 42\n");
    }
};
```

As with our previous example, we create two classes. The first class writes to a file while the second class uses the first class to write a string to said file. The difference is that we added the VIRTUAL macro. When the code is compiled into our application, VIRTUAL is set to nothing, meaning that it is removed from the code by the compiler. When the code is compiled in our test, however, it is set to virtual, which tells the compiler to give the class a vTable. Since this is only done during our tests, the added overhead is fine.

Now that our class supports inheritance in our test case, we can create a subclassed version of our file{} class as follows:

```
class mock_file : public file
{
public:
    void write(const std::string &str)
    {
        if (str == "The answer is: 42\n") {
            passed = true;
        }
        else {
            passed = false;
        }
    }

    bool passed{};
};
```

The preceding class defines our mock. Instead of writing to a file, our mock checks to see whether a specific string is written to our fake file and sets a global variable to true or false, depending on the results of the test.

We can then test our the_answer{} class as follows:

```
TEST_CASE("the answer")
{
    mock_file f;
    REQUIRE(f.passed == false);

    f.write("The answer is not: 43\n");
    REQUIRE(f.passed == false);
```

```
        the_answer{f};
        CHECK(f.passed);
}
```

When this is executed, we get the following:

As shown in the preceding screenshot, we can now check to make sure that our class writes to the file as expected. It should be noted that we use the REQUIRE() macro to ensure that the mock is in the false state prior to executing our test. This ensures that if our actual test registered as having passed, that it actually has passed, instead of registering as a pass because of a bug in our test logic.

Working with ASAN, the address sanitizer

In this recipe, we will learn how to leverage Google's **address sanitizer (ASAN)**—which is a dynamic analysis tool—to check for memory corruption errors in our code. This recipe is important because it provides a simple means to ensure that your code is both reliable and stable, with a minimal number of changes to your build system.

Getting ready

Before beginning, please ensure that all of the technical requirements are met, including the installation of Ubuntu 18.04 or higher and running the following in a Terminal window:

```
> sudo apt-get install build-essential git cmake
```

This will ensure that your operating system has the proper tools to compile and execute the examples in this recipe. Once this is complete, open a new Terminal. We will use this Terminal to download, compile, and run our examples.

How to do it...

Go through the following steps to follow the recipe:

1. From a new Terminal, run the following to download the source code:

```
> cd ~/
> git clone
https://github.com/PacktPublishing/Advanced-CPP-CookBook.git
> cd Advanced-CPP-CookBook/chapter07
```

2. To compile the source code, run the following:

```
> cmake -DCMAKE_BUILD_TYPE=ASAN ..
> make recipe02_examples
```

3. Once the source code is compiled, you can execute each example in this recipe by running the following commands:

```
> ./recipe02_example01
...

> ./recipe02_example02
...

> ./recipe02_example03
...

> ./recipe02_example04
...

> ./recipe02_example05
...
```

In the next section, we will go through each of these examples and explain what each example program does and how it relates to the lessons that are being taught in this recipe.

How it works...

Google's address sanitizer is a set of modifications to the GCC and LLVM compilers, as well as a set of libraries that must be linked into your application when testing. To accomplish this, we must add the following compiler flags when compiling code for testing (but do not add these flags to production releases):

```
-fsanitize=address
-fno-optimize-sibling-calls
```

```
-fsanitize-address-use-after-scope
-fno-omit-frame-pointer
-g -O1
```

The most important flag to pay attention to here is the `-fsanitize=address` flag, which tells the compiler to enable ASAN. The rest of the flags are required by the sanitizer to function properly, with the most notable flags being `-g` and `-O1`. The `-g` flag enables debugging and the `-O1` flag sets the optimization level to 1 to provide some performance improvements. Note that once the ASAN tool is enabled, the compiler will automatically attempt to link to the ASAN libraries, which must be present on your machine.

To demonstrate how this sanitizer works, let's look at a few examples.

Memory leak error

`AddressSanitizer` is a dynamic analysis tool that is designed to identify memory corruption errors. It is similar to Valgrind, but is built directly into your executable. The easiest example to demonstrate this with (and sadly one of the most common types of errors) is a memory leak, which is shown in the following code:

```
int main(void)
{
    new int;
}
```

This results in the following output:

```
[~/book/chapter07/build]: ./recipe02_example01

==============================================================
==65910==ERROR: LeakSanitizer: detected memory leaks

Direct leak of 4 byte(s) in 1 object(s) allocated from:
    #0 0x7fbf70d459d7 in operator new(unsigned long) (/lib64/libasan.so.5+0x10f9d7)
    #1 0x401153 in main /home/user/book/chapter07/recipe02.cpp:27
    #2 0x7fbf7073a1a2 in __libc_start_main (/lib64/libc.so.6+0x271a2)

SUMMARY: AddressSanitizer: 4 byte(s) leaked in 1 allocation(s).
[~/book/chapter07/build]:
```

In the preceding example, we allocate an integer in our program using the `new` operator, but we will never free this allocated memory prior to exiting the program. The ASAN tool is capable of detecting this issue and outputs an error when the application completes its execution.

Memory deleted twice

The ability to detect memory leaks is extremely helpful, but it is not the only type of error that can be detected by ASAN. Another common type of error is deleting memory twice. For example, consider the following code snippet:

```
int main(void)
{
    auto p = new int;
    delete p;

    delete p;
}
```

When executed, we see the following output:

In the preceding example, we allocate an integer using the `new` operator and then `delete` the integer using the delete operator. Since the pointer to the previously allocated memory is still in our `p` variable, we can delete it again, which we do before we exit the program. On some systems, this would generate a segmentation fault as it is undefined behavior. The ASAN tool is capable of detecting this issue and outputs an error message stating that a `double-free` error has occurred.

Accessing invalid memory

Another type of error is attempting to access memory that was never allocated. This is usually caused by the code attempting to dereference a null pointer, but it could also occur when a pointer is corrupt, as follows:

```
int main(void)
{
    int *p = (int *)42;
    *p = 0;
}
```

This results in the following output:

In the preceding example, we create a pointer to an integer and then provide it with a corrupt value of 42 (which is not a valid pointer). We then attempt to dereference the corrupt pointer, which results in a segmentation fault. It should be noted that the ASAN tool is capable of detecting this issue, but it is not capable of providing any useful information. This is because the ASAN tool is a library that hooks into memory allocation routines, keeping track of each allocation and how the allocations are used. If an allocation never occurs, it will not have any information about what happened above and beyond what a typical Unix signal handler could already provide, something that other dynamic analysis tools, such as Valgrind, are better suited to handle.

Using memory after deleting it

To further demonstrate how the address sanitizer works, let's look at the following example:

```
int main(void)
{
    auto p = new int;
    delete p;
```

```
    *p = 0;
}
```

When we execute this, we see the following:

The preceding example allocates an integer and then deletes the integer. We then attempt to use the previously deleted memory. Since this memory location was originally allocated, ASAN has the address cached. When the dereference to the previously deleted memory occurs, ASAN is capable of detecting the issue as a `heap-use-after-free` error. It is only capable of detecting this issue because the memory was previously allocated.

Deleting memory that was never allocated

As a final example, let's look at the following:

```
int main(void)
{
    int *p = (int *)42;
    delete p;
}
```

This results in the following:

```
user@localhost:~/book/chapter07/build
[~/book/chapter07/build]: ./recipe02_example05
AddressSanitizer:DEADLYSIGNAL
=================================================================
==65985==ERROR: AddressSanitizer: SEGV on unknown address 0x00000000001a (pc 0x7f49e0df3c7f bp 0x000000000004 sp 0x7ffdf
5ea3200 T0)
==65985==The signal is caused by a WRITE memory access.
==65985==Hint: address points to the zero page.
    #0 0x7f49e0df3c7e  (/lib64/libasan.so.5+0x28c7e)
    #1 0x7f49e0edc07c in operator delete(void*, unsigned long) (/lib64/libasan.so.5+0x11107c)
    #2 0x401158 in main /home/user/book/chapter07/recipe02.cpp:114
    #3 0x7f49e08cf1a2 in __libc_start_main (/lib64/libc.so.6+0x271a2)
    #4 0x40108d in _start (/home/user/book/chapter07/build/recipe02_example05+0x40108d)

AddressSanitizer can not provide additional info.
SUMMARY: AddressSanitizer: SEGV (/lib64/libasan.so.5+0x28c7e)
==65985==ABORTING
[~/book/chapter07/build]:
```

In the preceding example, we create an integer to a pointer and then provide it with a corrupt value again. Unlike our previous example, in this example, we attempt to delete the corrupt pointer, which results in a segmentation fault. Once again, ASAN is able to detect this issue, but doesn't have any useful information as an allocation never occurred.

It should be noted that the C++ Core Guidelines—which is a coding standard for modern C++—are incredibly helpful at preventing the types of issues that we previously described. Specifically, the Core Guidelines state that `new()`, `delete()`, `malloc()`, `free()`, and friends should never be used directly, but instead, `std::unique_ptr` and `std::shared_ptr` should be used for *all memory allocations*. These APIs allocate and free memory for you, automatically. If we look at the previous examples again, it is easy to see how using these APIs to allocate memory instead of using `new()` and `delete()` manually can prevent these types of issues from occurring as most of the preceding examples were all related to the invalid use of `new()` and `delete()`.

Working with UBSAN, the undefined behavior sanitizer

In this recipe, we will learn how to use the UBSAN dynamic analysis tool with our C++ applications, which is capable of detecting undefined behavior. There are many different types of errors that can be introduced in our applications, and undefined behavior is likely the most common type, as the C and C++ specifications define several instances where undefined behavior is possible.

This recipe is important because it will teach you how to enable this simple feature and how it can be used in your applications.

Getting ready

Before beginning, please ensure that all of the technical requirements are met, including the installation of Ubuntu 18.04 or higher and running the following in a Terminal window:

```
> sudo apt-get install build-essential git cmake
```

This will ensure that your operating system has the proper tools to compile and execute the examples in this recipe. Once this is complete, open a new Terminal. We will use this Terminal to download, compile, and run our examples.

How to do it...

Go through the following steps to work through the recipe:

1. From a new Terminal, run the following to download the source code:

   ```
   > cd ~/
   > git clone
   https://github.com/PacktPublishing/Advanced-CPP-CookBook.git
   > cd Advanced-CPP-CookBook/chapter07
   ```

2. To compile the source code, run the following:

   ```
   > cmake -DCMAKE_BUILD_TYPE=UBSAN .
   > make recipe03_examples
   ```

3. Once the source code is compiled, you can execute each example in this recipe by running the following commands:

   ```
   > ./recipe03_example01
   Floating point exception (core dumped)

   > ./recipe03_example02
   Segmentation fault (core dumped)

   > ./recipe03_example03
   Segmentation fault (core dumped)

   > ./recipe03_example04
   ```

In the next section, we will go through each of these examples and explain what each example program does and how it relates to the lessons being taught in this recipe.

How it works...

The UBSAN tool is capable of detecting several types of undefined behavior, including the following:

- Out-of-bounds errors
- Floating-point errors
- Division by zero
- Integer overflows
- Null-pointer dereferencing
- Missing returns
- Signed-/unsigned-conversion errors
- Unreachable code

In this recipe, we will look at a couple of these examples, but to start, we must first enable the UBSAN tool in our application. To do this, we must enable the following flag in our application's build system:

```
-fsanitize=undefined
```

This flag will tell GCC or LLVM to use the UBSAN tool, which adds additional logic to our application as well as links to a UBSAN library. It should be noted that the UBSAN tool grows in its capability over time. For this reason, both GCC and LLVM have different levels of support for UBSAN. To get the most out of this tool, your application should be compiled against both GCC and LLVM, and you should use the most up-to-date compiler possible for both of these.

Divide-by-zero errors

One of the easiest examples to demonstrate with UBSAN is the divide-by-zero error, as follows:

```
int main(void)
{
    int n = 42;
    int d = 0;

    auto f = n/d;
}
```

When this is run, we see the following:

```
user@localhost:~/book/chapter07/build
[~/book/chapter07/build]: ./recipe03_example01
/home/user/book/chapter07/recipe03.cpp:30:15: runtime error: division by zero
Floating point exception (core dumped)
[~/book/chapter07/build]:
```

In the preceding example, we create two integers (a numerator and a denominator) with the denominator set to 0. We then divide the numerator and the denominator resulting in a divide-by-zero error, which UBSAN detects and outputs as the program crashes.

Null-pointer dereferences

A more common type of problem in C++ is a null-pointer dereference, as follows:

```
int main(void)
{
    int *p = 0;
    *p = 42;
}
```

This results in the following:

```
user@localhost:~/book/chapter07/build
[~/book/chapter07/build]: ./recipe03_example02
/home/user/book/chapter07/recipe03.cpp:44:8: runtime error: store to null pointer of type 'int'
Segmentation fault (core dumped)
[~/book/chapter07/build]:
```

In the preceding example, we create a pointer to an integer and set it to 0 (that is, a NULL pointer). We then dereference the NULL pointer and set its value, resulting in a segmentation fault, which UBSAN is capable of detecting as the program crashes.

Out-of-bounds errors

Both of the preceding examples could have been detected using a Unix signal handler. In the next example, we will access an array out of bounds, which is undefined in the C++ specification and is a lot more difficult to detect:

```
int main(void)
{
    int numbers[] = {4, 8, 15, 16, 23, 42};
    numbers[10] = 0;
}
```

When executed, we get the following:

As shown in the preceding example, we create an array with 6 elements and then attempt to access the 10th element in the array, which doesn't exist. Attempting to access this element in the array is not guaranteed to generate a segmentation fault. Regardless, UBSAN is capable of detecting this type of error and outputs the issue to `stderr` on exiting.

Overflow errors

Finally, we can also detect signed integer overflow errors, which are undefined in C++, but highly unlikely to generate a crash, and instead will cause the program to enter a corrupt state (often producing endless loops, out-of-bounds errors, and so on). Consider the following code:

```
#include <climits>

int main(void)
{
    int i = INT_MAX;
    i++;
}
```

This results in the following:

As shown in the preceding example, we create an integer and set it to its maximum value. We then attempt to increase this integer, which would normally flip the integer's sign, an error that UBSAN is capable of detecting.

Using #ifndef NDEBUG to conditionally execute additional checks

In this recipe, we will learn how to leverage the NDEBUG macro, which stands for *no debug*. This recipe is important because most build systems automatically define this macro when a *release* or *production* build is compiled, which can be leveraged to disable debug logic when such a build is created.

Getting ready

Before beginning, please ensure that all of the technical requirements are met, including the installation of Ubuntu 18.04 or higher and running the following in a Terminal window:

```
> sudo apt-get install build-essential git cmake
```

This will ensure that your operating system has the proper tools to compile and execute the examples in this recipe. Once this is complete, open a new Terminal. We will use this Terminal to download, compile, and run our examples.

How to do it...

Go through the following steps to work through the recipe:

1. From a new Terminal, run the following to download the source code:

```
> cd ~/
> git clone
https://github.com/PacktPublishing/Advanced-CPP-CookBook.git
> cd Advanced-CPP-CookBook/chapter07
```

2. To compile the source code, run the following:

```
> cmake .
> make recipe04_examples
```

3. Once the source code is compiled, you can execute each example in this recipe by running the following commands:

```
> ./recipe04_example01
The answer is: 42
```

```
> ./recipe04_example02
recipe04_example02: /home/user/book/chapter07/recipe04.cpp:45: int
main(): Assertion `42 == 0' failed.
Aborted (core dumped)
```

In the next section, we will step through each of these examples and explain what each example program does and how it relates to the lessons being taught in this recipe.

How it works...

The NDEBUG macro originates from C and was used to change the behavior of the assert() function. The assert() function can be written as follows:

```
void __assert(int val, const char *str)
{
    if (val == 0) {
        fprintf(stderr, "Assertion '%s' failed.\n", str);
        abort();
    }
}

#ifndef NDEBUG
    #define assert(a) __assert(a, #a)
#else
```

```
        #define assert(a)
    #endif
```

As shown in the preceding code, if the __assert() function is given a Boolean that evaluates to false (written in C, this is an integer that is equal to 0), an error message is outputted to stderr and the application is aborted. The NDEBUG macro is then used to determine whether the assert() function exists, and if the application is in release mode, then all of the assert logic is removed, reducing the size of the application. When using CMake, we can enable the NDEBUG flag using the following:

```
> cmake -DCMAKE_BUILD_TYPE=Release ..
```

This will automatically define the NDEBUG macro and enable optimizations. To prevent this macro from being defined, we can do the opposite:

```
> cmake -DCMAKE_BUILD_TYPE=Debug ..
```

The preceding CMake code will *not* define the NDEBUG macro, and instead will enable debugging, as well as disable most optimizations (although this depends on the compiler).

In our own code, the assert macro can be used as follows:

```
#include <cassert>

int main(void)
{
    assert(42 == 0);
}
```

This results in the following:

As shown in the preceding example, we create an application that uses the assert() macro to check a false statement, which results in the application aborting.

Although the NDEBUG macro is used by the assert() function, you can also use it yourself as follows:

```
int main(void)
{
#ifndef NDEBUG
    std::cout << "The answer is: 42\n";
#endif
}
```

As shown in the preceding code, if the application is not compiled in *release* mode (that is, if the NDEBUG macro is not defined on the command line when compiling), then the application will output to stdout. This same logic can be used throughout your code to create your own debug macros and functions to ensure that your debug logic is removed in *release* mode, allowing you to add as much debug logic as you need without modifying the resulting application that you deliver to your customers.

8
Creating and Implementing Your Own Container

In this chapter, you will learn how to create your own custom container in C++ by leveraging an existing container that the C++ Standard Template Library already provides. This chapter is important because, in a lot of cases, your code will have common operations that are performed on a Standard Template Library container that are duplicated throughout the code (as is the case with implementing thread safety). The recipes in this chapter will teach you how to easily encapsulate this duplicated code into a custom container without having to write your own container from scratch or littering your code with duplicated logic that is hard to test and validate.

Throughout this chapter, you will learn the skills needed to implement a custom wrapper container, capable of ensuring that `std::vector` is maintained in sorted order at all times. The first recipe will teach you the basics of how to create this wrapper. The second recipe will expand upon the first, teaching you how to redefine the interface of a container based on how the container operates. In this case, since the container is always in sorted order, you will learn why providing a `push_back()` function doesn't make sense, even though all we are doing is creating a wrapper (the addition of the wrapper changes the concept of the container itself). In the third recipe you will learn the skills to work with iterators and why, in this example, `const` iterators can only be supported. Finally, we will add several additional APIs to our container to provide a complete implementation.

The recipes in this chapter are as follows:

- Using a simple wrapper around std::vector
- Adding the relevant parts of the std::set API
- Working with iterators
- Adding the relevant parts of the std::vector API

Technical requirements

To compile and run the examples in this chapter, the reader must have administrative access to a computer running Ubuntu 18.04 with a functional internet connection. Prior to running these examples, the reader must install the following:

```
> sudo apt-get install build-essential git cmake
```

If this is installed on any operating system other than Ubuntu 18.04, then GCC 7.4 or higher and CMake 3.6 or higher will be required.

The code files for the chapter can be found at `https://github.com/PacktPublishing/Advanced-CPP-CookBook/tree/master/chapter08`.

Using a simple wrapper around std::vector

In this recipe, we will learn how to create our own custom container by wrapping an existing Standard Template Library container to provide custom functionality as needed. In the later recipes, we will build upon this custom container to eventually create a complete container based on `std::vector`.

This recipe is important because oftentimes, code that leverages an existing container is accompanied by common logic that is duplicated each time the container is used. This recipe (and this entire chapter) will teach you how to encapsulate this duplicated logic into your own container so that it can be independently tested.

Getting ready

Before beginning, please ensure that all of the technical requirements are met, including installing Ubuntu 18.04 or higher and running the following in a terminal window:

```
> sudo apt-get install build-essential git cmake
```

This will ensure that your operating system has the proper tools to compile and execute the examples in this recipe. Once this is complete, open a new terminal. We will use this terminal to download, compile, and run our examples.

How to do it...

Go through the following steps to try out the recipe:

1. From a new terminal, run the following to download the source code:

```
> cd ~/
> git clone
https://github.com/PacktPublishing/Advanced-CPP-CookBook.git
> cd Advanced-CPP-CookBook/chapter08
```

2. To compile the source code, run the following:

```
> cmake .
> make recipe01_examples
```

3. Once the source code is compiled, you can execute each example in this recipe by running the following commands:

```
> ./recipe01_example01
1
2
3
4
5
6
7
8

> ./recipe01_example02
1
2
3

> ./recipe01_example03
3
elements:  4 42
3
elements:  4 8 15 42
3
elements:  4 8 15 16 23 42
```

In the next section, we will step through each of these examples and explain what each one does and how it relates to the lessons being taught in this recipe.

How it works...

In this recipe, we will learn how to create a simple wrapper container around
std::vector. Most of the time, the **Standard Template Library** (**STL**) containers are
sufficient to perform the tasks that your applications might need, and, in general, creating
your own containers should be avoided as they are complicated to get right.

From time to time, however, you might find yourself repeatedly performing the same
actions on a container. When this occurs, it is often helpful to wrap these common
operations into a wrapper container that can be independently unit tested to ensure that the
container works as expected. For example, the STL containers are not thread safe. If you
need a container to function with thread safety each time you access the container, you
will first need to ensure that you have exclusive access to the container (for example, by
locking a std::mutex) before the container operation can take place. This pattern will be
repeated throughout your code, increasing the chances of entering deadlock. This issue can
be prevented by creating a container wrapper that adds a std::mutex to each public
member of the container.

In this recipe, let's consider an example where we create a vector (that is, an array of
elements in contiguous memory that you must have direct access to) that must remain in
sorted order at all times. To start, we will need some headers:

```
#include <vector>
#include <algorithm>
#include <iostream>
```

To implement our container, we will leverage std::vector. Although we could
implement our own container from scratch, most of the time this is not needed, and should
be avoided, as such a task is extremely time consuming and complicated. We will need the
algorithm header for std::sort and iostream for testing. So let's add this as follows:

```
template<
    typename T,
    typename Compare = std::less<T>,
    typename Allocator = std::allocator<T>
    >
class container
{
    using vector_type = std::vector<T, Allocator>;
    vector_type m_v;

public:
```

The container's definition will start with its template definition, which is the same as the definition of the std::vector with an added Compare type that will be used to define the order in which we would like our container to be sorted. By default, the container will be sorted in ascending order, but this can be changed as needed. Finally, the container will have one private member variable that is an instance of the std::vector that this container is wrapping.

For the container to function properly with C++ utilities, template functions, and even some key language features, the container will need to define the same aliases as std::vector, shown as follows:

```
using value_type = typename vector_type::value_type;
using allocator_type = typename vector_type::allocator_type;
using size_type = typename vector_type::size_type;
using difference_type = typename vector_type::difference_type;
using const_reference = typename vector_type::const_reference;
using const_pointer = typename vector_type::const_pointer;
using compare_type = Compare;
```

As you can see, there is no need to manually define the aliases ourselves. Instead, we can simply forward the declaration of the aliases from the std::vector itself. The exception to this is the compare_type alias, as this is an alias that we are adding to our wrapper container that represents the type used by the template class for the comparison operation that will ultimately be given to std::sort.

We also do not include the non-const versions of the reference aliases. The reason for this is that our container must keep the std::vector in sorted order at all times. If we provide the user with direct write access to the elements stored within std::vector, the user could put std::vector into an unordered state without our custom container having the ability to reorder as needed.

Next, let's define our constructors (which map to the same constructors that std::vector provides).

Default constructor

The following defines our default constructor:

```
container() noexcept(noexcept(Allocator()))
{
    std::cout << "1\n";
}
```

Since the default constructor for `std::vector` produces an empty vector, there is no additional logic that we must add as an empty vector is sorted by default. Next, we must define a constructor that takes a custom allocator.

Custom allocator constructor

Our custom allocator constructor is defined as follows:

```
explicit container(
    const Allocator &alloc
) noexcept :
    m_v(alloc)
{
    std::cout << "2\n";
}
```

As with the previous constructor, this constructor creates an empty vector, but with an allocator that already exists.

Count constructors

The next two constructors allow the user of the API to set the minimum size of the vector as follows:

```
container(
    size_type count,
    const T &value,
    const Allocator &alloc = Allocator()
) :
    m_v(count, value, alloc)
{
    std::cout << "3\n";
}

explicit container(
    size_type count,
    const Allocator &alloc = Allocator()
) :
    m_v(count, alloc)
{
    std::cout << "4\n";
}
```

The first constructor will create the vector of `count` elements, all initialized with a value of `value`, while the second creates the elements with their default values (for example, a vector of integers would be initialized to zero).

Copy/move constructors

To support the ability to copy and move our container, we will need to implement a copy and move constructor as follows:

```
container(
    const container &other,
    const Allocator &alloc
) :
    m_v(other.m_v, alloc)
{
    std::cout << "5\n";
}

container(
    container &&other
) noexcept :
    m_v(std::move(other.m_v))
{
    std::cout << "6\n";
}
```

Since our custom wrapper container must always remain in sorted order, copying or moving one container to another doesn't change the order of the elements in the container, meaning that no sort operation is needed for these constructors either. We do, however, take special care to ensure that a copy and a move occur properly by copying or moving the internal `std::vector` that our container encapsulates.

For completeness, we also provide a move constructor that allows us, just like the `std::vector`, to move while providing a custom allocator, as follows:

```
container(
    container &&other,
    const Allocator &alloc
) :
    m_v(std::move(other.m_v), alloc)
{
    std::cout << "7\n";
}
```

Next, we will provide a constructor that takes an initializer list.

Initializer list constructor

Finally, we will also add a constructor that takes an initializer list, as follows:

```
container(
    std::initializer_list<T> init,
    const Allocator &alloc = Allocator()
) :
    m_v(init, alloc)
{
    std::sort(m_v.begin(), m_v.end(), compare_type());
    std::cout << "8\n";
}
```

As shown in the preceding code, the initializer list could provide the initial elements for the std::vector in any order. As a result, we must sort the list after the vector is initialized.

Usage

Let's test this container to ensure that each constructor works as expected:

```
int main(void)
{
    auto alloc = std::allocator<int>();

    container<int> c1;
    container<int> c2(alloc);
    container<int> c3(42, 42);
    container<int> c4(42);
    container<int> c5(c1, alloc);
    container<int> c6(std::move(c1));
    container<int> c7(std::move(c2), alloc);
    container<int> c8{4, 42, 15, 8, 23, 16};

    return 0;
}
```

As shown in the preceding code block, we test our constructors by calling each one, which results in the following output:

As you can see, each constructor was successfully executed as expected.

Adding elements to our container

With our constructors in place, we will also need to provide the ability to manually add data to our container (for example, if we initially created our container using the default constructor).

To start, let's focus on the push_back() function that std::vector provides:

```
void push_back(const T &value)
{
    m_v.push_back(value);
    std::sort(m_v.begin(), m_v.end(), compare_type());

    std::cout << "1\n";
}

void push_back(T &&value)
{
    m_v.push_back(std::move(value));
    std::sort(m_v.begin(), m_v.end(), compare_type());

    std::cout << "2\n";
}
```

As shown in the preceding code snippet, the push_back() function has the same function signatures as the version std::vector provides, allowing us to simply forward the function call to std::vector. The problem is, pushing a value to the end of std::vector could result in std::vector entering an unordered state, requiring us to reorder std::vector on every single push (the result of requiring std::vector to remain in sorted order at all times).

---

[253]

One way to resolve this issue is by adding another member variable to the container wrapper that tracks when the `std::vector` is tainted. Another way to implement these functions is to add the elements in a sorted order (that is, traverse the vector sorted order and place the element in the proper position, shifting the remaining elements as needed). If elements are rarely added to the `std::vector`, then this approach might outperform a call to `std::sort`. If, however, elements are added to the `std::vector` a lot, then the tainted approach might perform better.

One of the key benefits of creating a container wrapper is that these types of optimizations can be implemented and tested without changing the code that relies on the container itself. Both implementations (or others) can be implemented, tested, and compared to determine which optimization is best suited to your particular needs, while the code that uses the container never changes. Not only does this declutter the code, but this added encapsulation strikes at the heart of object-oriented design, ensuring that each object in your code has only one purpose. In the case of the container wrapper, the purpose is to encapsulate the operation of maintaining `std::vector` in sorted order.

For completeness, we will also add the `emplace_back()` version of `push_back()`, just like `std::vector`:

```
template<typename... Args>
void emplace_back(Args&&... args)
{
    m_v.emplace_back(std::forward<Args>(args)...);
    std::sort(m_v.begin(), m_v.end(), compare_type());

    std::cout << "3\n";
}
```

The difference with the `emplace_back()` function compared to the `std::vector` equivalent is that our version does not return a reference to the element created. This is because of the fact that the sort would invalidate the reference, making it impossible to return a valid reference.

Usage of push/emplace

Finally, let's test our `push_back()` and `emplace` functions to ensure that they are called properly, as follows:

```
int main(void)
{
    int i = 42;
    container<int> c;
```

```
        c.push_back(i);
        c.push_back(std::move(i));
        c.emplace_back(42);

        return 0;
}
```

As shown in the preceding code snippet, we call each version of `push_back()` as well as the `emplace_back()` function to ensure that they are properly called as expected, which results in the following:

We can take this a step further and add better test data to our test container, as follows:

```
int main(void)
{
    int i = 42;
    container<int> c;

    c.emplace_back(4);
    c.push_back(i);
    c.emplace_back(15);
    c.push_back(8);
    c.emplace_back(23);
    c.push_back(std::move(16));

    return 0;
}
```

As shown in the preceding code snippet, we add the integers 4, 42, 15, 8, 23, and 16 to our vector. In the next recipe, we will steal APIs from `std::set` to provide better `push` and `emplace` APIs to our container, as well as an output function to get a better idea of what `std::vector` contains and the order in which it contains its elements.

Adding the relevant parts of the std::set API

In this recipe, we will learn how to add APIs from `std::set` to the custom container we created in the first recipe. Specifically, we will learn why `std::vector::push_back()` and `std::vector::emplace_back()` do not make sense when used with our custom container that always maintains its internal elements in sorted order.

Getting ready

Before beginning, please ensure that all of the technical requirements are met, including the installation of Ubuntu 18.04 or higher and running the following in a terminal window:

```
> sudo apt-get install build-essential git cmake
```

This will ensure that your operating system has the proper tools to compile and execute the examples in this recipe. Once this is complete, open a new terminal. We will use this terminal to download, compile, and run our examples.

How to do it...

Go through the following steps to try out the recipe:

1. From a new terminal, run the following to download the source code:

   ```
   > cd ~/
   > git clone
   https://github.com/PacktPublishing/Advanced-CPP-CookBook.git
   > cd Advanced-CPP-CookBook/chapter08
   ```

2. To compile the source code, run the following:

   ```
   > cmake .
   > make recipe02_examples
   ```

3. Once the source code is compiled, you can execute each example in this recipe by running the following commands:

```
> ./recipe02_example01
elements:  4
elements:  4  42
elements:  4  15  42
elements:  4  8  15  42
elements:  4  8  15  23  42
elements:  4  8  15  16  23  42
```

In the next section, we will step through each of these examples and explain what each example program does and how it relates to the lessons being taught in this recipe.

How it works...

In the first recipe of this chapter, we created a custom container wrapper that mimics a `std::vector`, but which ensures that elements in the vector remain in sorted order at all times, including the addition of the `std::vector::push_back()` function and the `std::vector::emplace_back()` function. In this recipe, we will add the `std::set::insert()` and `std::set::emplace()` functions to our custom container.

Since our container wrapper always ensures that `std::vector` is in sorted order, there is no difference between adding an element to the front, back, or middle of the vector. No matter which position an element is added to the vector, it must be sorted prior to the vector being accessed, which means that the order in which the element is added will likely change regardless of which position it is added in.

This lack of concern for where an element is added is similar to that of `std::set`. The `std::set` adds elements to a set, and then later returns `true` or `false`, depending on whether the element being tested is a member of the set. The `std::set` provides the `insert()` and `emplace()` functions for adding elements to the set. Let's add these same APIs to our custom container, as follows:

```
void insert(const T &value)
{
    push_back(value);
}

void insert(T &&value)
{
    push_back(std::move(value));
}
```

```
template<typename... Args>
void emplace(Args&&... args)
{
    emplace_back(std::forward<Args>(args)...);
}
```

As you can see in the preceding code snippet, we have added an `insert()` function (both the copy and the move), as well as an `emplace()` function, which does nothing more than call their `push_back()` and `emplace_back()` equivalents, ensuring that the parameters passed to these functions are properly forwarded. The only difference between these APIs and the APIs that we added in the previous recipe, *Using a simple wrapper around std::vector*, is the name of the function itself.

Although such a change might seem trivial, this is important as it redefines the concept between the container's APIs with the user. The `push_back()` and `emplace_back()` functions suggest that the element is added to the back of the vector when, in fact, it is not. Instead, they are simply added to the `std::vector`, and the order of the `std::vector` is changed based on the value of the element added. For this reason, the `push_back()` and `emplace_back()` functions are needed, but should either be renamed or marked as private to ensure that the user only uses the `insert()` and `emplace()` versions to properly manage expectations. When writing your own containers (even for wrappers), it is important that you adhere to the principle of least surprise, which ensures that the APIs that a user is using will work the way that the APIs might suggest.

Working with iterators

In this recipe, we will learn how to add iterator support to the custom container we started in the first recipe, which wraps a `std::vector`, ensuring that its contents remain in sorted order at all times.

To add iterator support, we will learn how to forward the iterators already provided by the `std::vector` (we will not be implementing iterators from scratch as that is a topic way outside the scope of this book, as implementing a container from scratch is incredibly difficult).

Getting ready

Before beginning, please ensure that all of the technical requirements are met, including installing Ubuntu 18.04 or higher and running the following in a terminal window:

```
> sudo apt-get install build-essential git cmake
```

This will ensure that your operating system has the proper tools to compile and execute the examples in this recipe. Once this is complete, open a new terminal. We will use this terminal to download, compile, and run our examples.

How to do it...

You need to go through the following steps to try out this recipe:

1. From a new terminal, run the following to download the source code:

```
> cd ~/
> git clone
https://github.com/PacktPublishing/Advanced-CPP-CookBook.git
> cd Advanced-CPP-CookBook/chapter08
```

2. To compile the source code, run the following:

```
> cmake .
> make recipe03_examples
```

3. Once the source code is compiled, you can execute each example in this recipe by running the following commands:

```
> ./recipe03_example01
elements: 4 8 15 16 23 42

> ./recipe03_example02
elements: 4 8 15 16 23 42
elements: 4 8 15 16 23 42
elements: 42 23 16 15 8 4
elements: 1 4 8 15 16 23 42
elements: 4 8 15 16 23 42
elements:
```

In the next section, we will step through each of these examples and explain what each example program does and how it relates to the lessons being taught in this recipe.

How it works...

The `std::vector` that our custom container wraps already provides an efficient implementation of iterators that can be used to work with our container. We will, however, need to forward specific parts of the APIs that `std::vector` provides to ensure the iterators work properly, including key C++ features, such as range-based for loops.

To start, let's add the last remaining constructor that `std::vector` provides to our custom container:

```
template <typename Iter>
container(
    Iter first,
    Iter last,
    const Allocator &alloc = Allocator()
) :
    m_v(first, last, alloc)
{
    std::sort(m_v.begin(), m_v.end(), compare_type());
}
```

As shown in the preceding code snippet, the iterator type that we are given is not defined. The iterator could come from another instance of our container or it could come from `std::vector` directly, which does not store its elements in sorted order. Even if the iterator came from an instance of our custom container, the order in which the iterator stores elements might not be the same as the order of the container elements. As a result, we must sort `std::vector` after it is initialized.

In addition to construction, it is important that our custom container also includes the iterator-based alias that `std::vector` provides, as these aliases are required for the container to properly work with C++ APIs. The following is an example code snippet for it:

```
using const_iterator = typename vector_type::const_iterator;
using const_reverse_iterator = typename
vector_type::const_reverse_iterator;
```

As shown in the preceding code snippet, like the aliases defined in the first recipe, we only need to forward declare the aliases that the `std::vector` already provided so that our custom container can leverage them as well. The difference is that we do not include the non-const versions of these iterator aliases. Since our custom container must leave the data in sorted order at all times, we must restrict the user's ability to modify the iterator's contents directly as this could result in changing the order of the container's elements, without the ability for our container to reorder as needed. Instead, modifications to the container should be made through the use of `insert()`, `emplace()`, and `erase()`.

C++ template-based functions rely on these aliases to properly implement their features, which also include range-based for loops.

Finally, there are a series of member functions, based on iterators, that `std::vector` provides that should also be forwarded through our custom container. The following code depicts this:

```
const_iterator begin() const noexcept
{
    return m_v.begin();
}

const_iterator cbegin() const noexcept
{
    return m_v.cbegin();
}
```

The first set of member functions are the `begin()` functions, which provide an iterator representing the first element in the `std::vector`. As with the aliases, we do not forward the non-const versions of these member functions. In addition, we include the `c` versions of these functions for completeness. In C++17, these are optional, as you can use `std::as_const()` instead if preferred. The next set of iterators is the `end()` iterators, which provide an iterator that represents the end of the `std::vector` (not to be confused with the iterator that represents the last element in the `std::vector`). The following code shows this:

```
const_iterator end() const noexcept
{
    return m_v.end();
}

const_iterator cend() const noexcept
{
    return m_v.cend();
}
```

As shown in the preceding code snippet, and as with most of these member functions, we simply need to forward the APIs to the private `std::vector` that our custom container encapsulates. This same process can be repeated for `rbegin()`, and `rend()`, which provide the same APIs as earlier, but return a reverse iterator, which traverses the `std::vector` in reverse order.

Next, we implement the iterator-based `emplace()` function, as follows:

```
template <typename... Args>
void emplace(const_iterator pos, Args&&... args)
{
    m_v.emplace(pos, std::forward<Args>(args)...);
    std::sort(m_v.begin(), m_v.end(), compare_type());
}
```

Although providing the `emplace()` API provides a more complete implementation, it should be noted that it would only be useful if further optimizations were made to take advantage of the intended position in the way the element is added to the container. This is in combination with a better approach to sorting the `std::vector`.

Although the preceding implementation works, it is likely to perform similarly to the version of `emplace()` we implemented in the first recipe. Since the custom container always remains in sorted order, where the element is inserted into the `std::vector` is irrelevant as the new order of the `std::vector` will change the position of the element being added. This is, of course, unless the addition of the position argument provides some additional support to the API to better optimize the addition, which our implementation doesn't do. For this reason, unless the `pos` argument is used for optimizations, the preceding function is likely redundant and unnecessary.

Like the previous `emplace()` functions, we do not attempt to return the iterator that represents the element that was added to the container, as this iterator becomes invalid after the sort, and there isn't enough information about what was added to the `std::vector` to relocate the iterator (for example, if duplicates exist, there is no way to know which element was actually just added).

Finally, we implement the `erase` functions, as follows:

```
const_iterator erase(const_iterator pos)
{
    return m_v.erase(pos);
}

const_iterator erase(const_iterator first, const_iterator last)
{
    return m_v.erase(first, last);
}
```

Unlike the `emplace()` function, removing an element from the `std::vector` does not change the order of the `std::vector`, so no sort is needed. It should also be noted that our version of the `erase()` functions return the `const` versions. Once again, this is because we cannot support the non-const versions of the iterators.

Finally, now that we have the ability to access the elements stored in the container, let's create some test logic to ensure that our container works as expected:

```
int main(void)
{
    container<int> c{4, 42, 15, 8, 23, 16};
```

To start, we will create a container from an initializer list that contains integers with no order. After this container is created, the `std::vector` that is storing these elements should be in sorted order. To prove this, let's loop through the container and output the results:

```
std::cout << "elements: ";

for (const auto &elem : c) {
    std::cout << elem << ' ';
}

std::cout << '\n';
```

As shown in the preceding code snippet, we start by outputting a label to `stdout` and then we use a ranged-based for loop to iterate over our container, outputting each element one at a time. Finally, we output a new line after all of the elements have been outputted to `stdout`, which results in the following output:

```
elements: 4 8 15 16 23 42
```

This output is in sorted order, as expected.

It should be noted that our ranged for loop must define each element as `const`. This is because we do not support the non-const versions of the iterators. Any attempt to use the non-const versions of these iterators would result in a compiler error, as in the following example:

```
for (auto &elem : c) {
    elem = 42;
}
```

The preceding code results in the following compiler error (which is intended):

```
/home/user/book/chapter08/recipe03.cpp: In function 'int main()':
/home/user/book/chapter08/recipe03.cpp:396:14: error: assignment of read-
only reference 'elem'
  396 |    elem = 42;
```

The reason that this compiler error occurs is because the ranged for loop can also be written as the following:

```
std::cout << "elements: ";

for (auto iter = c.begin(); iter != c.end(); iter++) {
    auto &elem = *iter;
    std::cout << elem << ' ';
}

std::cout << '\n';
```

As shown in the preceding code snippet, the element is not labeled as const, as the ranged for loop uses the begin() and end() member functions, resulting in a read-write iterator (unless you explicitly state const).

We can also create a test for our new emplace() function, as follows:

```
c.emplace(c.cend(), 1);

std::cout << "elements: ";
for (const auto &elem : c) {
    std::cout << elem << ' ';
}
std::cout << '\n';
```

This results in the following output:

```
elements: 1 4 8 15 16 23 42
```

As shown in the preceding output, the number 1 was added to our container in sorted order, even though we told the container to add our element to the end of the std::vector.

We can also reverse the preceding operation and validate that our erase() functions work properly, as follows:

```
c.erase(c.cbegin());

std::cout << "elements: ";
for (const auto &elem : c) {
    std::cout << elem << ' ';
}
std::cout << '\n';
```

This results in the following output:

```
elements: 4 8 15 16 23 42
```

As you can see, the newly added 1 has successfully been removed.

Adding the relevant parts of the std::vector API

In this recipe, we will complete the custom container that we have been building in the first three recipes of this chapter by adding the remaining APIs that the std::vector already provides. Along the way, we will remove the APIs that do not make sense, or that we cannot support because our custom container must keep the elements in the std::vector in sorted order.

This recipe is important as it will show you how to properly create a wrapper container that can be used to encapsulate an existing container with logic that is needed from the container (for example, thread-safety, or in our case, element order).

Getting ready

Before beginning, please ensure that all of the technical requirements are met, including the installation of Ubuntu 18.04 or higher and running the following in a terminal window:

```
> sudo apt-get install build-essential git cmake
```

This will ensure that your operating system has the proper tools to compile and execute the examples in this recipe. Once this is complete, open a new terminal. We will use this terminal to download, compile, and run our examples.

How to do it...

Go through the following steps to try out the recipe:

1. From a new terminal, run the following to download the source code:

```
> cd ~/
> git clone
https://github.com/PacktPublishing/Advanced-CPP-CookBook.git
> cd Advanced-CPP-CookBook/chapter08
```

2. To compile the source code, run the following:

```
> cmake .
> make recipe04_examples
```

3. Once the source code is compiled, you can execute each example in this recipe by running the following commands:

```
> ./recipe04_example01
elements: 4 8 15 16 23 42
elements: 4 8 15 16 23 42
elements: 4 8 15 16 23 42
elements: 42
elements: 4 8 15 16 23 42
elements: 4 8 15 16 23 42
c1.at(0): 4
c1.front(): 4
c1.back(): 42
c1.data(): 0xc01eb0
c1.empty(): 0
c1.size(): 6
c1.max_size(): 2305843009213693951
c1.capacity(): 42
c1.capacity(): 6
c1.size(): 0
c1.size(): 42
c1.size(): 0
c1.size(): 42
elements: 4 8 15 16 23
==: 0
!=: 1
 <: 1
<=: 1
 >: 0
>=: 0
```

In the next section, we will step through each of these examples and explain what each example program does and how it relates to the lessons being taught in this recipe.

How it works...

Currently, our custom container is capable of being constructed, added to, iterated over, and erased. The container does not, however, support the ability to directly access the container or support simple operations, such as a std::move() or comparison. To address these issues, let's start by adding the operator=() overloads that are missing:

```
constexpr container &operator=(const container &other)
{
    m_v = other.m_v;
    return *this;
}

constexpr container &operator=(container &&other) noexcept
{
    m_v = std::move(other.m_v);
    return *this;
}
```

The first operator=() overload provides support for a copy assignment, while the second overload provides support for a move assignment. Since we only have a single private member variable that already provides proper copy and move semantics, we do not need to worry about self assignment (or moving), as the std::vector function's implementation of copy and move will handle this for us.

If your own custom containers have additional private elements, self-assignment checks are likely needed. For example, consider the following code:

```
constexpr container &operator=(container &&other) noexcept
{
    if (&other == this) {
        return *this;
    }

    m_v = std::move(other.m_v);
    m_something = other.m_something;

    return *this;
}
```

The remaining operator=() overload takes an initializer list, shown as follows:

```
constexpr container &operator=(std::initializer_list<T> list)
{
    m_v = list;
    std::sort(m_v.begin(), m_v.end(), compare_type());
```

```
        return *this;
    }
```

As shown in the preceding code snippet, like the initializer list constructor, we must reorder the `std::vector` after the assignment, as the initializer list could be provided in any order.

The next member functions to implement are the `assign()` functions. The following code snippet shows this:

```
constexpr void assign(size_type count, const T &value)
{
    m_v.assign(count, value);
}

template <typename Iter>
constexpr void assign(Iter first, Iter last)
{
    m_v.assign(first, last);
    std::sort(m_v.begin(), m_v.end(), compare_type());
}

constexpr void assign(std::initializer_list<T> list)
{
    m_v.assign(list);
    std::sort(m_v.begin(), m_v.end(), compare_type());
}
```

These functions are similar to the `operator=()` overloads, but do not provide return values or support additional functionality. Let's see how:

- The first `assign()` function fills the `std::vector` with a specific `value` count number of times. Since the value never changes, the `std::vector` will always be in sorted order, in which case there is no need to sort the list.
- The second `assign()` function takes an iterator range similar to the constructor version of this function. Like that function, the iterator that is passed to this function could come from a raw `std::vector` or another instance of our custom container, but with a different sort order. For this reason, we must sort the `std::vector` after assignment.
- Finally, the `assign()` function also provides an initializer list version that is the same as our `operator=()` overload.

It should also be noted that we have added `constexpr` to each of our functions. This is because most of the functions in our custom container do nothing more than forward a call from the custom container to the `std::vector`, and, in some cases, make a call to `std::sort()`. The addition of `constexpr` tells the compiler to treat the code as a compile-time expression, enabling it to optimize out the additional function call when optimizations are enabled (if possible), ensuring that our custom wrapper has the smallest possible overhead.

In the past, this type of optimization was performed using the `inline` keyword. The `constexpr`, which was added in C++11, is not only capable of providing `inline` hints to the compiler, but it also tells the compiler that this function can be used at compile time instead of runtime (meaning that the compiler can execute the function while the code is being compiled to perform custom compile-time logic). In our example here, however, the runtime use of a `std::vector` is not possible as allocations are needed. As a result, the use of `constexpr` is simply for optimizations, and, on most compilers, the `inline` keyword would provide a similar benefit.

There are a number of additional functions that the `std::vector` also supports, such as `get_allocator()`, `empty()`, `size()`, and `max_size()`, all of which are just direct forwards. Let's focus on the accessors that, until now, have been missing from our custom container:

```
constexpr const_reference at(size_type pos) const
{
    return m_v.at(pos);
}
```

The first function that we provide to access the `std::vector` directly is the `at()` function. As with most of our member functions, this is a direct forward. Unlike a `std::vector`, however, we have no plans to add the `operator[]()` overloads that a `std::vector` provides. The difference between the `at()` function and the `operator[]()` overload is that the `operator[]()` does not check to ensure that the index that is provided is in bounds (that is, that it does not access elements outside the bounds of the `std::vector`).

The `operator[]()` overload is designed to function similarly to a standard C array. The problem with this operator (called the subscript operator) is that the lack of a bounds check opens the door for reliability and security bugs to make their way into your program. For this reason, the C++ core guidelines discourage the use of the subscript operator or any other forms of pointer arithmetic (anything that attempts to calculate the position of data through the use of a pointer without an explicit bounds check).

To prevent the use of the `operator[]()` overload from being used, we do not include it.

Like `std::vector`, we can also add the `front()` and `back()` accessors as follows:

```
constexpr const_reference front() const
{
    return m_v.front();
}

constexpr const_reference back() const
{
    return m_v.back();
}
```

The preceding additional accessors provide support for getting the first and last elements in our `std::vector`. As with the `at()` function, we only support the use of the `const_reference` versions of these functions that the `std::vector` already provides.

Let's now see the code snippet `data()` function:

```
constexpr const T* data() const noexcept
{
    return m_v.data();
}
```

The same goes for the `data()` function. We can only support the `const` versions of these member functions, as providing the non-const versions of these functions would provide the user direct access to the `std::vector`, allowing them to insert unordered data without the container having the ability to reorder as needed.

Let's now focus on the comparison operators. We start by defining the comparison operator's prototypes as friends of our container. This is needed as the comparison operators are typically implemented as non-member functions, and, as a result, will need private access to the container to compare the instances of `std::vector` that they contain.

For example, consider the following code snippet:

```
template <typename O, typename Alloc>
friend constexpr bool operator==(const container<O, Alloc> &lhs,
                                 const container<O, Alloc> &rhs);

template <typename O, typename Alloc>
friend constexpr bool operator!=(const container<O, Alloc> &lhs,
                                 const container<O, Alloc> &rhs);

template <typename O, typename Alloc>
friend constexpr bool operator<(const container<O, Alloc> &lhs,
```

```
                                   const container<O, Alloc> &rhs);

    template <typename O, typename Alloc>
    friend constexpr bool operator<=(const container<O, Alloc> &lhs,
                                     const container<O, Alloc> &rhs);

    template <typename O, typename Alloc>
    friend constexpr bool operator>(const container<O, Alloc> &lhs,
                                    const container<O, Alloc> &rhs);

    template <typename O, typename Alloc>
    friend constexpr bool operator>=(const container<O, Alloc> &lhs,
                                     const container<O, Alloc> &rhs);
```

Finally, we implement the comparison operators as follows:

```
template <typename O, typename Alloc>
bool constexpr operator==(const container<O, Alloc> &lhs,
                          const container<O, Alloc> &rhs)
{
    return lhs.m_v == rhs.m_v;
}

template <typename O, typename Alloc>
bool constexpr operator!=(const container<O, Alloc> &lhs,
                          const container<O, Alloc> &rhs)
{
    return lhs.m_v != rhs.m_v;
}
```

As with the member functions, we only need to forward the calls to the `std::vector`, as there is no need to implement custom logic. The same applies to the remaining comparison operators.

For example, we can implement the >, <, >=, and <= comparison operators as follows:

```
template <typename O, typename Alloc>
bool constexpr operator<(const container<O, Alloc> &lhs,
                         const container<O, Alloc> &rhs)
{
    return lhs.m_v < rhs.m_v;
}

template <typename O, typename Alloc>
bool constexpr operator<=(const container<O, Alloc> &lhs,
                          const container<O, Alloc> &rhs)
{
    return lhs.m_v <= rhs.m_v;
```

```
    }

    template <typename O, typename Alloc>
    bool constexpr operator>(const container<O, Alloc> &lhs,
                             const container<O, Alloc> &rhs)
    {
        return lhs.m_v > rhs.m_v;
    }

    template <typename O, typename Alloc>
    bool constexpr operator>=(const container<O, Alloc> &lhs,
                              const container<O, Alloc> &rhs)
    {
        return lhs.m_v >= rhs.m_v;
    }
```

That is it! That is how you implement your own container by leveraging an existing container.

As we saw, in most cases, there is no need to implement a container from scratch unless the container you need cannot be implemented using one of the containers that the C++ Standard Template Library already provides.

Using this approach, it is possible to not only create your own containers, but, more importantly, it is possible to encapsulate functionality that is duplicated throughout your code into a single container that can be independently tested and verified. This not only improves the reliability of your applications, but it makes them easier to read and maintain as well.

In the next chapter, we will explore how to use smart pointers in C++.

Exploring Type Erasure

9

In this chapter, you will learn what type erasure (also known as type erasing) is as well as how to use it in your own applications. This chapter is important because type erasing provides the ability to work with objects of different types without the need for the object to share a common base class.

This chapter starts with a simple explanation of type erasure by explaining how type erasure works in the C language as well as how to perform type erasure in C++ using inheritance. The next recipe will provide a different approach to type erasure using C++ templates, which will teach you how C++ concepts are used to define a type's specifications instead of the type itself.

Next, we will walk through the classic C++ type erasure pattern. This recipe will teach you the skills to erase type information, providing the ability to create type-safe, generic code. Finally, we will conclude with a comprehensive example of using type erasure to implement the delegate pattern, which is a pattern that provides the ability to wrap callable objects of any type and is used heavily by languages such as ObjC.

The recipes in this chapter are as follows:

- How to erase a type with inheritance
- Using C++ templates to write generic functions
- Learning the C++ type eraser pattern
- Implementing the delegate pattern

Technical requirements

To compile and run the examples in this chapter, you must have administrative access to a computer running Ubuntu 18.04 with a functional internet connection. Before running these examples, you must install the following:

```
> sudo apt-get install build-essential git cmake
```

If this is installed on any operating system other than Ubuntu 18.04, then GCC 7.4 or higher and CMake 3.6 or higher will be required.

Code files for this chapter can be found at `https://github.com/PacktPublishing/Advanced-CPP-CookBook/tree/master/chapter09`.

How to erase a type with inheritance

In this recipe, we will learn how to erase types using inheritance. When type erasing is discussed, inheritance is not usually considered, but in reality, it is the most common form of type erasing used in C++. This recipe is important because it will discuss what type erasing is and why it is so useful in everyday applications without simply removing type information—a practice that is common in C.

Getting ready

Before beginning, please ensure that all of the technical requirements are met, including installing Ubuntu 18.04 or higher and running the following in a Terminal window:

```
> sudo apt-get install build-essential git cmake
```

This will ensure your operating system has the proper tools to compile and execute the examples in this recipe. Once this is complete, open a new Terminal. We will use this Terminal to download, compile, and run our examples.

How to do it...

Let's try this recipe with the following steps:

1. From a new Terminal, run the following to download the source code:

```
> cd ~/
> git clone
https://github.com/PacktPublishing/Advanced-CPP-CookBook.git
> cd Advanced-CPP-CookBook/chapter09
```

2. To compile the source code, run the following:

```
> cmake .
> make recipe01_examples
```

3. Once the source code is compiled, you can execute each example in this recipe by running the following commands:

```
> ./recipe01_example01
1
0
```

In the next section, we will step through each of these examples and explain what each example program does and how it relates to lessons being taught in this recipe.

How it works...

Type erasure (or type erasing) is simply the act of removing, hiding, or reducing type information about an object, function, and so on. In the C language, type erasure is used all the time. Check out this example:

```
int array[10];
memset(array, 0, sizeof(array));
```

In the preceding example, we create an array of 10 elements, and then we use the memset() function to clear the array to all zeros. The memset() function in C looks something like this:

```
void *memset(void *ptr, int value, size_t num)
{
    size_t i;
    for (i = 0; i < num; i++) {
        ((char *)ptr)[i] = value;
    }

    return ptr;
}
```

As shown in the preceding code snippet, the first parameter the memset() function takes is void*. The array in our preceding example, however, is an array of integers. The memset() function doesn't actually care what type you provide, so long as you provide a pointer to the type and a size that represents the total size of the type in bytes. The memset() function then proceeds to type cast the provided pointer to a type that represents a byte (in C, this is usually char or unsigned char), and then sets the value of the type, byte by byte.

The use of `void*` in C is a form of type erasure. This type (pun intended) of erasure in C++ is typically discouraged as the only way to get the type information back is to use `dynamic_cast()`, which is slow (it requires a runtime type information lookup). Although there are many ways to perform type erasure in C++ without the need for a `void *`, let's focus on inheritance.

Inheritance is not generally described as type erasure in most literature, but it is likely the most widely used form of it. To better explore how this works, let's look at a common example. Suppose we are creating a game with multiple superheroes the user can choose from. Each superhero at some point has to attack the bad guy, but how the superhero attacks the bad guy varies from hero to hero.

For example, consider the following code snippet:

```
class spiderman
{
public:
    bool attack(int x, int) const
    {
        return x == 0 ? true : false;
    }
};
```

As shown in the preceding code snippet, our first hero doesn't care whether the bad guy is on the ground or in the air (that is, the hero will successfully hit the bad guy regardless of the bad guy's vertical distance), but will miss the bad guy if they are not in a specific horizontal position. Likewise, we might also have another hero as follows:

```
class captain_america
{
public:
    bool attack(int, int y) const
    {
        return y == 0 ? true : false;
    }
};
```

The second hero is the complete opposite of our first. This hero can successfully hit the bad guy anywhere on the ground but will miss if the bad guys is anywhere above the ground (the hero probably cannot reach them).

In the following example, both superheroes are fighting the bad guy at the same time:

```
for (const auto &h : heroes) {
    std::cout << h->attack(0, 42) << '\n';
}
```

Although we could call each superhero one at a time during the fight, it would be a lot more convenient if we could just loop through each hero in the fight and check to see which hero hits the bad guy versus which hero misses the bad guy.

In the preceding example, we have a hypothetical array of heroes that we loop through, checking to see which hero hits versus which hero misses. In this example, we don't care about the hero's type (that is, we don't care whether the hero is specifically our first or second hero), we simply care that each hero is actually a hero (and not an inanimate object) and that the hero is capable of attacking the bad guy. In other words, we need a way to erase each superhero's type so that we can put both heroes into a single array (which is not possible unless each hero is the same).

As you probably have already guessed, the most common way to accomplish this in C++ is to use inheritance (but as we will show later on in this chapter, it is not the only way). To start, we must first define a base class called `hero`, which each hero will inherit from, as follows:

```
class hero
{
public:
    virtual ~hero() = default;
    virtual bool attack(int, int) const = 0;
};
```

In our example, the only common function between each hero is that they both can attack the bad guy, the `attack()` function is the same for all heroes. As a result, we have created a pure virtual base class with a single pure virtual function called `attack()` that each hero must implement. It should also be noted that for a class to be pure virtual all member functions must be set to `0`, and the class's destructor must be explicitly labeled as `virtual`.

Now that we have defined what a hero is, we can modify our heroes to inherit this pure virtual base class, as follows:

```
class spiderman : public hero
{
public:
    bool attack(int x, int) const override
    {
        return x == 0 ? true : false;
```

```
        }
};

class captain_america : public hero
{
public:
    bool attack(int, int y) const override
    {
        return y == 0 ? true : false;
    }
};
```

As shown, both heroes inherit from the pure virtual definition of a hero and override the `attack()` function as required. With this modification, we can now create our list of heroes as follows:

```
int main(void)
{
    std::array<std::unique_ptr<hero>, 2> heros {
        std::make_unique<spiderman>(),
        std::make_unique<captain_america>()
    };

    for (const auto &h : heros) {
        std::cout << h->attack(0, 42) << '\n';
    }

    return 0;
}
```

From the preceding code, we observe the following:

- We create an array of `hero` pointers (using `std::unique_ptr` to store the lifetime of the hero, a topic that will be discussed in the next chapter).
- This array is then initialized to contain two heroes (one of each).
- Finally, we loop through each hero to see whether the hero successfully attacks the bad guy or misses.
- When the `hero::attack()` function is called, the call is routed automatically to the correct `spiderman::attack()` and `captain_america::attack()` functions as needed through the use of inheritance.

The array is erasing the type information of each hero in a type-safe manner to place each hero into a single container.

Using C++ templates to write generic functions

In this recipe, we will learn how to erase (or ignore) type information leveraging C++ templates. You will learn how C++ templates can be used to implement a C++ concept and how this type of erasure is used in the C++ Standard Library. This recipe is important as it will teach you how to better design your APIs as specifications that do not rely on specific types (or, in other words, how to write generic code).

Getting ready

Before beginning, please ensure that all of the technical requirements are met, including installing Ubuntu 18.04 or higher and running the following in a Terminal window:

```
> sudo apt-get install build-essential git cmake
```

This will ensure your operating system has the proper tools to compile and execute the examples in this recipe. Once this is complete, open a new Terminal. We will use this Terminal to download, compile, and run our examples.

How to do it...

Let's try this recipe with the following steps:

1. From a new Terminal, run the following to download the source code:

   ```
   > cd ~/
   > git clone https://github.com/PacktPublishing/Advanced-CPP-CookBook.git
   > cd Advanced-CPP-CookBook/chapter09
   ```

2. To compile the source code, run the following:

   ```
   > cmake .
   > make recipe02_examples
   ```

3. Once the source code is compiled, you can execute each example in this recipe by running the following commands:

   ```
   > ./recipe02_example01
   hero won fight
   hero lost the fight :(
   ```

In the next section, we will step through each of these examples and explain what each example program does and how it relates to the lessons being taught in this recipe.

How it works...

One of the oldest and most widely used features of C++ is C++ templates. Like inheritance, C++ templates are not generally described as a form of type erasure, but they are. Type erasure is nothing more than the act of removing or, in this case, ignoring type information.

Unlike the C language, however, type erasure in C++ generally attempts to avoid removing type information in favor of working around a type's strict definition while retaining type safety. One way to accomplish this is through the use of C++ templates. To better explain this, let's start with a simple example of a C++ template:

```
template<typename T>
T pow2(T t)
{
    return t * t;
}
```

In the preceding example, we have created a simple function that calculates the power of two for any given input. For example, we can call this function as follows:

```
std::cout << pow2(42U) << '\n'
std::cout << pow2(-1) << '\n'
```

When the compiler sees the use of the pow2() function, it automatically generates the following code for you (behind the scenes):

```
unsigned pow2(unsigned t)
{
    return t * t;
}

int pow2(int t)
{
    return t * t;
}
```

As shown in the preceding code snippet, the compiler creates two versions of the pow2() function: a version that takes an unsigned value and returns an unsigned one, and a version that takes an integer and returns an integer. The compiler created these two versions because the first time we used the pow2() function, we provided it with an unsigned value, while the second time we used the pow2() function, we provided it with int.

As far as our code is concerned, however, we don't actually care what type the function is provided, so long as the type that is provided can successfully execute operator*(). In other words, both the user of the pow2() function and the author of the pow2() function are safely ignoring (or erasing) the type information that is passed to and returned from the function from a conceptual point of view. The compiler, however, is very much aware of the types that are being provided and must safely handle each type as needed.

This form of type erasure performs the erasure at the specification of the API, and in C++, this specification is called a concept. Unlike most APIs that dictate both input and output types (for example, the sleep() function takes an unsigned integer and only an unsigned integer), a concept specifically ignores the type in favor of defining, instead, what properties a given type must provide.

For example, the preceding pow2() function has the following requirements:

- The provided type must either be an integer type or provide an operator *().
- The provided type must be either copy-constructible or move-constructible.

As shown in the previous code snippet, the pow2() function doesn't care what type it is given so long as the type provided meets certain minimum requirements. Let's examine a more complicated example to demonstrate how C++ templates can be used as a form of type erasure. Suppose we have two different heroes that are fighting a bad guy, and each hero provides the ability to attack the bad guy, which is shown with the following code:

```
class spiderman
{
public:
    bool attack(int x, int) const
    {
        return x == 0 ? true : false;
    }
};

class captain_america
{
public:
    bool attack(int, int y) const
    {
        return y == 0 ? true : false;
    }
};
```

As shown in the preceding code snippet, each hero provides the ability to attack a bad guy, but neither hero shares anything in common other than the fact that both happen to provide an `attack()` function with the same function signature. We also do not have the ability to add inheritance to each hero (maybe our design cannot handle the extra `vTable` overhead that inheritance adds, or maybe the hero definition is provided to us).

Now suppose we have a complicated function that must call the `attack()` function for each hero. We could write the same logic for each hero (that is, manually duplicate the logic), or we could write a C++ template function to handle this for us, which is shown as follows:

```cpp
template<typename T>
auto attack(const T &t, int x, int y)
{
    if (t.attack(x, y)) {
        std::cout << "hero won fight\n";
    }
    else {
        std::cout << "hero lost the fight :(\n";
    }
}
```

As shown in the preceding code snippet, we can leverage the type erasing properties of C++ templates to encapsulate our attack logic into a single template function. The preceding code doesn't care about what type it is provided so long as the type provides an `attack()` function that takes two integer types and returns an integer type (preferably `bool`, but any integer would work). In other words, so long as the type provided adheres to an agreed-upon concept, this template function will work, providing the compiler with a means to handle the type-specific logic for us.

We can call the preceding function as follows:

```cpp
int main(void)
{
    attack(spiderman{}, 0, 42);
    attack(captain_america{}, 0, 42);

    return 0;
}
```

This results in the following output:

Although this example shows how C++ templates can be used as a form of type erasure (at least for a specification to create a concept), when type erasure is discussed, there is a specific pattern called the type erasure pattern or just type erasure. In the next recipe, we will explore how we can leverage what we have learned in the first two recipes to erase type information generically while still supporting simple things such as containers.

There's more...

In this recipe, we learned how concepts can be used to ignore (or erasing) type-specific knowledge in favor of requiring a type to implemented a minimum set of features. These features can be enforce using SFINAE, a topic we discussed in greater detail in Chapter 4, *Using Templates for Generic Programming*.

See also

In Chapter 13, *Bonus – Using C++20 Features*, we will also discuss how the enforcement of a concept can be done using new features being added to C++20.

Learning the C++ type eraser pattern

In this recipe, we will learn what the type erasure pattern is in C++, and how we can leverage it to generically erase type information without sacrificing type-safety or requiring our types to inherit pure virtual base classes. This recipe is important as the type erasure pattern is used heavily in the C++ Standard Library and provides a simple way to encapsulate data types that do not share anything in common, other than providing a similar set of APIs, while still supporting things such as containers.

Getting ready

Before beginning, please ensure that all of the technical requirements are met, including installing Ubuntu 18.04 or higher and running the following in a Terminal window:

```
> sudo apt-get install build-essential git cmake
```

This will ensure your operating system has the proper tools to compile and execute the examples in this recipe. Once this is complete, open a new Terminal. We will use this Terminal to download, compile, and run our examples.

How to do it...

Let's try this recipe with the following steps:

1. From a new Terminal, run the following to download the source code:

```
> cd ~/
> git clone
https://github.com/PacktPublishing/Advanced-CPP-CookBook.git
> cd Advanced-CPP-CookBook/chapter09
```

2. To compile the source code, run the following:

```
> cmake .
> make recipe03_examples
```

3. Once the source code is compiled, you can execute each example in this recipe by running the following commands:

```
> ./recipe03_example01
1
0
```

In the next section, we will step through each of these examples and explain what each example program does and how it relates to the lessons being taught in this recipe.

How it works...

When we typically think of C++ type erasure, this is the example we think of. The type erasure pattern is needed when we must leverage a set of objects as if they are related, that may or may not share a common base class (that is, they either do not use inheritance or if they do use inheritance, it is possible they do not inherit from the same set of classes).

For example, suppose we have the following classes:

```
class spiderman
{
public:
    bool attack(int x, int) const
    {
        return x == 0 ? true : false;
    }
};

class captain_america
{
public:
    bool attack(int, int y) const
    {
        return y == 0 ? true : false;
    }
};
```

As shown in the preceding code snippet, each class defines a different type of hero. We would like to do something like this:

```
for (const auto &h : heros) {
    // something
}
```

The problem is, each class doesn't inherit from a similar base class, so we cannot just create an instance of each class and add them to `std::array` as the compiler would complain about the classes not being the same. We could store a raw `void *` pointer of each class in `std::array`, but then when it comes time to use `void *`, we would have to `dynamic_cast()` back to each type to do anything useful, like the following:

```
std::array<void *, 2> heros {
    new spiderman,
    new captain_america
};

for (const auto &h : heros) {
    if (ptr = dynamic_cast<spiderman>(ptr)) {
        // something
    }

    if (ptr = dynamic_cast<captain_america>(ptr)) {
        // something
    }
}
```

The use of `void *` is a form of type erasure, but this is far from ideal as the use of `dynamic_cast()` is slow, each new type that we add would only increase the number of `if` statements, and this implementation is far from C++ Core Guideline compliant.

There is another way, however, that we can address this problem. Suppose we wish to run the `attack()` function, which happens to be the same between each hero class (that is, each hero class at least adheres to a shared concept). If each class had used the following base class, we could just use inheritance, as follows:

```
class base
{
public:
    virtual ~base() = default;
    virtual bool attack(int, int) const = 0;
};
```

The problem is, our hero classes do not inherit from this base class. So, instead, let's create a wrapper class that does, as follows:

```
template<typename T>
class wrapper :
    public base
{
    T m_t;

public:
    bool attack(int x, int y) const override
    {
        return m_t.attack(x, y);
    }
};
```

As shown in the preceding code snippet, we have created a template wrapper class that inherits from our base class. This wrapper stores an instance to whatever type it is given, and then overrides the `attack()` function that is defined in the pure virtual base class, which forwards a call to it, to the instance that the wrapper is storing.

Now, we can create our array as follows:

```
std::array<std::unique_ptr<base>, 2> heros {
    std::make_unique<wrapper<spiderman>>(),
    std::make_unique<wrapper<captain_america>>()
};
```

`std::array` stores `std::unique_ptr` to our base class, and then we create our wrapper class (which inherits the base class) with each type we need, to store in the array. The compiler creates a version of the wrapper for each type that we need to store in the array, and since the wrapper inherits the base class, no matter what type we give the wrapper, the array can always store the resulting wrapper as needed.

Now, from this array, we can do the following:

```
for (const auto &h : heros) {
    std::cout << h->attack(0, 42) << '\n';
}
```

And there you have it: type erasure in C++. This pattern leverages C++ templates to give an object the same properties of inheritance even if the object doesn't directly use inheritance itself.

Implementing delegates with type erasing

In this recipe, we will learn how to implement the delegate pattern, which is a pattern that has been around for years (and is heavily used by some other languages, such as ObjC). This recipe is important as it will teach you what a delegate is, and how to leverage this pattern in your own applications to provide better extensibility without requiring your APIs to use inheritance.

Getting ready

Before beginning, please ensure that all of the technical requirements are met, including installing Ubuntu 18.04 or higher and running the following in a Terminal window:

```
> sudo apt-get install build-essential git cmake
```

This will ensure your operating system has the proper tools to compile and execute the examples in this recipe. Once this is complete, open a new Terminal. We will use this Terminal to download, compile, and run our examples.

How to do it...

Let's try this recipe with the following steps:

1. From a new Terminal, run the following to download the source code:

   ```
   > cd ~/
   > git clone
   https://github.com/PacktPublishing/Advanced-CPP-CookBook.git
   > cd Advanced-CPP-CookBook/chapter09
   ```

2. To compile the source code, run the following:

   ```
   > cmake .
   > make recipe04_examples
   ```

3. Once the source code is compiled, you can execute each example in this recipe by running the following commands:

   ```
   > ./recipe04_example01
   1
   0

   > ./recipe04_example02
   1
   0

   > ./recipe04_example03
   1
   0

   > ./recipe04_example04
   0
   1
   0
   ```

In the next section, we will step through each of these examples and explain what each example program does and how it relates to the lessons being taught in this recipe.

How it works...

If you have ever read a book on C++, you have likely seen the apples and oranges example, which demonstrates how object-oriented programming works. The idea goes as follows:

- An apple is a fruit.
- An orange is a fruit.
- An apple is not an orange but both are fruit.

This example is meant to teach how to organize your code into logical objects using inheritance. A logic that is shared by both an apple and an orange is written into an object called `fruit` while logic that is specific to an apple or an orange is written into the `apple` or `orange` objects that inherit from the base `fruit` object.

This example is also, however, showing how to extend the functionality of a fruit. By subclassing a fruit, I can create an apple that is capable of doing more than the `fruit` base class. This idea of *extending* the functionality of a class is common in C++, and oftentimes, we think of using inheritance to implement it. In this recipe, we will explore how to do this without the need for the apple or the orange to leverage inheritance with something called a delegate.

Suppose you are creating a game, and you wish to implement a battlefield where heroes and bad guys are fighting. At some point in your code, each hero in the battle will need to attack the bad guys. The problem is heroes come and go within the fight as they need time to recover, and so you really need to maintain a list of heroes that are capable of attacking the bad guys, and you simply need to loop through this dynamically changing list of heroes to see whether their attacks succeed or not.

Each hero could store a list of heroes that subclass a common base class and then run an `attack()` function that each hero overrides, but this would require the use of inheritance, which might not be desired. We could also use the type erasure pattern to wrap each hero and then store pointers to our wrapper's base class, but this would be specific to our `attack()` function, and we believe there will be other instances where these types of extensions will be needed.

Enter the delegate pattern, which is an extension to the type erasure pattern. With the delegate pattern, we can write code like the following:

```
int main(void)
{
    spiderman s;
    captain_america c;
```

```
    std::array<delegate<bool(int, int)>, 3> heros {
        delegate(attack),
        delegate(&s, &spiderman::attack),
        delegate(&c, &captain_america::attack)
    };

    for (auto &h : heros) {
        std::cout << h(0, 42) << '\n';
    }

    return 0;
}
```

As shown in the preceding code snippet, we have defined an instance of two different classes that are not alike, and then we have created an array that stores three delegates. The delegate's template parameter takes a function signature of bool(int, int), while the delegate itself appears to be created from a function pointer as well as two member function pointers from the class instances we created earlier. We are then able to loop through each of the delegates and call them, effectively calling the function pointer and each member function pointer independently.

The delegate pattern provides the ability to encapsulate different callable objects into a single object with a common type that is capable of calling the callable objects so long as they share the same function signature. More importantly, delegates can encapsulate both function pointers and member function pointers, providing the user of the API with the ability to store a private state if needed.

To explain how this works, we will start simple and then build upon our example until we reach the final implementation. Let's start with a base class as follows:

```
template<
    typename RET,
    typename... ARGS
    >
class base
{
public:
    virtual ~base() = default;
    virtual RET func(ARGS... args) = 0;
};
```

As shown in the preceding code snippet, we have created a template of a pure virtual base class. The template arguments are RET (which defines a return value) and ARGS... (which define a variadic list of arguments). We then create a function called func(), which takes our list of arguments and returns the template return type.

Next, let's define a wrapper that inherits from the base class using the type erasure pattern (if you have not read the previous recipe, please do so now):

```
template<
    typename T,
    typename RET,
    typename... ARGS
    >
class wrapper :
    public base<RET, ARGS...>
{
    T m_t{};
    RET (T::*m_func)(ARGS...);

public:

    wrapper(RET (T::*func)(ARGS...)) :
        m_func{func}
    { }

    RET func(ARGS... args) override
    {
        return std::invoke(m_func, &m_t, args...);
    }
};
```

Just like the type eraser pattern, we have a wrapper class that stores an instance of our type and then provides a function that the wrapper can call. The difference is the function that can be called is not statically defined and instead is defined by the template arguments that are provided. Furthermore, we also store a function pointer with the same function signature, which is initialized by the wrapper's constructor and called in the func() function using std::invoke.

This additional logic, compared to the typical type erasure example, provides the ability to define any function signature that we wish to call from the object we are storing in the wrapper instead of defining it ahead of time (meaning the function we wish to call can be determined at runtime and not compile time).

We can then create our delegate class as follows:

```
template<
    typename RET,
    typename... ARGS
    >
class delegate
{
    std::unique_ptr<base<RET, ARGS...>> m_wrapper;
```

```
public:

    template<typename T>
    delegate(RET (T::*func)(ARGS...)) :
        m_wrapper{
            std::make_unique<wrapper<T, RET, ARGS...>>(func)
        }
    { }

    RET operator()(ARGS... args)
    {
        return m_wrapper->func(args...);
    }
};
```

As with the type erasure pattern, we store a pointer to the wrapper, which is created from the constructor of the delegate. The important detail to recognize here is the T type is not defined in the delegate itself. Instead, the T type is only known during the construction of the delegate which is used to create an instantiation of the wrapper. This means that each instance of a delegate is the same, even if the delegate is storing a wrapper that wraps different types. This allows us to use the delegate as follows.

Suppose we have two heroes that do not share a common base, but do provide an attack() function with the same signature:

```
class spiderman
{
public:
    bool attack(int x, int)
    {
        return x == 0 ? true : false;
    }
};

class captain_america
{
public:
    bool attack(int, int y)
    {
        return y == 0 ? true : false;
    }
};
```

We can leverage our delegate class to store an instance of our hero classes and call their attack functions as follows:

```
int main(void)
{
    std::array<delegate<bool, int, int>, 2> heros {
        delegate(&spiderman::attack),
        delegate(&captain_america::attack)
    };

    for (auto &h : heros) {
        std::cout << h(0, 42) << '\n';
    }

    return 0;
}
```

This results in the following output:

Although we have already made significant progress in creating our delegate (it at least works), there are a few issues with this early implementation:

- The delegate's signature is `bool, int, int`, which is misleading as we really want a function signature such as `bool(int, int)` so that the code is self-documenting (the delegate's type is a single function signature, not three different types).
- This delegate cannot handle functions marked `const`.
- We have to store an instance of the delegated object inside our wrapper, which prevents us from creating delegates to more than one function for the same object.
- We do not have support for non-member functions.

Let's address each of these.

Adding a function signature to our delegate

Although adding a function signature to our delegate as the template parameter can be done without the need for C++17, user-defined type deduction in C++17 makes this process simple. The following code snippet shows this:

```
template<
    typename T,
    typename RET,
    typename... ARGS
    >
delegate(RET(T::*)(ARGS...)) -> delegate<RET(ARGS...)>;
```

As shown in the preceding code snippet, the user-defined type deduction tells the compiler how to take our delegate constructor and convert it into the template signature that we wish to use. Without this user-defined type deduction guide, the `delegate(RET(T::*)(ARGS...))` constructor would result in the delegate being deduced as `delegate<RET, ARGS...>`, which is not what we want. Instead, we would like the compiler to deduce `delegate<RET(ARGS...)>`. Nothing else about our delegate implementation needs to change. We simply need to tell the compiler how to perform type deduction.

Adding const support to our delegate

Our delegate currently cannot take a member function marked as `const` as we have not provided our delegate with a wrapper capable of doing so. For example, our heroes' `attack()` function currently looks like this:

```
class spiderman
{
public:
    bool attack(int x, int)
    {
        return x == 0 ? true : false;
    }
};
```

We would, however, like our hero `attack()` functions to look like the following since they do not modify any private member variables:

```
class spiderman
{
public:
    bool attack(int x, int) const
    {
```

```
            return x == 0 ? true : false;
    }
};
```

To support this change, we must create a wrapper that supports this, shown as follows:

```
template<
    typename T,
    typename RET,
    typename... ARGS
    >
class wrapper_const :
    public base<RET, ARGS...>
{
    T m_t{};
    RET (T::*m_func)(ARGS...) const;

public:

    wrapper_const(RET (T::*func)(ARGS...) const) :
        m_func{func}
    { }

    RET func(ARGS... args) override
    {
        return std::invoke(m_func, &m_t, args...);
    }
};
```

As shown in the preceding, this wrapper is the same as our previous wrapper with the difference being that the function signature that we store has an added const instance. For the delegate to use this additional wrapper, we must also provide an additional delegate constructor as follows:

```
template<typename T>
delegate(RET (T::*func)(ARGS...) const) :
    m_wrapper{
        std::make_unique<wrapper_const<T, RET, ARGS...>>(func)
    }
{ }
```

This means we will also need an additional user-defined type deduction guide, as follows:

```
template<
    typename T,
    typename RET,
    typename... ARGS
    >
delegate(RET(T::*)(ARGS...) const) -> delegate<RET(ARGS...)>;
```

With these modifications, we can now support member functions marked with `const`.

Adding support for one-to-many to our delegate

Currently, our wrappers store an instance to each type. This approach is often used with type erasure, but in our case, it prevents the ability to create many delegates for the same object (that is, no support for one-to-many). To fix this, we will store a pointer to an object in our wrappers instead of the object itself, as follows:

```
template<
    typename T,
    typename RET,
    typename... ARGS
    >
class wrapper :
    public base<RET, ARGS...>
{
    const T *m_t{};
    RET (T::*m_func)(ARGS...);

public:

    wrapper(const T *t, RET (T::*func)(ARGS...)) :
        m_t{t},
        m_func{func}
    { }

    RET func(ARGS... args) override
    {
        return std::invoke(m_func, m_t, args...);
    }
};
```

As shown in the preceding, the only change we have made is we store a pointer to the object we are wrapping instead of the object itself, which also means we need to initialize this pointer in our constructor. To use this new wrapper, we must modify our delegate constructor as follows:

```
template<typename T>
delegate(const T *t, RET (T::*func)(ARGS...)) :
    m_wrapper{
        std::make_unique<wrapper<T, RET, ARGS...>>(t, func)
    }
{ }
```

This, in turn, means we must update our user-defined type deduction guides as follows:

```
template<
    typename T,
    typename RET,
    typename... ARGS
    >
delegate(const T *, RET(T::*)(ARGS...)) -> delegate<RET(ARGS...)>;
```

With these modifications, we can now create our delegates as follows:

```
int main(void)
{
    spiderman s;
    captain_america c;

    std::array<delegate<bool(int, int)>, 2> heros {
        delegate(&s, &spiderman::attack),
        delegate(&c, &captain_america::attack)
    };

    for (auto &h : heros) {
        std::cout << h(0, 42) << '\n';
    }

    return 0;
}
```

As shown in the preceding, the delegate takes a pointer to each object, which means we can create as many of these delegates as we wish, including the ability to create delegates to other member function pointers if needed.

Adding support for non-member functions to our delegate

Finally, we need to modify the delegate to add support for non-member functions. Check out this example:

```
bool attack(int x, int y)
{
    return x == 42 && y == 42 ? true : false;
}
```

To do this, we simply need to add another wrapper as follows:

```
template<
    typename RET,
    typename... ARGS
    >
class fun_wrapper :
    public base<RET, ARGS...>
{
    RET (*m_func)(ARGS...);

public:

    fun_wrapper(RET (*func)(ARGS...)) :
        m_func{func}
    { }

    RET func(ARGS... args) override
    {
        return m_func(args...);
    }
};
```

As shown in the preceding, as with our original wrapper, we store a pointer to the function we wish to call, but in this case, we do not need to store a pointer to an object as there is no object (as this is a non-member function wrapper). To use this new wrapper, we must add another delegate constructor as follows:

```
delegate(RET (func)(ARGS...)) :
    m_wrapper{
        std::make_unique<fun_wrapper<RET, ARGS...>>(func)
    }
{ }
```

This means we must also provide another user-defined type deduction guide as follows:

```
template<
    typename RET,
    typename... ARGS
    >
delegate(RET(*)(ARGS...)) -> delegate<RET(ARGS...)>;
```

With all of the modifications, we are finally able to use our delegate as defined at the beginning of this recipe:

```
int main(void)
{
    spiderman s;
    captain_america c;

    std::array<delegate<bool(int, int)>, 3> heros {
        delegate(attack),
        delegate(&s, &spiderman::attack),
        delegate(&c, &captain_america::attack)
    };

    for (auto &h : heros) {
        std::cout << h(0, 42) << '\n';
    }

    return 0;
}
```

When this is executed, we get the following output:

This delegate could further be extended to support lambda functions by adding yet another set of wrappers, and the need for `std::unique_pointer` in the delegate could be removed in favor of a placement new, using a small buffer the size of the member function wrapper (or, in other words, removing the dynamic memory allocation), which is sometimes referred to as a small size optimization.

10
An In-Depth Look at Dynamic Allocation

In this chapter, you will learn how to work with dynamic memory allocation. This chapter is important because not all variables can be defined globally or on the stack (that is, from within a function), as global memory should be avoided where possible and stack memory is usually far more limited than heap memory (the memory that's used for dynamic memory allocations). The use of heap memory, however, has lead to numerous bugs over the years with respect to leaking and dangling pointers.

This chapter will teach you not only how this dynamic memory allocation works but also how to allocate memory from the heap correctly in a C++ Core Guideline compliant manner.

Beginning with why we use smart pointers as well as the difference between them, conversions, and other references, we will conclude this chapter with a brief explanation of how the heap works under Linux and why dynamic memory allocation is so slow.

In this chapter, we will cover the following recipes:

- Comparing std::shared_ptr and std::unique_ptr
- Converting from a unique_ptr into a shared_ptr
- Working with circular references
- Typecasting with smart pointers
- The heap under a microscope

Technical requirements

To compile and run the examples in this chapter, you must have administrative access to a computer running Ubuntu 18.04 with a functional internet connection. Prior to running these examples, you must install Valgrind using the following command:

```
> sudo apt-get install build-essential git cmake valgrind
```

If this is installed on any operating system other than Ubuntu 18.04, then GCC 7.4 or higher and CMake 3.6 or higher will be required.

The code files for this chapter can be found at https://github.com/PacktPublishing/ Advanced-CPP-CookBook/tree/master/chapter10.

Comparing std::shared_ptr and std::unique_ptr

In this recipe, we will learn about why the C++ Core Guidelines discourage the use of manually calling new and delete and why, instead, they recommend the use of std::unique_ptr and std::shared_ptr. We will also learn about the differences between a std::unique_ptr and a std::shared_ptr and why a std::shared_ptr should only be used in certain scenarios (that is, why std::unique_ptr is likely to be the smart pointer type that you should be using in most scenarios). This recipe is important as it will teach you how to properly allocate dynamic (heap) memory in modern C++.

Getting ready

Before beginning, please ensure that all of the technical requirements have been met, including installing Ubuntu 18.04 or higher and running the following in a Terminal window:

```
> sudo apt-get install build-essential git cmake
```

Once you have done this, open a new Terminal. We will use this Terminal to download, compile, and run our examples.

How to do it...

Follow these steps to complete this recipe:

1. From a new Terminal, run the following to download the source code:

```
> cd ~/
> git clone
https://github.com/PacktPublishing/Advanced-CPP-CookBook.git
> cd Advanced-CPP-CookBook/chapter10
```

2. To compile the source code, run the following command:

```
> cmake .
> make recipe01_examples
```

3. Once the source code has been compiled, you can execute each example in this recipe by running the following commands:

```
> ./recipe01_example01

> ./recipe01_example02
free(): double free detected in tcache 2
Aborted (core dumped)

> ./recipe01_example03

> ./recipe01_example04

> ./recipe01_example05

> ./recipe01_example06
count: 42

> ./recipe01_example07
count: 33320633

> ./recipe01_example08
count: 42
```

In the next section, we will step through each of these examples and explain what each example program does and how it relates to the lessons being taught in this recipe.

How it works...

In C++, there are three different ways to declare a variable:

- **Global variables**: These are variables that are globally accessible. On Linux, these usually exist in the `.data`, `.rodata`, or `.bss` sections of your executable.
- **Stack variables**: These are variables that you define inside functions and reside in your application's stack memory, which is managed by the compiler.
- **Heap variables**: These are variables that are created using `malloc()`/`free()` or `new()`/`delete()` and use heap memory that is managed by a dynamic memory management algorithm (for example, `dlmalloc`, `jemalloc`, `tcmalloc`, and so on).

In this chapter, we will focus on the latter, that is, heap style memory allocation. You might already know that, in C++, memory is allocated using `new()` and `delete()`, as follows:

```
int main(void)
{
    auto ptr = new int;
    *ptr = 42;
}
```

As we can see, an integer pointer (that is, a pointer that points to an integer) is allocated and then set to `42`. We use `new()` in C++ and not `malloc()` for the following reasons:

- `malloc()` returns `void *` and not the type that we care about. This can lead to allocation mismatch bugs (that is, you intend to allocate a car, and instead you allocate an orange). In other words, `malloc()` does not provide type safety.
- `malloc()` requires a size parameter. In order to allocate memory, we are required to know how many bytes to allocate for the type that we care about. This can lead to allocation size mismatch bugs (that is, you intend to allocate enough bytes for a car, but instead you only allocate enough bytes for an orange).
- `malloc()` returns `NULL` on error, requiring `NULL` checks on every allocation.

The `new()` operator addresses all of these issues:

- `new()` returns `T*`. As shown in the preceding example, this even allows for the use of `auto`, preventing redundancy, as C++'s type system has enough information to properly allocate and track the desired type.

- `new()` doesn't take a size argument. Instead, you tell it what type you want to allocate, which already has the size information about the type implicitly. Once again, by simply stating what you want to allocate, you get what you want to allocate, including the proper pointer and size.
- `new()` throws an exception if the allocation fails. This prevents the need for NULL checks. If the next line of code executes, you are guaranteed that the allocation succeeds (assuming you do not have exceptions disabled).

There is, however, still one issue with the `new()` operator; `new()` doesn't track ownership. Like `malloc()`, the `new()` operator returns a pointer, and this pointer can be passed around from function to function with no concept of who actually owns the pointer, which means it should delete the pointer when it is no longer needed.

This concept of ownership is a key component of the C++ Core Guidelines (in addition to memory spans) that attempts to address common bugs in C++ that result in instability, reliability, and security bugs. Let's take a look at an example of this:

```
int main(void)
{
    auto p = new int;
    delete p;

    delete p;
}
```

In the preceding example, we allocate an integer pointer and then delete the pointer twice. In the previous example, we never actually delete the integer pointer prior to exiting the program. Now, consider the following code block:

```
int main(void)
{
    auto p = new int;
    delete p;

    *p = 42;
}
```

In the preceding example, we allocate an integer pointer, delete it, and then use it. Although these examples seem simple and obvious to avoid, in large, complex projects, these types of bugs occur often enough that the C++ community has developed static and dynamic analysis tools to identify these type of bugs automatically for us (although they are not perfect), as well as the C++ Core Guidelines themselves, in an attempt to prevent these types of bugs in the first place.

In C++11, the standards committee introduced `std::unique_ptr` to address this ownership issue with `new()` and `delete()`. Here is how it works:

```cpp
#include <memory>

int main(void)
{
    auto ptr = std::make_unique<int>();
    *ptr = 42;
}
```

In the preceding example, we allocate an integer pointer using the `std::make_unique()` function. This function creates a `std::unique_ptr` and gives it a pointer that's allocated using `new()`. Here, the resulting pointer (for the most part) looks and behaves like a regular pointer, with the exception that the pointer is deleted automatically when `std::unique_ptr` loses scope. That is to say, `std::unique_ptr` owns the pointer that was allocated using `std::make_unique()` and is responsible for the lifetime of the pointer itself. In this example, we don't need to run `delete()` manually as `delete()` is run for us when the `main()` function is complete (as that is when `std::unique_ptr` loses scope).

Using this simple trick of managing ownership, all of the bugs shown in the preceding code can be avoided (for the most part, which we will get to later). Although the following code is not C++ Core Guideline compliant (as the subscript operator is discouraged), you can also allocate arrays using `std::unique_ptr`, as follows:

```cpp
#include <memory>
#include <iostream>

int main(void)
{
    auto ptr = std::make_unique<int[]>(100);
    ptr[0] = 42;
}
```

As shown in the preceding code, we allocate a C-style array of size `100` and then set the first element in the array. In general, the only pointer type that you will ever need is `std::unique_ptr`. There are, however, some issues that can still arise:

- Not tracking the lifetime of a pointer properly, for example, allocating `std::unique_ptr` in a function and returning the resulting pointer. Once the function returns, `std::unique_ptr` loses scope and thus deletes the pointer you just returned. `std::unique_ptr` *does not* implement automatic garbage collection. You are still required to understand the lifetime of the pointer and how that affects your code.

- It is still possible to leak memory (although far more difficult) by never providing `std::unique_ptr` with an opportunity to lose scope; for example, adding `std::unique_ptr` to a global list or allocating `std::unique_ptr` in a class that you manually allocate with `new()` and then leak. Once again, `std::unique_ptr` *does not* implement automatic garbage collection and you are still required to ensure `std::unique_ptr` loses scope when needed.
- `std::unique_ptr` is also not capable of supporting shared ownership. Although this is an issue, this type of scenario rarely occurs. In most scenarios, `std::unique_ptr` is all that you need to ensure proper ownership.

One question that is raised often is, *once the pointer is allocated, how do we safely pass this pointer to other functions?* The answer is, you use the `get()` function and pass the pointer as a regular, C-style pointer. `std::unique_ptr` defines ownership, not `NULL` pointer safety. `NULL` pointer safety is provided by the Guideline Support Library with the `gsl::not_null` wrapper and `expects()` macros.

How these are used depends on your pointer philosophy:

- Some believe any function that takes a pointer as an argument should be checked for a `NULL` pointer. The advantage of this approach is a `NULL` pointer can be identified quickly and safely handled, while the disadvantage is the extra branch logic you are introducing to your code, which reduces performance and readability.
- Some believe *public* functions that take a pointer as an argument should be checked for a `NULL` pointer. The advantage of this approach is an improvement in performance as not all functions need `NULL` pointer checks. The disadvantage of this approach is that the public interfaces still have extra branch logic.
- Some believe a function should simply document its expectations (called a contract). The benefit to this approach is that the `assert()` and `expects()` macros can be used to check for `NULL` pointers in debug mode to enforce this contract, while in release mode, there are no performance penalties. The disadvantage of this approach is that, in release mode, all bets are off.

Which approach you take will largely depend on the type of application you are writing. If you are writing the next Crush game, you will likely care more about the latter approach as it performs the best. If you are writing an application that will automatically pilot an aircraft, we all hope you are using the first approach.

To demonstrate how to pass a pointer using `std::unique_ptr`, let's look at the following example:

```
std::atomic<int> count;

void inc(int *val)
{
    count += *val;
}
```

Suppose you have a super critical function that is executed as a thread, taking an integer pointer as an argument, and adding the provided integer to a global counter. The preceding implementation of this thread is an *all bets off*, cross your fingers, and hope for the best approach. This function can be implemented as follows:

```
void inc(int *val)
{
    if (val != nullptr) {
        count += *val;
    }
    else {
        std::terminate();
    }
}
```

The preceding function calls `std::terminate()` (not a very fault-tolerant approach) if the provided pointer is a NULL pointer. As we can see, this approach is hard to read as there is a lot of extra logic here. We could implement this as follows:

```
void inc(gsl::not_null<int *> val)
{
    count += *val;
}
```

This does the same thing as a NULL pointer check (depending on how you define `gsl::not_null` to work, as this could also throw an exception). You could also implement this as follows:

```
void inc(int *val)
{
    expects(val);
    count += *val;
}
```

The previous example always checks for NULL pointers while the preceding approach uses the contract approach, allowing the check to be removed in release modes. You could also use assert() as well (if you are not using the GSL... which jokingly, of course, should never be the case).

It should also be noted that the C++ standards committee is working to add expects() logic as a core component of the language through the use of C++ contracts, a feature that was sadly removed from C++20, but will hopefully be added in future versions of the standard, as we might be able to write the preceding function as follows (and tell the compiler which approach we wish to use instead of having to manually write it):

```
void inc(int *val) [[expects: val]]
{
    count += *val;
}
```

We can use this function as follows:

```
int main(void)
{
    auto ptr = std::make_unique<int>(1);
    std::array<std::thread, 42> threads;

    for (auto &thread : threads) {
        thread = std::thread{inc, ptr.get()};
    }

    for (auto &thread : threads) {
        thread.join();
    }

    std::cout << "count: " << count << '\n';

    return 0;
}
```

From the preceding code example, we can observe the following:

- We allocate an integer pointer from the heap using std::make_unique(), which returns std::unique_ptr().
- We create an array of threads and execute each thread, passing the newly allocated pointer to each one.
- Finally, we wait for all of the threads to finish and output the resulting count. Since std::unique_ptr is scoped to the main() function, we must ensure that the threads finish prior to returning from the main() function.

The preceding example results in the following output:

As we mentioned previously, the preceding example defines `std::unique_ptr` as scoped to the `main()` function, which means we must ensure the threads are done before the `main()` function returns. This type of scenario is not always the case. Let's look at the following example:

```
std::atomic<int> count;

void inc(int *val)
{
    count += *val;
}
```

Here, we create a function that adds to a count when given an integer pointer:

```
int main(void)
{
    std::array<std::thread, 42> threads;

    {
        auto ptr = std::make_unique<int>(1);

        for (auto &thread : threads) {
            thread = std::thread{inc, ptr.get()};
        }
    }

    for (auto &thread : threads) {
        thread.join();
    }

    std::cout << "count: " << count << '\n';

    return 0;
}
```

As shown in the preceding code, the `main()` function is also identical to our previous example, with the exception that `std::unique_ptr` is created in its own scope, which is released before the threads are required to complete. This results in the following output:

```
user@localhost:~/book/ch10/build
[~/book/chapter10/build]: ./recipe01_example07
count: 35615129
[~/book/chapter10/build]:
```

As shown in the preceding screenshot, the resulting output is garbage as the threads attempted to read from memory that has been deleted (that is, the threads were given a dangling pointer).

Although this is a simple example, this type of scenario can occur in more complex scenarios and the root of the issue is shared ownership. In this example, each thread owns the pointer. In other words, no one thread attempts to take sole ownership of the pointer (including the main thread that allocates and executes the other threads). Although this type of issue usually occurs in multithreaded applications that have this no master thread design, this can also occur in asynchronous logic where the pointer is allocated and then passed to multiple, asynchronous jobs whose lifetime and point of execution are unknown.

To handle these specific types of issues, C++ provides `std::shared_ptr`. This is a wrapper around a managed object. Each time `std::shared_ptr` is copied, the managed object increases an internal counter, which is used to track how many owners the pointer (which the managed object stores) has. Each time `std::shared_ptr` loses scope, the managed object decreases the internal counter and deletes the pointer once this count reaches `0`. Using this approach, `std::shared_ptr` is capable of supporting a one-to-many ownership model, which can handle the scenarios we defined previously.

Let's look at the following example:

```
std::atomic<int> count;

void inc(std::shared_ptr<int> val)
{
    count += *val;
}
```

As shown in the preceding code, we have the same thread function that increments a counter, but the difference is that it takes `std::shared_ptr` instead of a regular integer pointer. Now, we can implement our preceding example as follows:

```
int main(void)
{
    std::array<std::thread, 42> threads;

    {
        auto ptr = std::make_shared<int>(1);

        for (auto &thread : threads) {
            thread = std::thread{inc, ptr};
        }
    }

    for (auto &thread : threads) {
        thread.join();
    }

    std::cout << "count: " << count << '\n';

    return 0;
}
```

As shown in the preceding code, the pointer is created in its own scope, which is removed before the threads are required to complete. Unlike the previous example, however, this code results in the following:

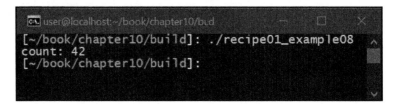

The reason the preceding code executes properly is the pointer's ownership is shared between all of the threads and the pointer itself is not deleted (even though the scope is lost) until all of the threads complete.

One final note: it might be tempting to use `std::shared_ptr` for all pointer types when `std::unique_ptr` should be used instead as it has nice typecasting APIs and, in theory, ensures that a function has a valid pointer. The reality is, regardless of the use of `std::shared_ptr` or `std::unique_ptr`, a function must perform its NULL checks as defined by your application's needs as `std::shared_ptr` can still be created as a NULL pointer.

`std::shared_ptr` also has added overhead, as it must store the deleter that it needs internally. It also requires an additional heap allocation for the managed object. Both `std::shared_ptr` and `std::unique_ptr` define pointer ownership. They do not provide automatic garbage collection (that is, they do not automatically handle pointer lifetime), nor do they guarantee a pointer is not NULL. `std::shared_ptr` should only be used when more than one thing must own the lifetime of a pointer to ensure the proper execution of your application; otherwise, use `std::unique_ptr`.

Converting from a std::unique_ptr into a std::shared_ptr

In this recipe, we will learn how to convert from a `std::unique_ptr` into a `std::shared_ptr`. This recipe is important as it is often convenient to define an API as accepting `std::unique_ptr` when the API itself really needs `std::shared_ptr` for internal use. A good example of this is when creating a GUI API. You might pass a widget to the API to store and own, without knowing if, later on down the road, the implementation of your GUI might need to add threads, in which case `std::shared_pointer` might be a better option. This recipe will provide you with the skills to convert a `std::unique_ptr` into a `std::shared_ptr` if needed, without having to modify the API itself.

Getting ready

Before beginning, please ensure that all of the technical requirements have been met, including installing Ubuntu 18.04 or higher and running the following in a Terminal window:

```
> sudo apt-get install build-essential git cmake
```

Once you have done this, open a new Terminal. We will use this Terminal to download, compile, and run our examples.

How to do it...

Follow these steps to complete this recipe:

1. From a new Terminal, run the following to download the source code:

```
> cd ~/
> git clone
https://github.com/PacktPublishing/Advanced-CPP-CookBook.git
> cd Advanced-CPP-CookBook/chapter10
```

2. To compile the source code, run the following command:

```
> cmake .
> make recipe02_examples
```

3. Once the source code has been compiled, you can execute each example in this recipe by running the following commands:

```
> ./recipe02_example01
count: 42
```

In the next section, we will step through each of these examples and explain what each example program does and how it relates to the lessons being taught in this recipe.

How it works...

`std::shared_ptr` is used to manage a pointer when more than one thing must own the pointer for the application to execute properly. Suppose, however, that you provide an API that must accept an integer pointer, as follows:

```
void execute_threads(int *ptr);
```

The preceding API suggests that whoever calls this function owns the integer pointer. That is, whoever calls this function is required to allocate the integer pointer, as well as delete it once the function is complete. If, however, we intend for the preceding API to own the pointer, we really should write this API as follows:

```
void execute_threads(std::unique_ptr<int> ptr);
```

This API says, *please allocate me an integer pointer, but I own it once it's passed and will ensure it is deleted when needed.* Now, suppose this function will use this pointer in a one-to-many ownership scenario. What do you do? You could write your API as follows:

```
void execute_threads(std::shared_ptr<int> ptr);
```

This would, however, prevent your API from optimizing the one-to-many relationship in the future (that is, if you were able to remove this relationship in the future, you would still be stuck with `std::shared_ptr`, even though it is suboptimal without having to modify the API's function signature).

To solve this, the C++ APIs provide the ability to convert a `std::unique_ptr` into a `std::shared_ptr`, as follows:

```
std::atomic<int> count;

void
inc(std::shared_ptr<int> val)
{
    count += *val;
}
```

Suppose we have an internal function that, for now, takes an integer pointer as a `std::shared_ptr`, uses its value to increment `count`, and executes it as a thread. Then, we provide a public API for it to use this internal function, as follows:

```
void
execute_threads(std::unique_ptr<int> ptr)
{
    std::array<std::thread, 42> threads;
    auto shared = std::shared_ptr<int>(std::move(ptr));

    for (auto &thread : threads) {
        thread = std::thread{inc, shared};
    }

    for (auto &thread : threads) {
        thread.join();
    }
}
```

As shown in the preceding code, our API claims ownership of a previously allocated integer pointer. Then, it creates a series of threads, executing each one and waiting for each thread to finish. The problem is that our internal function requires a `std::shared_ptr` (for example, maybe this internal function is used somewhere else in the code where there is a one-to-many ownership scenario that we cannot remove at the moment).

To prevent the need to define our public API with `std::shared_ptr`, we can convert `std::unique_ptr` into `std::shared_ptr` by moving `std::unique_ptr` into a new `std::shared_ptr` and then calling our threads from there.

`std::move()` is required, as the only way to pass ownership of `std::unique_ptr` is through the use of `std::move()` (as only one `std::unique_ptr` can own the pointer at any given time).

Now, we can execute this public API as follows:

```
int main(void)
{
    execute_threads(std::make_unique<int>(1));
    std::cout << "count: " << count << '\n';

    return 0;
}
```

This results in the following output:

In the future, we might be able to remove the need for `std::shared_ptr` and pass `std::unique_ptr` to our internal function using the `get()` function, and, when that time comes, we won't have to modify the public API.

Working with circular references

In this recipe, we will learn how to work with circular references. A circular reference occurs when we're using more than one `std::shared_ptr`, where each `std::shared_ptr` owns a reference to the other. This recipe is important as this type of circular reference can occur when we're working with circularly dependent objects (although this should be avoided whenever possible). If it does occur, the shared nature of `std::shared_ptr` results in a memory leak. This recipe will provide you with the skills to avoid said memory leak using `std::weak_ptr`.

Getting ready

Before beginning, please ensure that all of the technical requirements have been met, including installing Ubuntu 18.04 or higher and running the following in a Terminal window:

```
> sudo apt-get install build-essential git cmake valgrind
```

Once you have done this, open a new Terminal. We will use this Terminal to download, compile, and run our examples.

How to do it...

To work with circular references, perform the following steps:

1. From a new Terminal, run the following to download the source code for this recipe:

    ```
    > cd ~/
    > git clone
    https://github.com/PacktPublishing/Advanced-CPP-CookBook.git
    > cd Advanced-CPP-CookBook/chapter10
    ```

2. To compile the source code, run the following command:

    ```
    > cmake .
    > make recipe03_examples
    ```

3. Once the source code has been compiled, you can execute each example in this recipe by running the following commands:

    ```
    > valgrind ./recipe03_example01
    . . .
    ==7960== HEAP SUMMARY:
    ==7960==    in use at exit: 64 bytes in 2 blocks
    ==7960==  total heap usage: 3 allocs, 1 frees, 72,768 bytes
    allocated
    . . .

    > valgrind ./recipe03_example02
    . . .
    ==7966== HEAP SUMMARY:
    ==7966==    in use at exit: 64 bytes in 2 blocks
    ==7966==  total heap usage: 4 allocs, 2 frees, 73,792 bytes
    allocated
    . . .
    ```

```
> valgrind ./recipe03_example03
...
==7972== HEAP SUMMARY:
==7972== in use at exit: 0 bytes in 0 blocks
==7972== total heap usage: 4 allocs, 4 frees, 73,792 bytes
allocated
...

> valgrind ./recipe03_example04
...
==7978== HEAP SUMMARY:
==7978== in use at exit: 0 bytes in 0 blocks
==7978== total heap usage: 4 allocs, 4 frees, 73,792 bytes
allocated
...
```

In the next section, we will step through each of these examples and explain what each example program does and how it relates to the lessons being taught in this recipe.

How it works...

Although they should be avoided, circular references are likely to occur as your projects grow more and more complex and in size. If shared smart pointers are leveraged when these circular references occur, a hard to find memory leak can occur. To understand how this is possible, let's look at the following example:

```
class car;
class engine;
```

As shown in the preceding code, we start with two class prototypes. Circular references almost always start in this fashion as one class depends on another and vice versa, requiring the use of a class prototype.

Let's define a `car` as follows:

```
class car
{
    friend void build_car();
    std::shared_ptr<engine> m_engine;

public:
    car() = default;
};
```

As shown in the preceding code, this is a simple class that stores a shared pointer to an engine and friends a function named build_car(). Now, we can define an engine as follows:

```
class engine
{
    friend void build_car();
    std::shared_ptr<car> m_car;

public:
    engine() = default;
};
```

As shown in the preceding code, an engine is similar to a car with the difference that the engine stores a shared pointer to a car. Both, however, friend a build_car() function. Both also create default constructed shared pointers, meaning their shared pointers are NULL pointers at the time of construction.

The build_car() function is used to complete the construction of each object, as follows:

```
void build_car()
{
    auto c = std::make_shared<car>();
    auto e = std::make_shared<engine>();

    c->m_engine = e;
    e->m_car = c;
}
```

As shown in the preceding code, we create each object and then set the car's engine and vice versa. Since both the car and the engine are scoped to the build_car() function, we expect that these pointers will be deleted once the build_car() function returns. Now, we can execute this build_car() function as follows:

```
int main(void)
{
    build_car();
    return 0;
}
```

This seems like a simple program, but it has a hard to find memory leak. To demonstrate this, let's run this application in `valgrind`, which is a dynamic memory analysis tool that's capable of detecting memory leaks:

```
[~/book/chapter10/build]: valgrind ./recipe03_example01
==250833== Memcheck, a memory error detector
==250833== Copyright (C) 2002-2017, and GNU GPL'd, by Julian Seward et al.
==250833== Using Valgrind-3.15.0 and LibVEX; rerun with -h for copyright info
==250833== Command: ./recipe03_example01
==250833==
==250833==
==250833== HEAP SUMMARY:
==250833==     in use at exit: 64 bytes in 2 blocks
==250833==   total heap usage: 3 allocs, 1 frees, 72,768 bytes allocated
==250833==
==250833== LEAK SUMMARY:
==250833==    definitely lost: 32 bytes in 1 blocks
==250833==    indirectly lost: 32 bytes in 1 blocks
==250833==      possibly lost: 0 bytes in 0 blocks
==250833==    still reachable: 0 bytes in 0 blocks
==250833==         suppressed: 0 bytes in 0 blocks
==250833== Rerun with --leak-check=full to see details of leaked memory
==250833==
==250833== For lists of detected and suppressed errors, rerun with: -s
==250833== ERROR SUMMARY: 0 errors from 0 contexts (suppressed: 0 from 0)
[~/book/chapter10/build]:
```

As shown in the preceding screenshot, `valgrind` says that memory was leaked. If we run `valgrind` with `--leak-check=full`, it will tell us that the memory leaks are with the car and engine shared pointers. The reason this memory leak occurs is that the car holds a shared reference to an engine. This same engine holds a shared reference to the car itself.

For example, consider the following code:

```cpp
void build_car()
{
    auto c = std::make_shared<car>();
    auto e = std::make_shared<engine>();

    c->m_engine = e;
    e->m_car = c;

    std::cout << c.use_count() << '\n';
    std::cout << e.use_count() << '\n';
}
```

As shown in the preceding code, we have added a call to `use_count()`, which outputs the number of owners `std::shared_ptr` contains. If this is executed, we'll see the following output:

```
user@localhost:~/book/chapter10/build
[~/book/chapter10/build]: ./recipe03_example02
2
2
[~/book/chapter10/build]:
```

The reason we can see two owners is because the `build_car()` function holds a reference to a car and an engine here:

```
auto c = std::make_shared<car>();
auto e = std::make_shared<engine>();
```

The car holds a second reference to an engine because of this:

```
c->m_engine = e;
```

This is also the same for the engine and the car. When the `build_car()` function completes, the following loses scope first:

```
auto e = std::make_shared<engine>();
```

The engine, however, is not deleted because the car still holds a reference to the engine. Then, the car loses scope:

```
auto c = std::make_shared<car>();
```

However, the car is not deleted because the engine (which hasn't been deleted yet) also holds a reference to the car. This results in `build_car()` returning with neither the car nor the engine being deleted because both still hold a reference to each other, with no means of telling either object to remove their references.

This type of circular memory leak, although easy to identify in our example, can be extremely difficult to identify in complex code, which is one of many reasons why shared pointers and circular dependencies should be avoided (usually a better design can remove the need for both). If this cannot be avoided, `std::weak_ptr` can be used instead, as follows:

```
class car
{
    friend void build_car();
```

```
        std::shared_ptr<engine> m_engine;

public:
        car() = default;
};
```

As shown in the preceding code, we still define our car as holding a shared reference to an engine. We do this as we assume a car has a longer lifetime (that is, in our model, you can have a car without an engine, but you cannot have an engine without a car). The engine, however, is defined as follows:

```
class engine
{
        friend void build_car();
        std::weak_ptr<car> m_car;

public:
        engine() = default;
};
```

As shown in the preceding code, the engine now stores a weak reference to the car. Our build_car() function is defined as follows:

```
void build_car()
{
        auto c = std::make_shared<car>();
        auto e = std::make_shared<engine>();

        c->m_engine = e;
        e->m_car = c;

        std::cout << c.use_count() << '\n';
        std::cout << e.use_count() << '\n';
}
```

As shown in the preceding code, the build_car() function doesn't change. The difference now is that, when we execute this application using valgrind, we see the following output:

```
[~/book/chapter10/build]: valgrind ./recipe03_example03
==250915== Memcheck, a memory error detector
==250915== Copyright (C) 2002-2017, and GNU GPL'd, by Julian Seward et al.
==250915== Using Valgrind-3.15.0 and LibVEX; rerun with -h for copyright info
==250915== Command: ./recipe03_example03
==250915==
1
2
==250915==
==250915== HEAP SUMMARY:
==250915==     in use at exit: 0 bytes in 0 blocks
==250915==   total heap usage: 4 allocs, 4 frees, 73,792 bytes allocated
==250915==
==250915== All heap blocks were freed -- no leaks are possible
==250915==
==250915== For lists of detected and suppressed errors, rerun with: -s
==250915== ERROR SUMMARY: 0 errors from 0 contexts (suppressed: 0 from 0)
[~/book/chapter10/build]:
```

As shown in the preceding screenshot, there are no memory leaks, and the `use_count()` for the car is 1, while the `use_count()` for the engine is still 2 compared to the previous example. In the engine class, we use `std::weak_ptr`, which has access to the managed object `std::shared_ptr` manages, but doesn't increase the managed object's internal count when created. This provides `std::weak_ptr` with the ability to query whether `std::shared_ptr` is valid without having to hold a strong reference to the pointer itself.

The reason the memory leak is removed is that, when the engine loses scope, its use count is decreased from 2 to 1. Once the car loses scope, which only has a use count of 1, it gets deleted, which in turn decrements the engine's use count to 0, which causes the engine to be deleted as well.

The reason we use `std::weak_ptr` instead of a C-style pointer in the engine is because `std::weak_ptr` provides us with the ability to query the managed object to see if the pointer is still valid. For example, suppose we need to check whether the car still exists, as follows:

```
class engine
{
    friend void build_car();
    std::weak_ptr<car> m_car;

public:
    engine() = default;

    void test()
    {
        if (m_car.expired()) {
```

```
            std::cout << "car deleted\n";
        }
    }
};
```

Using the `expired()` function, we can test to see whether the car still exists before using it, which is something that isn't possible with a C-style pointer. Now, we can write our `build_car()` function as follows:

```
void build_car()
{
  auto e = std::make_shared<engine>();

  {
  auto c = std::make_shared<car>();

  c->m_engine = e;
  e->m_car = c;
  }

  e->test();
}
```

In the preceding example, we create an engine and then create a new scope that creates our car. Then, we create our circular reference and lose scope. This causes the car to be deleted as expected. The difference is that our engine isn't deleted yet as we still hold a reference to it. Now, we can run our test function, which results in the following output when it's run with `valgrind`:

```
user@localhost:~/book/chapter10/build
[~/book/chapter10/build]: valgrind ./recipe03_example04
==250945== Memcheck, a memory error detector
==250945== Copyright (C) 2002-2017, and GNU GPL'd, by Julian Seward et al.
==250945== Using Valgrind-3.15.0 and LibVEX; rerun with -h for copyright info
==250945== Command: ./recipe03_example04
==250945==
car deleted
==250945==
==250945== HEAP SUMMARY:
==250945==     in use at exit: 0 bytes in 0 blocks
==250945==   total heap usage: 4 allocs, 4 frees, 73,792 bytes allocated
==250945==
==250945== All heap blocks were freed -- no leaks are possible
==250945==
==250945== For lists of detected and suppressed errors, rerun with: -s
==250945== ERROR SUMMARY: 0 errors from 0 contexts (suppressed: 0 from 0)
[~/book/chapter10/build]:
```

As shown in the preceding screenshot, there are no memory leaks. std::weak_ptr successfully removed the chicken and egg problem that was introduced by the circular reference. As a result, std::shared_ptr is able to function as expected, releasing memory in the right order. In general, circular references and dependencies should be avoided whenever possible, but, if they cannot be avoided, std::weak_ptr, as shown in this recipe, can be used to prevent memory leaks.

Typecasting with smart pointers

In this recipe, we will learn how to typecast using std::unique_ptr and std::shared_ptr. Typecasting allows you to convert one type into another. This recipe is important as it demonstrates the proper way of handling typecasting with std::unique_ptr and std::shared_ptr when attempting to convert the smart pointer's type (for example, when upcasting or downcasting with virtual inheritance).

Getting ready

Before beginning, please ensure that all of the technical requirements have been met, including installing Ubuntu 18.04 or higher and running the following in a Terminal window:

```
> sudo apt-get install build-essential git cmake
```

Once you have done this, open a new Terminal. We will use this Terminal to download, compile, and run our examples.

How to do it...

To see how typecasting works, perform the following steps:

1. From a new Terminal, run the following to download the source code:

```
> cd ~/
> git clone
https://github.com/PacktPublishing/Advanced-CPP-CookBook.git
> cd Advanced-CPP-CookBook/chapter10
```

2. To compile the source code, run the following command:

```
> cmake .
> make recipe04_examples
```

3. Once the source code has been compiled, you can execute each example in this recipe by running the following commands:

```
> ./recipe04_example01
downcast successful!!
```

```
> ./recipe04_example02
downcast successful!!
```

In the next section, we will step through each of these examples and explain what each example program does and how it relates to the lessons being taught in this recipe.

How it works...

Typecasting with smart pointers is not as straightforward as you might expect.

To explain this better, let's look at a simple example of how to typecast from a base class to a subclass using `std::unique_ptr`:

```
class base
{
public:
    base() = default;
    virtual ~base() = default;
};
```

Let's see how this works:

1. We start with a virtual base class, as shown in the preceding code, and then we subclass the base class as follows:

```
class subclass : public base
{
public:
    subclass() = default;
    ~subclass() override = default;
};
```

2. Next, we create a `std::unique_ptr` in our `main()` function and pass the pointer to a `foo()` function:

```
int main(void)
{
    auto ptr = std::make_unique<subclass>();
    foo(ptr.get());

    return 0;
}
```

`std::unique_ptr` simply owns the lifetime of the pointer. Any use of the pointer requires the use of the `get()` function, which converts `std::unique_ptr` into a normal, C-style pointer from that point on. This is the intended use of `std::unique_ptr`, since it isn't designed to ensure pointer safety and is designed to ensure who owns the pointer is well-defined, ultimately determining when the pointer should be deleted.

3. Now, the `foo()` function can be defined as follows:

```
void foo(base *b)
{
    if (dynamic_cast<subclass *>(b)) {
        std::cout << "downcast successful!!\n";
    }
}
```

As shown in the preceding code, the `foo()` function can treat the pointer as a normal C-style pointer, using `dynamic_cast()` to downcast from the base pointer back to the original subclass.

This same style of typecasting, which is standard C++, does not work with `std::shared_ptr`. The reason why is because the code that needs a typecast version of `std::shared_ptr` might also need to hold a reference to the pointer (that is, a copy of `std::shared_ptr` to prevent deletion).

That is, it is not possible to go from `base *b` to `std::shared_ptr<subclass>` because `std::shared_ptr` doesn't hold a reference to the pointer; instead, it holds a reference to a managed object, which stores the reference to the actual pointer. Since `base *b` doesn't store a managed object, there is no way to create a `std::shared_ptr` from it.

C++ does, however, provide `std::shared_ptr` versions of `static_cast()`, `reinterpret_cast()`, `const_cast()`, and `dynamic_cast()` to perform the typecasting of shared pointers, which preserves the managed object when typecasting. Let's take a look at an example:

```
class base
{
public:
    base() = default;
    virtual ~base() = default;
};

class subclass : public base
{
public:
    subclass() = default;
    ~subclass() override = default;
};
```

As shown in the preceding code, we start with the same base and subclass. The difference occurs in our `foo()` function:

```
void foo(std::shared_ptr<base> b)
{
    if (std::dynamic_pointer_cast<subclass>(b)) {
        std::cout << "downcast successful!!\n";
    }
}
```

Instead of taking `base *b`, it takes `std::shared_ptr<base>`. Now, we can use the `std::dynamic_pointer_cast()` function instead of `dynamic_cast()` to downcast `std::shared_ptr<base>` to a `std::shared_ptr<subclass>`. The `std::shared_ptr` typecast functions provide us with the ability to typecast while still maintaining access to a `std::shared_ptr` as needed.

The resulting `main()` function will look like this:

```
int main(void)
{
    auto ptr = std::make_shared<subclass>();
    foo(ptr);

    return 0;
}
```

This results in the following output:

It should be noted that we don't need to explicitly upcast as this can be done automatically (similar to regular pointers). We are only required to downcast explicitly.

The heap under a microscope

In this recipe, we will learn how the heap works in Linux. We will take a deeper look into how Linux actually provides heap memory when you use `std::unique_ptr`.

Although this recipe is intended for those of you who have more advanced capabilities, it is important as it will teach you what your application does to allocate memory from the heap (that is, using `new()`/`delete()`), which, in turn, will show you why heap allocations should never be done from time critical code, since they are slow. This recipe will teach you the skills you'll need when heap allocations are safe to perform and when heap allocations should be avoided in your applications, even if some of the assembly code that we inspect is hard to follow.

Getting ready

Before beginning, please ensure that all of the technical requirements have been met, including installing Ubuntu 18.04 or higher and running the following in a Terminal window:

```
> sudo apt-get install build-essential git cmake
```

Once you have done this, open a new Terminal. We will use this Terminal to download, compile, and run our examples.

How to do it...

To try the code files for this chapter, go through the following steps:

1. From a new Terminal, run the following to download the source code:

```
> cd ~/
> git clone
https://github.com/PacktPublishing/Advanced-CPP-CookBook.git
> cd Advanced-CPP-CookBook/chapter10
```

2. To compile the source code, run the following command:

```
> cmake .
> make recipe05_examples
```

3. Once the source code has been compiled, you can execute each example in this recipe by running the following commands:

```
> ./recipe05_example01
```

In the next section, we will step through each of these examples and explain what each example program does and how it relates to the lessons being taught in this recipe.

How it works...

To better understand the extent to which code has to execute so as to allocate a variable on the heap, we will start with the following simple example:

```
int main(void)
{
    auto ptr = std::make_unique<int>();
}
```

As shown in the preceding example, we allocate an integer using `std::unique_ptr()`. We use `std::unique_ptr()` as our starting point, as this is how most C++ Core Guideline code will allocate memory on the heap.

The `std::make_unique()` function allocates a `std::unique_ptr` using the following pseudo logic (this is a simplified example as this doesn't show how custom deleters are handled):

```
namespace std
{
    template<typename T, typename... ARGS>
    auto make_unique(ARGS... args)
    {
        return std::unique_ptr(new T(std::forward<ARGS>(args)...));
    }
}
```

As shown in the preceding code, the `std::make_unique()` function creates a `std::unique_ptr` and gives it a pointer that it allocates with the `new()` operator. Once `std::unique_ptr` loses scope, it will delete the pointer using `delete()`.

When the compiler sees the new operator, it replaces the code with a call to operator `new(unsigned long)`. To see this, let's look at the following example:

```
int main(void)
{
    auto ptr = new int;
}
```

In the preceding example, we allocate a simple pointer using `new()`. Now, we can look at the resulting compiled assembly, which can be seen in the following screenshot:

```
[~/book/chapter10/build]: objdump -d recipe05_example02 | grep "<main>:" -A 13
0000000000401fc5 <main>:
  401fc5:       55                      push    %rbp
  401fc6:       48 89 e5                mov     %rsp,%rbp
  401fc9:       48 83 ec 10             sub     $0x10,%rsp
  401fcd:       bf 04 00 00 00          mov     $0x4,%edi
  401fd2:       e8 19 00 00 00          callq   401ff0 <_Znwm>
  401fd7:       48 89 45 f8             mov     %rax,-0x8(%rbp)
  401fdb:       b8 00 00 00 00          mov     $0x0,%eax
  401fe0:       c9                      leaveq
  401fe1:       c3                      retq
  401fe2:       66 2e 0f 1f 84 00 00    nopw    %cs:0x0(%rax,%rax,1)
  401fe9:       00 00 00
  401fec:       0f 1f 40 00             nopl    0x0(%rax)

[~/book/chapter10/build]:
```

As shown in the following screenshot, a call is made to _Znwm, which is mangled C++ code for `operator new(unsigned long)`, which is easy to demangle:

```
[~/book/chapter10/build]: c++filt _Znwm
operator new(unsigned long)
[~/book/chapter10/build]:
```

The `new()` operator itself looks like the following pseudocode (note that this doesn't take into account the ability to disable exception support or provide support for a new handler):

```cpp
void* operator new(size_t size)
{
    if (auto ptr = malloc(size)) {
        return ptr;
    }

    throw std::bad_alloc();
}
```

Now, we can look at the new operator to see `malloc()` being called:

```
[~/book/chapter10/build]: objdump -d recipe05_example02 | grep "_Znwm>:" -A 20
0000000000401ff0 <_Znwm>:
  401ff0:	f3 0f 1e fa          	endbr64
  401ff4:	53                   	push   %rbx
  401ff5:	48 85 ff             	test   %rdi,%rdi
  401ff8:	bb 01 00 00 00       	mov    $0x1,%ebx
  401ffd:	48 0f 45 df          	cmovne %rdi,%rbx
  402001:	48 89 df             	mov    %rbx,%rdi
  402004:	e8 87 51 02 00       	callq  427190 <__libc_malloc>
  402009:	48 85 c0             	test   %rax,%rax
  40200c:	74 02                	je     402010 <_Znwm+0x20>
  40200e:	5b                   	pop    %rbx
  40200f:	c3                   	retq
  402010:	e8 ab 12 00 00       	callq  4032c0 <_ZSt15get_new_handlerv>
  402015:	48 85 c0             	test   %rax,%rax
  402018:	0f 84 c2 f0 ff ff    	je     4010e0 <_Znwm.cold>
  40201e:	ff d0                	callq  *%rax
  402020:	eb df                	jmp    402001 <_Znwm+0x11>
  402022:	66 2e 0f 1f 84 00 00 	nopw   %cs:0x0(%rax,%rax,1)
  402029:	00 00 00
  40202c:	0f 1f 40 00          	nopl   0x0(%rax)

[~/book/chapter10/build]:
```

As shown in the preceding screenshot, `malloc()` is called. If the resulting pointer is not `NULL`, the operator returns; otherwise, it enters its error state, which involves calling a new handler and eventually throwing `std::bad_alloc()` (at least by default).

The call to `malloc()` itself is far more complicated. When an application itself is started, the first thing it does is reserve heap space. The operating system gives every application a contiguous block of virtual memory to operate from, and the heap on Linux is the last block of memory in the application (that is, the memory that `new()` returns comes from the end of the application's memory space). Placing the heap here provides the operating system with a way to add additional memory to the application as it is needed (as the operating simply extends the end of the application's virtual memory).

The application itself uses the `sbrk()` function to ask the operating system for more memory when it runs out. When this function is called, the operating system allocates pages of memory from its internal page pool and maps this memory into the application by moving the end of the application's memory space. The map process itself is slow as the operating system not only has to allocate pages from the pool, which requires some sort of search and reservation logic, but it must also walk the application's page tables to add this additional memory to its virtual address space.

Once `sbrk()` has provided the application with additional memory, the `malloc()` engine takes over. As we mentioned previously, the operating system simply maps pages of memory into the application. Each page can be as small as 4k bytes to anywhere from 2 MB to even 1 GB, depending on the request. In our example, however, we allocated a simple integer, which is only 4 bytes in size. To convert pages into small objects without wasting memory, `malloc()` itself has an algorithm that breaks the memory provided by the operating system up into small blocks. This engine must also handle when these blocks of memory are freed so that they can be used again. This requires complex data structures to manage all of the application's memory, and each call to `malloc()`, `free()`, `new()`, and `delete()` has to exercise this logic.

A simple call to create a `std::unique_ptr` using `std::make_unique()` has to create `std::unique_ptr` with memory allocated from `new()`, which actually calls `malloc()`, which must search through a complex data structure to find a free block of memory that can eventually be returned, that is, assuming `malloc()` has free memory and doesn't have to ask the operating system for more memory using `sbrk()`.

In other words, dynamic (that is, heap) memory is slow and should only be used when needed, and, ideally, not in time critical code.

Common Patterns in C++ 11

In this chapter, you will learn various design patterns in C++. Design patterns provide a common approach to solving different types of problems properly, and oftentimes, design patterns are discussed throughout the internet, at conferences, and in front of the water cooler at work regarding their advantages and disadvantages.

The goal of this chapter is to introduce you to some of the more popular, less popular, and even controversial patterns, giving you an idea of the different types of problems that design patterns attempt to solve. This is an important chapter as it will give you the skills to tackle hard problems by teaching you already existing approaches to common problems others have experienced in the past. Learning even a subset of these design patterns will lay the foundation for discovering other design patterns on your own as you run into problems in your own applications.

The recipes in this chapter are as follows:

- Learning the factory pattern
- Using the singleton pattern properly
- Extending your objects with the decorator pattern
- Adding communication with the observer pattern
- Improving performance with static polymorphism

Technical requirements

To compile and run the examples in this chapter, you must have administrative access to a computer running Ubuntu 18.04 with a functional internet connection. Before running these examples, you must install the following:

```
> sudo apt-get install build-essential git cmake
```

If this is installed on any operating system other than Ubuntu 18.04, then GCC 7.4 or higher and CMake 3.6 or higher will be required.

Code files for this chapter can be found at `https://github.com/PacktPublishing/Advanced-CPP-CookBook/tree/master/chapter11`.

Learning the factory pattern

In this recipe, we will learn what the factory pattern is, how to implement it, and when to use it. This recipe is important, especially when unit testing as the factory pattern provides the ability to add seams (that is, intentional places in your code that provide opportunities for making changes) capable of changing what type of object another object allocates, including the ability to allocate fake objects for testing.

Getting ready

Before beginning, please ensure that all of the technical requirements are met, including installing Ubuntu 18.04 or higher and running the following in a Terminal window:

```
> sudo apt-get install build-essential git cmake
```

This will ensure your operating system has the proper tools to compile and execute the examples in this recipe. Once this is complete, open a new Terminal. We will use this Terminal to download, compile, and run our examples.

How to do it...

Perform the following steps to try the code for the factory pattern:

1. From a new Terminal, run the following to download the source code:

   ```
   > cd ~/
   > git clone
   https://github.com/PacktPublishing/Advanced-CPP-CookBook.git
   > cd Advanced-CPP-CookBook/chapter11
   ```

2. To compile the source code, run the following:

   ```
   > cmake .
   > make recipe01_examples
   ```

3. Once the source code is compiled, you can execute each example in this recipe by running the following commands:

```
> ./recipe01_example01
```

```
> ./recipe01_example02
```

```
> ./recipe01_example03
correct answer: The answer is: 42
```

```
> ./recipe01_example04
wrong answer: Not sure
```

```
> ./recipe01_example05
correct answer: The answer is: 42
```

In the next section, we will go through each of these examples and explain what each example program does and how it relates to the lessons being taught in this recipe.

How it works...

The factory pattern provides an object that allocates resources with a means to change the types that the object allocates. To better understand how this pattern works and why it is so useful, let's look at the following example:

```cpp
class know_it_all
{
public:
    auto ask_question(const char *question)
    {
        (void) question;
        return answer("The answer is: 42");
    }
};
```

We start, as shown in the preceding code, with a class called know_it_all that provides an answer when asked a question. In this particular case, no matter what question is asked, it always returns the same answer. The answer is defined as the following:

```cpp
class answer
{
    std::string m_answer;

public:
    answer(std::string str) :
        m_answer{std::move(str)}
```

```
        { }
    };
```

As shown in the preceding, the answer is a simple class that is constructed given a string and stores the string internally. It is important to note in this case that the user of this API cannot actually extract the string that the answer class stores, meaning the use of these APIs is as follows:

```
int main(void)
{
    know_it_all universe;
    auto ___ = universe.ask_question("What is the meaning of life?");
}
```

As shown in the preceding, we can ask a question, and a result is provided, but we are not sure of what result was actually provided. This type of problem exists all of the time in object-oriented programming, and testing this sort of logic is one of the many reasons why entire books have been written on the subject of object mocking. A mock is a fake version of an object designed specifically to validate the output of a test (unlike a fake, which is nothing more than an object that provides test input). In the preceding example, however, a mock still needs a way to be created so that the output of a function can be verified. Enter the factory pattern.

Let's modify the answer class as follows:

```
class answer
{
    std::string m_answer;

public:
    answer(std::string str) :
        m_answer{std::move(str)}
    { }

    static inline auto make_answer(std::string str)
    { return answer(str); }
};
```

As shown in the preceding code, we have added a static function that allows the answer class to create instances of itself. We have not changed the fact that the answer class doesn't provide the ability to extract the content it holds within, just how the answer class is created. We can then modify the know_it_all class as follows:

```
template<factory_t factory = answer::make_answer>
class know_it_all
{
```

```
public:
    auto ask_question(const char *question)
    {
        (void) question;
        return factory("The answer is: 42");
    }
};
```

As shown in the preceding code, the only difference here is that the `know_it_all` class takes a template parameter for `factory_t` and uses it to create the answer class instead of creating the `answer` class directly. `factory_t` is defined as follows:

```
using factory_t = answer(*)(std::string str);
```

This defaults to the static `make_answer()` function that we added to the `answer` class. In its most simple form, the preceding example demonstrates the factory pattern. Instead of creating an object directly, we delegate the creation of an object to another object. The preceding implementation doesn't change anything about how the two classes are used, as follows:

```
int main(void)
{
    know_it_all universe;
    auto ___ = universe.ask_question("What is the meaning of life?");
}
```

As shown in the preceding, the `main()` logic remains unchanged, but this new approach ensures that the `know_it_all` class focuses on answering questions without worrying about how to create the `answer` class itself, leaving that task to a different object. The real power behind this subtle change is we can now provide the `know_it_all` class with a different factory, resulting in a different `answer` class being returned. To demonstrate this, let's create a new `answer` class as follows:

```
class expected_answer : public answer
{
public:
    expected_answer(std::string str) :
        answer{str}
    {
        if (str != "The answer is: 42") {
            std::cerr << "wrong answer: " << str << '\n';
            exit(1);
        }

        std::cout << "correct answer: " << str << '\n';
    }
```

```
    static inline answer make_answer(std::string str)
    { return expected_answer(str); }
};
```

As shown in the preceding, we have created a new `answer` class that sub-classes the original `answer` class. This new class checks the value it is given during construction and outputs success or failure based on the string it is provided. We can then use this new `answer` class as follows:

```
int main(void)
{
    know_it_all<expected_answer::make_answer> universe;
    auto ____ = universe.ask_question("What is the meaning of life?");
}
```

The following is the resulting output:

```
[~/book/chapter11/build]: ./recipe01_example03
correct answer: The answer is: 42
[~/book/chapter11/build]:
```

Using the preceding approach, we are not able to ask different questions to see whether the `know_it_all` class provides the right answers without having to modify the original `answer` class. For example, suppose the `know_it_all` class was implemented this way:

```
template<factory_t factory = answer::make_answer>
class know_it_all
{
public:
    auto ask_question(const char *question)
    {
        (void) question;
        return factory("Not sure");
    }
};
```

We tested this version of the `know_it_all` class, as follows:

```
int main(void)
{
    know_it_all<expected_answer::make_answer> universe;
    auto ____ = universe.ask_question("What is the meaning of life?");
}
```

The result would be the following:

```
[~/book/chapter11/build]: ./recipe01_example04
wrong answer: Not sure
[~/book/chapter11/build]:
```

It should be noted that there are several ways to implement the factory pattern. The preceding approach uses a template argument to change how the know_it_all class creates answers, but we could also use a runtime approach as well, as in this example:

```
class know_it_all
{
    std::function<answer(std::string str)> m_factory;

public:
    know_it_all(answer(*f)(std::string str) = answer::make_answer) :
        m_factory{f}
    { }

    auto ask_question(const char *question)
    {
        (void) question;
        return m_factory("The answer is: 42");
    }
};
```

As shown in the preceding, we start with a custom know_it_all constructor that stores a pointer to a factory function, which again, defaults to our answer class, but provides the ability to change the factory if we choose, which is shown as follows:

```
int main(void)
{
    know_it_all universe(expected_answer::make_answer);
    auto ___ = universe.ask_question("What is the meaning of life?");
}
```

If we wanted, we could also add a setter to this class to change this function pointer at runtime.

Using the singleton pattern properly

In this recipe, we will learn how to properly implement the singleton pattern in C++11 and above and when it is appropriate to use the singleton pattern. This recipe is important as it will teach you when to use the singleton pattern, which provides a clear definition of a single global resource, ensuring the resource is kept global without the possibility of multiple copies.

Getting ready

Before beginning, please ensure that all of the technical requirements are met, including installing Ubuntu 18.04 or higher and running the following in a Terminal window:

```
> sudo apt-get install build-essential git cmake
```

This will ensure your operating system has the proper tools to compile and execute the examples in this recipe. Once this is complete, open a new Terminal. We will use this Terminal to download, compile, and run our examples.

How to do it...

Perform the following steps to try the singleton pattern:

1. From a new Terminal, run the following to download the source code:

   ```
   > cd ~/
   > git clone
   https://github.com/PacktPublishing/Advanced-CPP-CookBook.git
   > cd Advanced-CPP-CookBook/chapter11
   ```

2. To compile the source code, run the following:

   ```
   > cmake .
   > make recipe01_examples
   ```

3. Once the source code is compiled, you can execute each example in this recipe by running the following commands:

   ```
   > ./recipe02_example01
   memory: 0x4041a0
   i1: 0x4041a0
   i2: 0x4041a4
   i3: 0x4041a8
   ```

```
i4: 0x4041ac

> ./recipe02_example02
memory: 0x4041a0
i1: 0x4041a0
i2: 0x4041a4
i3: 0x4041a0
i4: 0x4041a4

> ./recipe02_example03
memory: 0x4041a0
i1: 0x4041a0
i2: 0x4041a4
i3: 0x4041a8
i4: 0x4041ac

> ./recipe02_example04
memory: 0x4041a0
i1: 0x4041a0
i2: 0x4041a4
i3: 0x4041a8
i4: 0x4041ac
```

In the next section, we will step through each of these examples and explain what each example program does and how it relates to the lessons being taught in this recipe.

How it works...

The singleton pattern has been around in C++ for several years, and it is arguably one of the most controversial patterns in all of C++ as its global nature introduces coupling in your application (similar to how global variables introduce coupling). The singleton pattern implements a single, global resource. Specifically, it creates an object that maintains global scope, while ensuring no copies of itself can exist. The debate as to whether or not the singleton pattern should be used in your code will not be answered in this book as it depends on your use case, but let's at least cover some advantages and disadvantages of this pattern.

Advantages: The singleton pattern provides a clearly defined interface for global resources that can only contain a single instance. Whether we like it or not, global resources exist in all of our applications (for example, heap memory). If such a global resource is needed, and you have a mechanism to handle coupling (for example, a mocking engine such as Hippomocks), the singleton pattern is a great way to ensure the global resource is managed properly.

Disadvantages: The following are the disadvantages:

- The singleton pattern defines a global resource, and like any global resource (for example, a global variable), any code that uses a singleton object becomes tightly coupled with the singleton. Coupling, in objected-oriented design, should always be avoided as it prevents the ability to fake a resource your code might depend on, which limits flexibility when testing.
- The singleton pattern hides dependencies. When inspecting an object's interface, there is no way to determine that the object's implementation depends on a global resource. Most argue that this can be handled with good documentation.
- The singleton pattern maintains its state throughout the lifetime of the application. This is especially true (that is, the disadvantage is obvious) when unit testing as the singleton's state carries from one unit test to the next, which most consider a violation of what a unit test is.

In general, global resources should always be avoided. Period. To ensure that your code is properly written to enforce the singleton design pattern, if and when you need a single global resource. Let's discuss the following example.

Suppose you are writing an application for an embedded device, and your embedded device has an additional memory pool that you can map into your application (for example, device memory for a video or network device). Now, suppose you can only ever have one of these additional memory pools and you need to implement a set of APIs to allocate memory from this pool. In our example, we will implement this memory pool using the following:

```
uint8_t memory[0x1000] = {};
```

Next, we will implement a memory manager class to allocate memory from this pool, as follows:

```
class mm
{
    uint8_t *cursor{memory};

public:
    template<typename T>
    T *allocate()
    {
        if (cursor + sizeof(T) > memory + 0x1000) {
            throw std::bad_alloc();
        }

        auto ptr = new (cursor) T;
        cursor += sizeof(T);
```

```
            return ptr;
    }
};
```

As shown in the preceding code, we have created a memory manager class that stores a pointer to the memory buffer that contains our single, global resource. We then create a simple allocation function that handles this memory out as needed (with no ability to free, which keeps the algorithm really simple).

Since this is a global resource, we create the class globally as follows:

```
mm g_mm;
```

Finally, we can use our new memory manager as follows:

```
int main(void)
{
    auto i1 = g_mm.allocate<int>();
    auto i2 = g_mm.allocate<int>();
    auto i3 = g_mm.allocate<int>();
    auto i4 = g_mm.allocate<int>();

    std::cout << "memory: " << (void *)memory << '\n';
    std::cout << "i1: " << (void *)i1 << '\n';
    std::cout << "i2: " << (void *)i2 << '\n';
    std::cout << "i3: " << (void *)i3 << '\n';
    std::cout << "i4: " << (void *)i4 << '\n';
}
```

In the preceding example, we allocate four integer pointers and then output the address of our memory block and the addresses of the integer pointers to ensure the algorithm is working as intended, resulting in the following output:

As shown in the preceding, the memory manager properly allocates memory as needed.

The problem with the preceding implementation is that the memory manager is just a class like any other, meaning it can be created as many times as we want as well as copied. To better demonstrate why this is a problem, let's look at the following example. Instead of creating one memory manager, let's create two:

```
mm g_mm1;
mm g_mm2;
```

Next, let's use both of these memory managers as follows:

```
int main(void)
{
    auto i1 = g_mm1.allocate<int>();
    auto i2 = g_mm1.allocate<int>();
    auto i3 = g_mm2.allocate<int>();
    auto i4 = g_mm2.allocate<int>();

    std::cout << "memory: " << (void *)memory << '\n';
    std::cout << "i1: " << (void *)i1 << '\n';
    std::cout << "i2: " << (void *)i2 << '\n';
    std::cout << "i3: " << (void *)i3 << '\n';
    std::cout << "i4: " << (void *)i4 << '\n';
}
```

As shown in the preceding, the only difference is we are now using two memory managers instead of one. This results in the following output:

As shown in the preceding, memory has been double allocated, which will likely result in corruption and undefined behavior. The reason this occurs is the memory buffer itself is a global resource—something we cannot change. The memory manager itself does nothing to ensure this scenario cannot happen and, as a result, the user of this API might accidentally create a second memory manager. Note that, in our example, we explicitly created a second copy, but a second copy could occur by simply passing the memory manager around, inadvertently creating copies along the way.

To address this issue, we must handle two specific scenarios:

- Creating more than one instance of the memory manager
- Copying the memory manager

To address both of these issues, let's now show the singleton pattern:

```
class mm
{
    uint8_t *cursor{memory};
    mm() = default;
```

As shown in the preceding, we start with the constructor being marked as `private`. Marking the constructor as `private` prevents the use of the memory manager from creating their own instances of the memory manager. Instead, to get an instance of the memory manager, we will use the following `public` function:

```
static auto &instance()
{
    static mm s_mm;
    return s_mm;
}
```

This preceding function creates a static (that is, global) instance of the memory manager and then returns a reference to this instance. Using this function, the user of the API can only get an instance of the memory manager from this function, which always returns only a reference to the globally defined resource. In other words, there is no ability to create additional instances of the class without the compiler complaining.

The last step to creating the singleton class is the following:

```
mm(const mm &) = delete;
mm &operator=(const mm &) = delete;
mm(mm &&) = delete;
mm &operator=(mm &&) = delete;
```

As shown in the preceding, the copy and move constructors/operators are explicitly deleted. This addresses the second issue. By removing the copy constructor and operator, there is no ability to create a copy of the global resource, ensuring that the class only exists as a single global object.

To use this singleton class, we would do the following:

```
int main(void)
{
    auto i1 = mm::instance().allocate<int>();
```

```
    auto i2 = mm::instance().allocate<int>();
    auto i3 = mm::instance().allocate<int>();
    auto i4 = mm::instance().allocate<int>();

    std::cout << "memory: " << (void *)memory << '\n';
    std::cout << "i1: " << (void *)i1 << '\n';
    std::cout << "i2: " << (void *)i2 << '\n';
    std::cout << "i3: " << (void *)i3 << '\n';
    std::cout << "i4: " << (void *)i4 << '\n';
}
```

This results in the following output:

```
user@localhost:~/book/chapter11/build                    —    □    ×
[~/book/chapter11/build]: ./recipe02_example03
memory: 0x4041a0
i1: 0x4041a0
i2: 0x4041a4
i3: 0x4041a8
i4: 0x4041ac
[~/book/chapter11/build]:
```

If we attempt to create another instance of the memory manager ourselves, we would get an error similar to the following:

```
/home/user/book/chapter11/recipe02.cpp:166:4: error: 'constexpr mm::mm()' is
private within this context
   166 | mm g_mm;
```

Finally, since the singleton class is a single, global resource, we can create wrappers to remove the verbosity, as in the following:

```
template<typename T>
constexpr T *allocate()
{
    return mm::instance().allocate<T>();
}
```

This change can be used as follows:

```
int main(void)
{
    auto i1 = allocate<int>();
    auto i2 = allocate<int>();
    auto i3 = allocate<int>();
    auto i4 = allocate<int>();
```

```
std::cout << "memory: " << (void *)memory << '\n';
std::cout << "i1: " << (void *)i1 << '\n';
std::cout << "i2: " << (void *)i2 << '\n';
std::cout << "i3: " << (void *)i3 << '\n';
std::cout << "i4: " << (void *)i4 << '\n';
}
```

As shown in the preceding, the `constexpr` wrapper provides a simple means to remove the verbosity of our singleton class, something that would be difficult to do if the memory manager wasn't a singleton.

Extending your objects with the decorator pattern

In this recipe, we will learn how to implement the decorator pattern, which provides the ability to extend the functionality of a class without the need for inheritance, which by design is static in nature. This recipe is important because inheritance doesn't support the ability to extend a class at runtime, a problem the decorator pattern addresses.

Getting ready

Before beginning, please ensure that all of the technical requirements are met, including installing Ubuntu 18.04 or higher and running the following in a Terminal window:

```
> sudo apt-get install build-essential git cmake
```

This will ensure your operating system has the proper tools to compile and execute the examples in this recipe. Once this is complete, open a new Terminal. We will use this Terminal to download, compile, and run our examples.

How to do it...

Perform the following steps to try this recipe:

1. From a new Terminal, run the following to download the source code:

    ```
    > cd ~/
    > git clone
    https://github.com/PacktPublishing/Advanced-CPP-CookBook.git
    > cd Advanced-CPP-CookBook/chapter11
    ```

2. To compile the source code, run the following:

```
> cmake .
> make recipe03_examples
```

3. Once the source code is compiled, you can execute each example in this recipe by running the following commands:

```
> ./recipe03_example01
button width: 42

> ./recipe03_example02
button1 width: 10
button2 width: 42

> ./recipe03_example03
button width: 74

> ./recipe03_example04
button width: 42
button content width: 4
```

In the next section, we will step through each of these examples and explain what each example program does and how it relates to the lessons being taught in this recipe.

How it works...

In this recipe, we will learn how to implement the decorator pattern. To start, let's look at a simple example: suppose we are writing a C++ application that will host a website. In our website, we need to define a button that users can click on, but we need to calculate the width of the button given an extra margin that adds to the total size of the button:

```
class margin
{
public:
    int width()
    {
        return 32;
    }
};
```

As shown in the preceding, we have created a class called `margin` that returns the width of the margin in question (we will only focus on the width to simplify our example). We can then define our button as follows:

```
class button : public margin
{
public:
    int width()
    {
        return margin::width() + 10;
    }
};
```

As shown in the preceding, the total width of our button is the width of the button itself plus the width of the margin. We can then get the width of our button as follows:

```
int main()
{
    auto b = new button();
    std::cout << "button width: " << b->width() << '\n';
}
```

This results in the following output:

The problem with the preceding example is the button must always have a margin as the button directly inherits the margin class. There are ways to prevent this (for example, our button could have a configuration option that determines whether the button returns the width with the margin or not), but in this recipe, we will use the decorator pattern to solve this issue, allowing us to create two buttons: one button with a margin, and one button without a margin. Let's try this:

1. To start, let's define the following pure virtual base class as follows:

```
class base
{
public:
    virtual int width() = 0;
};
```

As shown in the preceding, the pure virtual base class defines the `width` function.

2. We can then implement our button as follows:

```
class button : public base
{
public:
    int width() override
    {
        return 10;
    }
};
```

As shown in the preceding, the button inherits the base class and returns a width of 10. Using the preceding, we can start that `button` is always a width of 10, and the button has no concept of a margin.

3. To add a margin to the button, we first must create a decorator class as follows:

```
class decorator : public base
{
    std::unique_ptr<base> m_base;

public:
    decorator(std::unique_ptr<base> b) :
        m_base{std::move(b)}
    { }

    int width()
    {
        return m_base->width();
    }
};
```

The decorator pattern starts with a private member to a `base` pointer, which is set in the decorator's constructor. The decorator also defines the `width` function but forwards the call to the base class.

4. Now, we can create a margin class, which is a decorator, as follows:

```
class margin : public decorator
{
public:
    margin(std::unique_ptr<base> b) :
        decorator{std::move(b)}
    { }
```

```
        int width()
        {
            return decorator::width() + 32;
        }
    };
```

As shown in the preceding, the margin class returns the width of the object it is decorating with an additional 32 added to it.

5. We can then create our two buttons as follows:

```
int main()
{
    auto button1 = std::make_unique<button>();
    auto button2 =
std::make_unique<margin>(std::make_unique<button>());

    std::cout << "button1 width: " << button1->width() << '\n';
    std::cout << "button2 width: " << button2->width() << '\n';
}
```

This results in the following output:

The biggest advantage to the decorator pattern is it allows us to extend a class at runtime. For example, we can create a button with two margins if we want:

```
int main()
{
    auto b =
        std::make_unique<margin>(
            std::make_unique<margin>(
                std::make_unique<button>()
            )
        );

    std::cout << "button width: " << b->width() << '\n';
}
```

We could otherwise create another decorator. To demonstrate this, let's extend our base class as follows:

```
class base
{
public:
    virtual int width() = 0;
    virtual int content_width() = 0;
};
```

The preceding base class now defines a width, and a content width (the amount of space inside our button that we can actually use). Now, we can create our button as follows:

```
class button : public base
{
public:
    int width() override
    {
        return 10;
    }

    int content_width() override
    {
        return width() - 1;
    }
};
```

As shown in the preceding, our button has a static width, and the content width is the same as the width itself minus 1 (to leave space for the button's border). We then define our decorator as follows:

```
class decorator : public base
{
    std::unique_ptr<base> m_base;

public:
    decorator(std::unique_ptr<base> b) :
        m_base{std::move(b)}
    { }

    int width() override
    {
        return m_base->width();
    }

    int content_width() override
    {
        return m_base->content_width();
```

```
        }
};
```

As shown in the preceding, the only difference is the decorator now has to forward the width and the content width functions. Our margin decorator looks like the following:

```
class margin : public decorator
{
public:
    margin(std::unique_ptr<base> b) :
        decorator{std::move(b)}
    { }

    int width() override
    {
        return decorator::width() + 32;
    }

    int content_width() override
    {
        return decorator::content_width();
    }
};
```

As is the case with web programming, a margin increases the size of an object. It doesn't change the space within an object for its internal contents, and hence, the margin returns the content width with no modifications. With the preceding changes, we can now add a padding decorator as follows:

```
class padding : public decorator
{
public:
    padding(std::unique_ptr<base> b) :
        decorator{std::move(b)}
    { }

    int width() override
    {
        return decorator::width();
    }

    int content_width() override
    {
        return decorator::content_width() - 5;
    }
};
```

The padding decorator is the opposite of the margin decorator. It doesn't change the size of an object, it reduces the total amount of space given to the internal contents of an object. As a result, it doesn't change the width, but it does decrease the size of the content.

To create a button using our new decorators, we can use the following:

```
int main()
{
    auto b =
        std::make_unique<margin>(
            std::make_unique<padding>(
                std::make_unique<button>()
            )
        );

    std::cout << "button width: " << b->width() << '\n';
    std::cout << "button content width: " << b->content_width() << '\n';
}
```

As shown in the preceding, we create a button that has an added margin and added padding, which results in the following output:

```
[~/book/chapter11/build]: ./recipe03_example04
button width: 42
button content width: 4
[~/book/chapter11/build]:
```

The decorator pattern provides the ability to create different buttons without the need for compile-time inheritance, which would require us to have a different button definition for every possible type of button we could think of. It should be noted, however, that the decorator pattern comes at a cost of added allocations and redirections of function calls, so this runtime flexibility does come at a cost.

Adding communication with the observer pattern

In this recipe, we will learn how to implement the observer pattern. The observer pattern provides the ability for a class to register with another class to receive notifications when an event occurs. The Qt language provides this feature through the use of its singles and slots mechanism while requiring a MOC compiler to make it work. This recipe is important as we will learn how to implement the observer pattern without the need for Qt, using standard C++.

Getting ready

Before beginning, please ensure that all of the technical requirements are met, including installing Ubuntu 18.04 or higher and running the following in a Terminal window:

```
> sudo apt-get install build-essential git cmake
```

This will ensure your operating system has the proper tools to compile and execute the examples in this recipe. Once this is complete, open a new Terminal. We will use this Terminal to download, compile, and run our examples.

How to do it...

Perform the following steps to try this recipe:

1. From a new Terminal, run the following to download the source code:

```
> cd ~/
> git clone https://github.com/PacktPublishing/Advanced-CPP-CookBook.git
> cd Advanced-CPP-CookBook/chapter11
```

2. To compile the source code, run the following:

```
> cmake .
> make recipe04_examples
```

3. Once the source code is compiled, you can execute each example in this recipe by running the following commands:

```
> ./recipe04_example01
mom's phone received alarm notification
dad's phone received alarm notification
```

In the next section, we will step through each of these examples and explain what each example program does and how it relates to the lessons being taught in this recipe.

How it works...

The observer pattern provides the ability for an observer to be notified when an event occurs. To explain how this works, let's start with the following pure virtual base class:

```
class observer
{
public:
    virtual void trigger() = 0;
};
```

As shown in the preceding, we have defined observer, which must implement a trigger() function. We can then create two different versions of this pure virtual base class as follows:

```
class moms_phone : public observer
{
public:
    void trigger() override
    {
        std::cout << "mom's phone received alarm notification\n";
    }
};

class dads_phone : public observer
{
public:
    void trigger() override
    {
        std::cout << "dad's phone received alarm notification\n";
    }
};
```

As shown in the preceding code, we have created two different classes, both of which subclass the observer pure virtual class, overriding the trigger function. We can then implement a class that produces an event the observer might be interested in, shown as follows:

```
class alarm
{
    std::vector<observer *> m_observers;

public:
    void trigger()
    {
        for (const auto &o : m_observers) {
            o->trigger();
        }
    }

    void add_phone(observer *o)
    {
        m_observers.push_back(o);
    }
};
```

As shown in the preceding code, we start with `std::vector`, which stores any number of observers. We then provide a trigger function, which represents our event. When this function is executed, we loop through all of the observers and notify them of the event by calling their `trigger()` functions. Finally, we provide a function that allows an observer to subscribe to the event in question.

The following demonstrates how these classes could be used:

```
int main(void)
{
    alarm a;
    moms_phone mp;
    dads_phone dp;

    a.add_phone(&mp);
    a.add_phone(&dp);

    a.trigger();
}
```

The output for this is as follows:

```
user@localhost:~/book/chapter11/build                    —    □    ✕
[~/book/chapter11/build]: ./recipe04_example01
mom's phone received alarm notification
dad's phone received alarm notification
[~/book/chapter11/build]:
```

As shown in the preceding, when the alarm class is triggered, the observers are notified of the event and process the notification as needed.

Improving performance with static polymorphism

In this recipe, we will learn how to create polymorphism without the need for virtual inheritance. Instead, we will use compile-time inheritance (called static polymorphism). This recipe is important because static polymorphism does not incur the same performance and memory usage penalties as runtime, virtual inheritance (as no vTable is required), at the expense of readability and the inability to leverage the runtime benefits of virtual subclassing.

Getting ready

Before beginning, please ensure that all of the technical requirements are met, including installing Ubuntu 18.04 or higher and running the following in a Terminal window:

```
> sudo apt-get install build-essential git cmake
```

This will ensure your operating system has the proper tools to compile and execute the examples in this recipe. Once this is complete, open a new Terminal. We will use this Terminal to download, compile, and run our examples.

How to do it...

Perform the following steps to try the recipe:

1. From a new Terminal, run the following to download the source code:

```
> cd ~/
> git clone
https://github.com/PacktPublishing/Advanced-CPP-CookBook.git
> cd Advanced-CPP-CookBook/chapter11
```

2. To compile the source code, run the following:

```
> cmake .
> make recipe05_examples
```

3. Once the source code is compiled, you can execute each example in this recipe by running the following commands:

```
> ./recipe05_example01
subclass1 specific
common
subclass2 specific
common
> ./recipe05_example02
subclass1 specific
common
subclass2 specific
common
```

In the next section, we will step through each of these examples and explain what each example program does and how it relates to the lessons being taught in this recipe.

How it works...

One of the main goals of polymorphism is that it provides the ability to override how an object executes a particular function while, at the same time, providing the ability to provide common logic across a set of objects. The problem with virtual inheritance is that the ability to override requires the use of a vTable (that is, a virtual table, which is an extra block of memory needed to handle virtual inheritance) if you wish to use the base class as your interface.

For example, consider the following code:

```
class base
{
public:
    virtual void foo() = 0;

    void common()
    {
        std::cout << "common\n";
    }
};
```

Let's start with the previously defined base class. It provides a `foo()` function as pure (that is, a subclass must implement this function) while also providing its own common logic. We can then create two subclasses as follows:

```
class subclass1 : public base
{
public:
    void foo() override
    {
        std::cout << "subclass1 specific\n";
    }
};

class subclass2 : public base
{
public:
    void foo() override
    {
        std::cout << "subclass2 specific\n";
    }
};
```

As shown in the preceding, we subclass the base class and override the `foo()` function with subclass-specific functionality. We can then call the subclass-specific `foo()` functions from our base class as follows:

```
int main(void)
{
    subclass1 s1;
    subclass2 s2;

    base *b1 = &s1;
    base *b2 = &s2;

    b1->foo();
```

```
        b1->common();

        b2->foo();
        b2->common();
    }
```

This results in the following output:

This type of runtime polymorphism requires the use of a vTable, which not only increases the memory footprint of each object but also incurs a performance penalty as each function call requires a vTable lookup. If the runtime properties of virtual inheritance are not needed, static polymorphism can provide the same functionality without the penalties.

To start, let's define the base class as follows:

```
template<typename T>
class base
{
public:
    void foo()
    { static_cast<T *>(this)->foo(); }

    void common()
    {
        std::cout << "common\n";
    }
};
```

Like our previous example, the base class doesn't implement the `foo()` function but instead requires a subclass to implement this function (which is what allows a static cast to cast this to type `T`).

We can then implement our subclasses as follows:

```
class subclass1 : public base<subclass1>
{
public:
    void foo()
    {
```

```
            std::cout << "subclass1 specific\n";
    }
};

class subclass2 : public base<subclass2>
{
public:
    void foo()
    {
        std::cout << "subclass2 specific\n";
    }
};
```

As with the previous example, the subclasses simply implement the `foo()` function. The difference, in this case, is the inheritance requires the use of the template parameter, which removes the need for the `foo()` function to override as the base class never uses a virtual function.

The preceding static polymorphism allows us to execute the `foo()` function from our base class as follows:

```
template<typename T>
void test(base<T> b)
{
    b.foo();
    b.common();
}
```

As shown in the preceding, the `test()` function does not have any information about each subclass. It only has information about the base (or interface) class. This `test()` function can be executed as follows:

```
int main(void)
{
    subclass1 c1;
    subclass2 c2;

    test(c1);
    test(c2);
}
```

This again results in the same output:

As shown in the preceding, if the polymorphic types are known at compile time, static polymorphism can be used to remove the need for `virtual`, removing the need of a vTable. This type of logic is especially helpful when working with template classes where the base type is known but the subclass type is not (and is provided), allowing the template function to only need the base interface.

12
A Closer Look at Type Deduction

In this chapter, you will learn all of the ins and outs of type deduction in C++, including some of the new additions in C++17. This chapter is important as it will teach you all of the ways in which the compiler will attempt to deduce type information automatically for you. Without a firm understanding of how type deduction works in C++, it is possible to create code that doesn't work as expected, especially when using `auto` and template programming. The knowledge gained from this chapter will provide you with the skills to properly leverage type deduction in your own applications.

The recipes in this chapter are as follows:

- Using auto and type deduction
- Learning how `decltype` type deduction rules work
- Working with template function type deduction
- Leveraging template class type deduction in C++17
- Working with user-defined type deduction in C++17

Technical requirements

To compile and run the examples in this chapter, you must have administrative access to a computer running Ubuntu 18.04 with a functional internet connection. Before running these examples, you must install the following:

```
> sudo apt-get install build-essential git cmake
```

If this is installed on any operating system other than Ubuntu 18.04, then GCC 7.4 or higher and CMake 3.6 or higher will be required.

Code files for this chapter can be found at `https://github.com/PacktPublishing/Advanced-CPP-CookBook/tree/master/chapter12`.

Using auto and type deduction

In this recipe, we will learn how the compiler handles the `auto` keyword, specifically for type deduction. This recipe is important because how `auto` is handled is not intuitive, and without a clear understanding of how `auto` works, your code will likely contain bugs and performance issues. The topics included in this recipe have a general description of `auto`, type deduction, forwarding (or universal) references, l-values, and r-values.

Getting ready

Before beginning, please ensure that all of the technical requirements are met, including installing Ubuntu 18.04 or higher and running the following in a Terminal window:

```
> sudo apt-get install build-essential git cmake
```

This will ensure your operating system has the proper tools to compile and execute the examples in this recipe. Once this is complete, open a new Terminal. We will use this Terminal to download, compile, and run our examples.

How to do it...

Perform the following steps to try the recipe:

1. From a new Terminal, run the following command to download the source code:

```
> cd ~/
> git clone
https://github.com/PacktPublishing/Advanced-CPP-CookBook.git
> cd Advanced-CPP-CookBook/chapter12
```

2. To compile the source code, run the following:

```
> cmake .
> make recipe01_examples
```

3. Once the source code is compiled, you can execute each example in this recipe by running the following commands:

```
> ./recipe01_example01
i1 = int
i2 = int
i3 = std::initializer_list<int>
i4 = std::initializer_list<int>
c = char
r = int

> ./recipe01_example02
i1 = int
i2 = const int
i3 = volatile int
i4 = const volatile int

> ./recipe01_example03
i1 = int
i2 = int&
a1 = int
a2 = int
a3 = int
a4 = int&
i3 = int&&
a5 = int&
a6 = int&
a7 = int&
a8 = int&
a9 = int&&
a10 = int&&

> ./recipe01_example04
i1 = int
i2 = const int&
i3 = const int&&
```

In the next section, we will step through each of these examples and explain what each example program does and how it relates to the lessons being taught in this recipe.

How it works...

The `auto` keyword is a feature added to C++11 called a **placeholder type specifier**. In other words, the `auto` keyword is used to tell the compiler a variable's type will be deduced from its initializer. Unlike other languages that use placeholder types, the `auto` keyword must still adhere to the strict type system of C++, meaning `auto` should not be confused with `std::any`.

For example, the following is possible with `std::any`:

```
std::any i = 42;
i = "The answer is: 42";
```

The following is not allowed with `auto`:

```
auto i = 42;
i = "The answer is: 42";
```

In the first example, we define `std::any`, which stores an integer. We then replace the integer inside `std::any` with a C-style string. With respect to `auto`, this is not possible as, once the compiler deduces the variable's type at initialization, the type cannot change (no different than any other variable in C++).

Let's look at a simple example of how to initialize a variable using `auto`:

```
int main(void)
{
    auto i1 = 42;
    auto i2{42};
    auto i3 = {42};
    auto i4 = {4, 8, 15, 16, 23, 42};

    show_type(i1);
    show_type(i2);
    show_type(i3);
    show_type(i4);

    char c = 0;
    auto r = c + 42;

    show_type(c);
    show_type(r);
}
```

Running this example results in the following output:

```
user@localhost:~/book/chapter12/build                          —    □    ×
[~/book/chapter12/build]: ./recipe01_example01
i1 = int
i2 = int
i3 = std::initializer_list<int>
i4 = std::initializer_list<int>
c = char
r = int
[~/book/chapter12/build]:
```

As shown in the preceding code, we create four variables using `auto`, initialize them, and then use a function called `show_type()` to return the output of the variable's type.

 For more information about how the `show_type()` function works, please see the code that comes with this chapter (the details of this function will make more sense after you finish reading this entire chapter).

The first variable in our example, `i1`, is deduced as an integer. This is because numeric types in C++ are always deduced as an integer, which we see with the `c` and `r` variables in our example as well. The reason is the compiler is allowed to increase the size of any variable during compilation, meaning, when the compiler sees `c + 42`, the first thing it does is store the value of `c` in a temporary integer before completing the addition.

The second variable, `i2`, in our example is also deduced as an integer as the `{}` notation is another form of initialization for any type in C++, with some additional rules. Specifically, `i3` and `i4` are deduced as `std::initializer_list` of integers since the last two use the `= {}` notation, which is defined by the C++ specification to always deduce to `std::initializer_list` in C++17. It should be noted that this assumes the compiler adheres to the specification, which is not always the case in this specific example, which is why critical system specifications such as AUTOSAR do not allow this type of initialization.

The `auto` keyword can also be combined with CV qualifiers (that is, `const`/`volatile`) as well. Check out this example:

```
int main(void)
{
    auto i1 = 42;
    const auto i2 = 42;
    volatile auto i3 = 42;
    const volatile auto i4 = 42;

    show_type(i1);
```

```
        show_type(i2);
        show_type(i3);
        show_type(i4);
}
```

The preceding examples results in the following output:

As shown in the preceding screenshot, each variable is decorated with the proper CV qualifiers as defined.

Up until now, in each example, we could have simply replaced the use of auto with int and nothing would have changed, which begs the question, why use auto in the first place? There are a couple of reasons why:

- Using something other than auto means your code is likely specifying a variable's type twice. For example, int *ptr = new int; states that the ptr variable is an integer twice: once in the variables declaration, and a second time in the variable's initialization.
- Some types in C++ are really long (for example, iterators), and the use of auto can greatly simplify the verbosity of your code, for example, auto i = v.begin().
- When writing template code, auto is required to properly handle reference types such as forwarding references.

Working with references is where the use of auto gets confusing, and where most people make mistakes. To better explain, let's look at the following example:

```
int main(void)
{
    int i = 42;

    int i1 = i;
    int &i2 = i;

    show_type(i1);
    show_type(i2);
```

```
        auto a1 = i1;
        auto a2 = i2;

        show_type(a1);
        show_type(a2);
}
```

This results in the following output:

```
i1 = int
i2 = int&
a1 = int
a2 = int
```

As shown in the preceding example, we create an integer, i, and set it to 42. We then create two more integers: one is a copy of i, while the second is a reference to i. As shown in the output, we get the expected types, int and int&. Using the auto keyword, we could expect that if we said something like auto a = i2, we would get an int& type as i2 is a reference to an integer, and since auto deduced its type based on how it is initialized, we should get int&. The problem is, we do not. Instead, we get int.

The reason for this is that auto gets its type based on how it is initialized without including the reference type. In other words, the use of auto in the example is only picking up on the i2 type, without paying attention to whether or not i2 is an integer or a reference to an integer. To force auto to be a reference to an integer, we must use the following syntax:

```
        auto a3 = i1;
        auto &a4 = i2;

        show_type(a3);
        show_type(a4);
```

This results in the following output:

```
a3 = int
a4 = int&
```

This output is as expected. The same rules apply to r-value references, but become even more complicated. For example, consider this code:

```
        int &&i3 = std::move(i);
        show_type(i3);
```

This results in the following output:

```
i3 = int&&
```

This output is again as expected. Based on what we have already learned, we would expect that the following would be required to get an r-value reference:

```
auto &&a5 = i3;
show_type(a6);
```

The problem is that this results in the following output:

a5 = int&

As shown in the preceding example, we did not get an r-value reference as expected. Anything labeled `auto &&` in C++ is considered a forwarding reference (this is also known as a universal reference, a term coined by Scott Meyers). The universal reference will deduce to either an l-value or r-value reference, depending on what the universal reference is initialized with.

So, for example, consider the following code:

```
auto &&a6 = i1;
show_type(a6);
```

This code results in the following:

a6 = int&

This is because `i1` was defined earlier as an integer, and so `a6` becomes an l-value reference to `i1`. The following is also true:

```
auto &&a7 = i2;
show_type(a7);
```

The preceding code results in the following:

a7 = int&

This is because `i2` was defined earlier as an l-value reference to an integer, which means that the universal reference becomes an l-value reference to an integer as well.

The confusing result is the following, as already shown in the preceding code snippet:

```
auto &&a8 = i3;
show_type(a8);
```

This again results in the following:

a8 = int&

Here, i3 was defined earlier as an r-value reference to an integer (proven by the resulting output), but the universal reference did not forward the r-valueness from i3. This is because, although i3 was defined as an r-value reference, once it is used, it becomes an l-value reference. As Scott Meyer has stated in the past, if a variable has a name (in our case, i3), it is an l-value, even if it starts off as an r-value. Another way to look at this is once a variable is used (as in accessed in any way), the variable is an l-value. So, the preceding code actually works as it should. i3, although defined as an r-value, is an l-value, and so the universal reference becomes an l-value reference to an integer, just the same as i1 and i2.

To get an r-value reference using auto, you must do the same thing as you would without the use of auto:

```
auto &&a9 = std::move(i3);
show_type(a9);
```

This results in the following:

```
a9 = int&&
```

As shown in the preceding code snippet, the best way to think about auto is to simply replace the word auto with the actual type (in this case, int), and whatever rules apply to the actual type also apply to auto. The difference is that if you attempted to write int &&blah = i, you would get an error as the compiler would recognize that you are attempting to create an r-value reference from an l-value reference, which is not possible (as you can only create an r-value reference from another r-value reference).

The reason the preceding examples are so important is that auto will not generate a complaint from the compiler. Instead, it will produce an l-value when you meant to create an r-value, which could result in inefficiencies or bugs. The most important thing to learn about the use of auto is that if it has a name, it is an l-value; otherwise, it is an r-value.

For example, consider the following code:

```
auto &&a10 = 42;
show_type(a10);
```

This code results in the following:

```
a10 = int&&
```

As the numeric value 42 does not have a variable name, it is a constant, and hence, the universal reference becomes an r-value reference to an integer.

It should also be noted that the use of `auto` confusingly does inherit CV qualifiers when dealing with references. Check out this example:

```
int main(void)
{
    const int i = 42;

    auto i1 = i;
    auto &i2 = i;
    auto &&i3 = std::move(i);

    show_type(i1);
    show_type(i2);
    show_type(i3);
}
```

This results in the following:

```
[~/book/chapter12/build]: ./recipe01_example04
i1 = int
i2 = const int&
i3 = const int&&
[~/book/chapter12/build]:
```

As shown in the preceding screenshot, the first integer remains an `int` type because a copy of `const int` is an `int`. Both `i2` and `i3`, however, become references to `const int`. If we were to replace `auto` with `int`, we would get a compiler error as you cannot create a non-const reference to `const int`, yet the use of `auto` will gladly convert your non-const variable into a `const` variable for you. The problem with this is that you will end up with odd error messages when you attempt to modify your variable, complaining that the variable is read-only when, in fact, you have not explicitly defined the variable as `const`. In general, it is good practice to always mark a variable defined with `auto` as `const` if you expect `const`, or non-const if you do not, preventing these sometimes hard-to-identify bugs.

Learning how decltype type deduction rules work

In this recipe, we will learn about how type deduction works with `decltype()` and `decltype(auto)`, and how to avoid the issues of referenceness with `auto` using `decltype(auto)` instead.

This recipe is important as `auto` has some strange behavior in how it handles references that `decltype()` addresses, providing C++ with a means to handle type deduction more predictably, especially when working with C++ templates.

Getting ready

Before beginning, please ensure that all of the technical requirements are met, including installing Ubuntu 18.04 or higher and running the following in a Terminal window:

```
> sudo apt-get install build-essential git cmake
```

This will ensure that your operating system has the proper tools to compile and execute the examples in this recipe. Once this is complete, open a new Terminal. We will use this Terminal to download, compile, and run our examples.

How to do it...

Perform the following steps to try this recipe:

1. From a new Terminal, run the following command to download the source code:

    ```
    > cd ~/
    > git clone
    https://github.com/PacktPublishing/Advanced-CPP-CookBook.git
    > cd Advanced-CPP-CookBook/chapter12
    ```

2. To compile the source code, run the following command:

    ```
    > cmake .
    > make recipe02_examples
    ```

3. Once the source code is compiled, you can execute each example in this recipe by running the following commands:

```
> ./recipe02_example01
i = int

> ./recipe02_example02
i = short int

> ./recipe02_example03
i = short int

> ./recipe02_example04
i1 = int
i2 = int

> ./recipe02_example05
i1 = int
i2 = const int
i3 = volatile int
i4 = const volatile int

> ./recipe02_example06
i1 = int
i2 = int&
i3 = int&&
a1 = int
a2 = int
a3 = int
a4 = int
a5 = int&
a6 = int&&
d1 = int
d2 = int&
d3 = int&&
```

In the next section, we will step through each of these examples and explain what each example program does and how it relates to the lessons being taught in this recipe.

How it works...

Neither `auto` nor `typename` in C++ provides the ability to get a variable's type and create new types using that information. To better explain why you might want to do this, let's look at the following example:

```
template<typename FUNC>
auto question(FUNC &&func)
{
    auto x = func() + 10;
    return x;
}
```

We start our example with a function that takes any function as an input and returns the result of this function plus `10`. We can then execute this function as follows:

```
short the_answer()
{
    return 32;
}

int main(void)
{
    auto i = question(the_answer);
    show_type(i);
}
```

As shown in the preceding example, we pass the `question()` function a pointer to another function that returns `short`. On executing this function, we store the results and then we use a function called `show_type()`, which is designed to output what type the provided type is. This results in the following:

```
[~/book/chapter12/build]: ./recipe02_example01
i = int
[~/book/chapter12/build]:
```

The problem with this example is the fact that the type that is returned is not the same type that we were given. C++ is allowed to increase the size of any variable as needed, and often does with shorts, especially when you attempt to perform arithmetic on a short with numeric values as numeric values are represented as integers.

Since we do not know what the return type of the provided function will be in the `question()` function, there is no way to fix this issue. Enter `decltype()`. To explain, let's update our example to address the preceding problem:

```
template<typename FUNC>
auto question(FUNC &&func)
{
    decltype(func()) x = func() + 10;
    return x;
}
```

As shown in the preceding example, we replaced `auto` with `decltype(func())`. This tells the compiler to get the return type of `func()` and use that type to define `x`. As a result, the compiler converts this template into the following function:

```
short question(short (*func)())
{
    short x = func() + 10;
    return x;
}
```

This happens instead of the following, which was expected initially:

```
int question(short (*func)())
{
    int x = func() + 10;
    return x;
}
```

This then results in the following output when executed:

```
[~/book/chapter12/build]: ./recipe02_example02
i = short int
[~/book/chapter12/build]:
```

As shown in the preceding screenshot, we are now getting the proper type returned from our `question()` function. With C++14, we can take this example a bit further and write it this way:

```
template<typename FUNC>
constexpr auto question(FUNC &&func) -> decltype(func())
{
    return func() + 10;
}
```

In the example in the preceding code snippet, we converted the `question()` function into `constexpr`, which allows the compiler to optimize out the function call, replacing a call to `question()` with the `func() + 10` statement. We also remove the need for a stack-based variable by explicitly telling the compiler what type we wish the function to return using the `-> decltype()` function return syntax. It should be noted that this syntax is needed as the following would not compile:

```
template<typename FUNC>
constexpr decltype(func()) question(FUNC &&func)
{
    return func() + 10;
}
```

The preceding code will not compile because the compiler does not have the definition of `func()` yet, and hence it doesn't know what its type is. The `->` syntax addresses this by placing the return type at the end of the function definition instead of at the front.

The `decltype()` specifier can also be used in place of `auto` as follows:

```
int main(void)
{
    decltype(auto) i1 = 42;
    decltype(auto) i2{42};

    show_type(i1);
    show_type(i2);
}
```

This results in the following output:

In this example, we create two integers using `decltype(auto)` and initialize them to 42. In this specific case, `decltype(auto)` and `auto` operate exactly the same. Both define the placeholder type as an integer as both are initialized using a numeric value, which, by default, is `int`.

Like `auto`, you can decorate `decltype(auto)` with CV qualifiers (that is, `const/volatile`) as follows:

```
int main(void)
{
    decltype(auto) i1 = 42;
    const decltype(auto) i2 = 42;
    volatile decltype(auto) i3 = 42;
    const volatile decltype(auto) i4 = 42;

    show_type(i1);
    show_type(i2);
    show_type(i3);
    show_type(i4);
}
```

This results in the following output:

The real magic of `decltype(auto)` is how it handles references. To demonstrate this, let's start with the following example:

```
int main(void)
{
    int i = 42;

    int i1 = i;
    int &i2 = i;
    int &&i3 = std::move(i);

    show_type(i1);
    show_type(i2);
    show_type(i3);
}
```

When executed, we see the following output:

```
i1 = int
i2 = int&
i3 = int&&
```

As shown in the preceding example, we have created an integer, an l-value reference to an integer, and an r-value reference to an integer. Let's see what happens if we attempt to use `auto` instead of `int` as follows:

```
auto a1 = i1;
auto a2 = i2;
auto a3 = std::move(i3);

show_type(a1);
show_type(a2);
show_type(a3);
```

We then see the following output:

```
a1 = int
a2 = int
a3 = int
```

As shown in the preceding example, we are only given integers. All of the references were removed. The only way to get references with `auto` is if we explicitly define them as follows:

```
auto a4 = i1;
auto &a5 = i2;
auto &&a6 = std::move(i3);

show_type(a4);
show_type(a5);
show_type(a6);
```

This results in the following, expected, output:

```
a4 = int
a5 = int&
a6 = int&&
```

The problem with having to add the extra `&` operators to explicitly define the reference type is that this assumes that, in our template code, we actually know what the references should be. If this information is not available, we would have no way of writing a template function and know whether we could create an l-value or r-value reference, likely resulting in a copy.

To overcome this, `decltype(auto)` not only inherits the type and CV qualifiers during initialization, it also inherits the references as follows:

```
decltype(auto) d1 = i1;
decltype(auto) d2 = i2;
decltype(auto) d3 = std::move(i3);

show_type(d1);
show_type(d2);
show_type(d3);
```

The preceding code, when executed, results in the following:

```
d1 = int
d2 = int&
d3 = int&&
```

As shown in the preceding example, `decltype(auto)` can be used to inherit all of the type information of the value it is being initialized to, including referenceness.

Working with template function type deduction

In this recipe, we will learn how template function type deduction works. Specifically, this recipe will teach you how template function type deduction works the same as `auto` type deduction, as well as how function type deduction can be used with some odd types (for example, C-style arrays).

This recipe is important as it will teach you how to write function templates properly, eliminating the need to explicitly define type information when invoking a function template.

Getting ready

Before beginning, please ensure that all of the technical requirements are met, including installing Ubuntu 18.04 or higher and running the following in a Terminal window:

```
> sudo apt-get install build-essential git cmake
```

This will ensure your operating system has the proper tools to compile and execute the examples in this recipe. Once this is complete, open a new Terminal. We will use this Terminal to download, compile, and run our examples.

How to do it...

Perform the following steps to try this recipe:

1. From a new Terminal, run the following command to download the source code:

```
> cd ~/
> git clone
https://github.com/PacktPublishing/Advanced-CPP-CookBook.git
> cd Advanced-CPP-CookBook/chapter12
```

2. To compile the source code, run the following command:

```
> cmake .
> make recipe03_examples
```

3. Once the source code is compiled, you can execute each example in this recipe by running the following commands:

```
> ./recipe03_example01
t = int
t = int

> ./recipe03_example02
t = const int&

> ./recipe03_example03
t = int&

> ./recipe03_example04
t = int&

> ./recipe03_example05
t = int&&

> ./recipe03_example06
t = int&&

> ./recipe03_example07
t = const int&

> ./recipe03_example08
```

```
t = const int&&

> ./recipe03_example09
t = int (&&)[6]
```

In the next section, we will step through each of these examples and explain what each example program does and how it relates to lessons being taught in this recipe.

How it works...

In C++11, the standards committee added the ability to automatically deduce a template function's type information based on the arguments that were passed to the function.

Check out this example:

```
template<typename T>
void foo(T t)
{
    show_type(t);
}
```

The preceding function creates a standard template function that executes a function called show_type() designed to output the type information that it is provided with.

Before C++11, we would use this function as follows:

```
int main(void)
{
    int i = 42;

    foo<int>(i);
    foo<int>(42);
}
```

The compiler already knows that the template should define the T type as an integer as that is what the function was provided for. C++11 removes this redundancy, allowing the following:

```
int main(void)
{
    int i = 42;

    foo(i);
    foo(42);
}
```

This results in the following output when executed:

```
user@localhost:~/book/chapter12/build                   —    □    ×
[~/book/chapter12/build]: ./recipe03_example01
t = int
t = int
[~/book/chapter12/build]:
```

Like `auto`, however, this type deduction gets interesting when r-value references are used, as follows:

```
template<typename T>
void foo(T &&t)
{
    show_type(t);
}
```

The preceding example defines `t` as a forwarding reference (also known as a universal reference). The universal reference takes on whatever reference type it is passed. For example, we call this function as follows:

```
int main(void)
{
    int i = 42;
    foo(i);
}
```

We get the following output:

```
user@localhost:~/book/chapter12/build                   —    □    ×
[~/book/chapter12/build]: ./recipe03_example04
t = int&
[~/book/chapter12/build]:
```

The preceding output shows that the template function was given an l-value reference to an integer. This is because i, in our main function, is an l-value, even though the function appears to be requesting an r-value reference. To get an r-value reference, we must provide an r-value, as follows:

```
int main(void)
{
    int i = 42;
    foo(std::move(i));
}
```

This results in the following output when executed:

As shown in the preceding screenshot, now that we have given the universal reference an r-value, we get an r-value. It should be noted that a universal reference only has the following signature:

```
template<typename T>
void foo(T &&t)
```

For example, the following is not a universal reference:

```
template<typename T>
void foo(const T &&t)
```

Neither is the following a universal reference:

```
void foo(int &&t)
```

Both of the preceding examples are r-value references, and hence require that an r-value be provided (in other words, both of these functions define move operations). A universal reference will accept both an l-value and an r-value reference. Although this seems like an advantage, it has the downside that it is sometimes difficult to know whether your template function has received an l-value or an r-value. Currently, the best way to ensure your template function acts like an r-value reference and not a universal reference is to use SFINAE:

```
std::is_rvalue_reference_v<decltype(t)>
```

Finally, it is also possible to perform type deduction on less common types such as C-style arrays, as in this example:

```
template<typename T, size_t N>
void foo(T (&&t)[N])
{
    show_type(t);
}
```

The preceding function states that we wish to have a C-style array of type `T` and size `N` passed to the function and then outputs its type when executed. We can use this function as follows:

```
int main(void)
{
    foo({4, 8, 15, 16, 23, 42});
}
```

This automatically deduces to an r-value reference of a C-style array of type `int` and size 6. As shown in this recipe, C++ provides several mechanisms for allowing the compiler to determine what types are leveraged in template functions.

Leveraging template class type deduction in C++17

In this recipe, we will learn how class type deduction works with class templates in C++17. This recipe is important as C++17 added the ability to deduce the type of a template class from its constructor, which reduces both the verbosity and redundancy of your code.

The knowledge gained from this recipe will provide you with the ability to write C++ classes that properly deduce their types from the class constructor without the need for explicit type declarations.

Getting ready

Before beginning, please ensure that all of the technical requirements are met, including installing Ubuntu 18.04 or higher and running the following in a Terminal window:

```
> sudo apt-get install build-essential git cmake
```

This will ensure that your operating system has the proper tools to compile and execute the examples in this recipe. Once this is complete, open a new Terminal. We will use this Terminal to download, compile, and run our examples.

How to do it...

Perform the following steps to try this recipe:

1. From a new Terminal, run the following command to download the source code:

   ```
   > cd ~/
   > git clone
   https://github.com/PacktPublishing/Advanced-CPP-CookBook.git
   > cd Advanced-CPP-CookBook/chapter12
   ```

2. To compile the source code, run the following command:

   ```
   > cmake .
   > make recipe04_examples
   ```

3. Once the source code is compiled, you can execute each example in this recipe by running the following commands:

   ```
   > ./recipe04_example01
   t = int
   t = int

   > ./recipe04_example02
   t = int&

   > ./recipe04_example03
   t = int&&
   t = int&&

   > ./recipe04_example04
   t = int&&
   u = int&

   > ./recipe04_example05
   t = int&&

   > ./recipe04_example06
   t = const char (&)[16]
   u = int&&
   ```

In the next section, we will step through each of these examples and explain what each example program does and how it relates to the lessons being taught in this recipe.

How it works...

Class template type deduction is a new feature added in C++17 that provides the ability to deduce the type of a template class from its constructor. Suppose we have the following class template:

```
template<typename T>
class the_answer
{

public:
    the_answer(T t)
    {
        show_type(t);
    }
};
```

As shown in the preceding code snippet, we have a simple class template that takes a type T during construction and uses a show_type() function to output whatever type it is given. Before C++17, this class would have been instantiated using the following:

```
int main(void)
{
    the_answer<int> is(42);
}
```

With C++17, we can now instantiate this class as follows:

```
int main(void)
{
    the_answer is(42);
}
```

The reason this works is that the constructor of the class takes a type T as an argument. Since we provided a numeric integer as the parameter, type T of the class is deduced as an integer. This type deduction includes support for references as well. Check out this example:

```
template<typename T>
class the_answer
{
```

```
public:
    the_answer(T &t)
    {
        show_type(t);
    }
};
```

In the preceding example, our class takes T& as a parameter in the constructor of the class, which allows us to instantiate the class as follows:

```
int main(void)
{
    int i = 42;
    the_answer is(i);
}
```

This results in the following when executed:

As shown in the preceding example, type T of the class was deduced as an l-value reference to an integer. Most of the type deduction rules that apply to function templates also apply to class templates, but there are some exceptions. For example, class template constructors do not support forwarding references (universal references). Consider the following code:

```
template<typename T>
class the_answer
{

public:
    the_answer(T &&t)
    {
        show_type(t);
    }
};
```

The preceding constructor is not a universal reference; it is an r-value reference, meaning we cannot do the following:

```
the_answer is(i);
```

This is not possible as it would be attempting to bind an l-value to an r-value, which is not allowed. Instead, like any other r-value reference, we must instantiate the class using the following:

```
the_answer is(std::move(i));
```

Or we can bind it with the following:

```
the_answer is(42);
```

The reason universal references are not supported for class template type deduction is the fact that class template type deduction uses the constructor to deduce the type and then fills in the type for the rest of the class based on whatever type was deduced, meaning by the time the constructor is compiled, it looks like this:

```
class the_answer
{

public:
    the_answer(int &&t)
    {
        show_type(t);
    }
};
```

This defines an r-value reference.

To get a universal reference in the constructor, or any other function, you must use a member function template, which itself can still support type deduction but is not used to deduce any of the class's types. Check out this example:

```
template<typename T>
class the_answer
{

public:

    template<typename U>
    the_answer(T &&t, U &&u)
    {
        show_type(t);
        show_type(u);
    }
};
```

In the preceding example, we create a class template with type T, and we define the constructor as a member function template. The constructor itself takes T &&t and U &&u. In this case, however, t is an r-value reference and u is a universal reference, even though they look identical. Both can be deduced by the compiler with C++17 as follows:

```
int main(void)
{
    int i = 42;
    the_answer is(std::move(i), i);
}
```

It should also be noted that the constructor does not have to have any of the types in any specific order for deduction to work. The only requirement is that all of the types are present in the constructor's arguments. For example, consider the following code:

```
template<typename T>
class the_answer
{

public:
    the_answer(size_t size, T &&t)
    {
        show_type(t);
    }
};
```

The preceding example can be instantiated as follows:

```
int main(void)
{
    the_answer is_2(42, 42);
}
```

Finally, type deduction also supports more than one template type, as in this example:

```
template<typename T, typename U>
class the_answer
{

public:
    the_answer(const T &t, U &&u)
    {
        show_type(t);
        show_type(u);
    }
};
```

The preceding example creates a class template with two generic types. The constructor for this class creates a `const` l-value reference to a type `T`, while also taking an r-value reference to a type `U`. This class can be instantiated as follows:

```
int main(void)
{
    the_answer is("The answer is: ", 42);
}
```

This results in the following output:

As shown in the preceding example, both `T` and `U` are successfully deduced.

Working with user-defined type deduction in C++17

In this recipe, we will learn how to help the compiler with class template type deduction using user-defined deduction guides. Most of the time, user-defined deduction guides are not needed, but in some cases, they might be to ensure the compiler deduces the proper types. This recipe is important because, without user-defined type deduction, certain types of template schemes are simply not possible, as will be shown.

Getting ready

Before beginning, please ensure that all of the technical requirements are met, including installing Ubuntu 18.04 or higher and running the following in a Terminal window:

```
> sudo apt-get install build-essential git cmake
```

This will ensure that your operating system has the proper tools to compile and execute the examples in this recipe. Once this is complete, open a new Terminal. We will use this Terminal to download, compile, and run our examples.

How to do it...

Perform the following steps to try this recipe:

1. From a new Terminal, run the following command to download the source code:

```
> cd ~/
> git clone
https://github.com/PacktPublishing/Advanced-CPP-CookBook.git
> cd Advanced-CPP-CookBook/chapter12
```

2. To compile the source code, run the following command:

```
> cmake .
> make recipe05_examples
```

3. Once the source code is compiled, you can execute each example in this recipe by running the following commands:

```
> ./recipe05_example01
t = unsigned int
t = int

> ./recipe05_example02
t = unsigned int

> ./recipe05_example03
t = std::__cxx11::basic_string<char>
```

In the next section, we will step through each of these examples and explain what each example program does and how it relates to the lessons being taught in this recipe.

How it works...

Class template type deduction is a much-needed feature in C++17 as it helps to reduce both the redundancy and verbosity of our C++. There are situations where, however, the compiler will deduce the wrong type—an issue that could be addressed if we didn't rely on type deduction. To better understand this type of issue, let's look at the following example:

```
template<typename T>
class the_answer
{

public:
    the_answer(T t)
```

```
        {
            show_type(t);
        }
    };
```

In the preceding example, we have created a simple class template whose constructor takes a type T and uses a `show_type()` function to output whatever type it is given. Now suppose that we wish to use this class to instantiate a version that takes an unsigned integer. There are two ways to do this:

```
the_answer<unsigned> is(42);
```

The preceding method is the most obvious as we are explicitly telling the compiler what type we wish to have, while not using type deduction at all. Another method to get an unsigned integer would be to use the proper numeric literal syntax as follows:

```
the_answer is(42U);
```

In the preceding example, we are leveraging type deduction, but we have to make sure we always add U to our integers. The advantage of this approach is that the code is explicit. The disadvantage to this approach is that if we forget to add U to state that we wish to have an unsigned integer, we could inadvertently create a class with the int type instead of the unsigned type.

To prevent this issue, we can leverage a user-defined type deduction to tell the compiler that if it sees an integer type, we really mean an unsigned type, as follows:

```
the_answer(int) -> the_answer<unsigned>;
```

The preceding statement tells the compiler that if it sees a constructor with an int type, int should produce a class with the unsigned type.

 The left-hand side takes a constructor signature, while the right-hand side takes a class template signature.

Using this method, we can take any constructor signature that we see and convert it into the class template type we wish, as in this example:

```
the_answer(const char *) -> the_answer<std::string>;
```

The user-defined type deduction guide tells the compiler that if it sees a C-style string, it should create std::string instead. We can then run our example with the following:

```
int main(void)
{
    the_answer is("The answer is: 42");
}
```

We then get the following output:

As shown in the preceding screenshot, the class was constructed with std::string (or at least GCC's internal representation of std::string) and not a C-style string.

Bonus - Using C++20 Features

13

In this chapter, you will take a quick look at some of the upcoming features being added to C++20. This chapter is important because, unlike C++14 and C++17, C++20 adds several game-changing features to the language that will alter C++ forever.

It begins with an introduction to C++20 Concepts, a new mechanism for defining the requirements of any arbitrary type. C++20 Concepts promises to change how we program using templates and `auto`, providing a mechanism for defining what is required of a type. We will then move to C++20 Modules, a new feature that removes the need for `#include`, changing how we define interfaces in C++. C++ Modules is a huge change to the language, requiring a complete overhaul of the entire Standard Library as well as our build tools. Next, we will take a quick look at `std::span` and C++ Ranges. Finally, we will briefly cover another game-changing addition to C++20 called Coroutines.

The recipes in this chapter are as follows:

- Looking at Concepts in C++20
- Working with Modules in C++20
- Introducing `std::span`, a new view on arrays
- Working with Ranges in C++20
- Learning how to use Coroutines in C++20

Technical requirements

To compile and run the examples in this chapter, you must have administrative access to a computer running Ubuntu 19.04 with a functional internet connection. Note that the rest of this book uses Ubuntu 18.04. Since we will be discussing C++20, which is still in development, we need the latest and greatest versions of GCC in this specific chapter. Before running these examples, you must install the following:

```
> sudo apt-get install build-essential git cmake
```

If this is installed on any operating system other than Ubuntu 18.04, then GCC 7.4 or higher and CMake 3.6 or higher will be required.

Code files for this chapter can be found at `//github.com/PacktPublishing/Advanced-CPP-CookBook/tree/master/chapter13`.

Looking at Concepts in C++20

In this recipe, we will discuss an upcoming addition to C++ that promises to completely change the way we think about template programming called C++20 Concepts. C++ today largely depends on the use of SFINAE to constrain the types that apply to any given template function. As seen in `Chapter 4`, *Using Templates for Generic Programming*, SFINAE is hard to write, confusing to read, and slow to compile. This recipe is important as template programming post-C++20 will not only be easier to code and debug, but will also reduce the human costs of template programming, making it easier to read and understand.

Getting ready

Before beginning, please ensure that all of the technical requirements are met, including installing Ubuntu 19.04 or higher and running the following in a Terminal window:

```
> sudo apt-get install build-essential git cmake
```

This will ensure your operating system has the proper tools to compile and execute the examples in this recipe. Once this is complete, open a new Terminal. We will use this Terminal to download, compile, and run our examples.

How to do it...

You will need to perform the following steps to try the recipe:

1. From a new Terminal, run the following to download the source code:

```
> cd ~/
> git clone
https://github.com/PacktPublishing/Advanced-CPP-CookBook.git
> cd Advanced-CPP-CookBook/chapter13
```

2. To compile the source code, run the following command:

```
> cmake .
> make recipe01_examples
```

3. Once the source code is compiled, you can execute each example in this recipe by running the following commands:

```
> ./recipe01_example01
The answer is: 42
The answer is not: 43

> ./recipe01_example02
The answer is: 42
The answer is not: 43
```

In the next section, we will step through each of these examples and explain what each example program does and how it relates to the lessons being taught in this recipe.

How it works...

To best explain how C++20 Concepts will aid in template programming, we will start with a simple example of programming an interface in C++ today. Interfaces define a contract between the implementation of an **Application Programming Interface** (**API**) and the user of the API and are heavily used in object-oriented programming to abstract away the interface of an API from its implementation details.

Let's start with the following pure virtual interface:

```
class interface
{
public:
    virtual ~interface() = default;
    virtual void foo() = 0;
};
```

The preceding pure virtual interface in C++ defines a `foo()` function. Clients of this API do not need to know how `foo()` is implemented. All they care about is the definition of the interface and the function signature of `foo()` to understand how `foo()` should behave. Using this interface, we can define an implementation of this interface, as follows:

```
class A :
    public interface
{
public:
```

```
        void foo() override
        {
            std::cout << "The answer is: 42\n";
        }
    };
```

As shown in the preceding example, we created a class called A that inherits the interface and override the `foo()` function to give it an implementation. We can do the same thing with another implementation, as follows:

```
class B :
    public interface
{
public:
    void foo() override
    {
        std::cout << "The answer is not: 43\n";
    }
};
```

As shown in the preceding example, the B class provides the interface with an alternative implementation of the interface. Clients of this interface can use the interface as follows:

```
class client
{
    interface &m_i;

public:
    client(interface &i) :
        m_i{i}
    { }

    void bar()
    {
        m_i.foo();
    }
};
```

The client doesn't actually need to know anything about A or B. It simply includes the definition of the interface and uses the interface to access any specific implementation. We can use this client as follows:

```
int main(void)
{
    A a;
    B b;
```

```
        client c1(a);
        client c2(b);

        c1.bar();
        c2.bar();
    }
```

As shown in the preceding example, we first create instances of both A and B, and we then create two different clients that are given implementations of the interface for both A and B. Finally, we execute the `bar()` functions for each client, resulting in the following output:

As shown in the preceding screenshot, the client is unaware that the interface was defined in two different ways as the client only concerns itself with the interface. This technique is demonstrated in a lot of C++ literature, specifically to implement what is known as the S.O.L.I.D object-oriented design principles. The S.O.L.I.D design principles stand for the following:

- **Single responsibility principle**: This ensures that if an object must change, it only changes for one reason (that is, an object doesn't provide more than one responsibility).
- **Open–closed principle**: This ensures that an object can be extended without being modified.
- **Liskov substitution principle**: This ensures that, when inheritance is used, subclasses implement the behavior of functions they override and not just the function's signature.
- **Interface segregation principle**: This ensures that an object has the smallest possible interface so that clients of the object are not forced to depend on APIs they do not use.
- **Dependency inversion principle**: This ensures that objects are only dependent on interfaces and not on implementations.

The combination of these principles is designed to ensure that your use of object-oriented programming in C++ is easier to understand and maintain over time. One issue, however, with the existing literature for S.O.L.I.D and C++ is that it advocates for the heavy use of pure virtual interfaces, which come at a cost. Each class must be given an extra virtual table (that is, vTable), and all function calls encounter the extra overhead of virtual function overloading.

One way to solve this is to use static interfaces (something that is not often talked about in existing literature). To best explain how this works, let's start with the definition of our interface, as follows:

```cpp
#include <iostream>

template<typename DERIVED>
class interface
{
public:
    constexpr void foo()
    {
        static_cast<DERIVED *>(this)->foo_override();
    }
};
```

As shown in the preceding example, we will leverage static polymorphism to implement our interface. The preceding class takes a type called DERIVED and casts an instance of the interface to the DERIVED class, calling a version of the foo function that has been overridden. The implementation of A now looks like this:

```cpp
class A :
    public interface<A>
{
public:
    void foo_override()
    {
        std::cout << "The answer is: 42\n";
    }
};
```

As shown in the preceding example, instead of inheriting the interface, A now inherits an interface of A. When the foo() function from the interface is called, the interface redirects the call to the foo_override() function for A. We can implement B using the same approach:

```cpp
class B :
    public interface<B>
{
public:
    void foo_override()
    {
        std::cout << "The answer is not: 43\n";
    }
};
```

As shown in the preceding example, B is capable of providing its own implementation of the interface. It should be noted that so far in this design pattern, we have yet to use virtual, meaning we have created an interface and implementations of that interface without the need for virtual inheritance, so there is no overhead associated with this design. In fact, the compiler is capable of removing the redirection of the call from foo() to foo_override(), ensuring that the use of abstraction doesn't provide any additional runtime costs compared to the use of pure virtual interfaces.

Clients of A and B can be implemented as follows:

```
template<typename T>
class client
{
    interface<T> &m_i;

public:
    client(interface<T> &i) :
        m_i{i}
    { }

    void bar()
    {
        m_i.foo();
    }
};
```

As shown in the preceding code snippet, the only difference between the client in this example and the one in the previous example is the fact that this client is a template class. Static polymorphism requires that the type of information about an interface is known at compile time. This tends to be fine in most designs as the use of pure virtual interfaces earlier was not because we wanted the ability to perform runtime polymorphism and type erasure, but instead to ensure that clients only adhere to interfaces and not implementations. In both cases, the implementation of each client is static and known at compile time.

To use the client, we can use some C++17 class type deduction to ensure that our main() function remains unchanged, as follows:

```
int main(void)
{
    A a;
    B b;

    client c1(a);
    client c2(b);
```

```
        c1.bar();
        c2.bar();
    }
```

Executing the preceding example results in the following:

As shown in the preceding screenshot, the code executes the same. The only difference between the two approaches is the fact that one uses pure virtual inheritance, which comes with a runtime cost, while the second approach uses static polymorphism, which comes with a human cost. Specifically, the preceding example for most beginners is difficult to understand. In large projects with nested dependencies, the use of static polymorphism can be extremely difficult to understand and read.

Another issue with the preceding example is the fact that the compiler does not have enough information about the interface and clients of that interface to provide a reasonable error message when the wrong type is given. Check out this example:

```
int main(void)
{
    client c(std::cout);
}
```

This results in the following compiler error:

```
/home/user/book/chapter13/recipe01.cpp: In function 'int main()':
/home/user/book/chapter13/recipe01.cpp:187:23: error: class template
argument deduction failed:
  187 | client c(std::cout);
      |         ^
/home/user/book/chapter13/recipe01.cpp:187:23: error: no matching function
for call to 'client(std::ostream&)'
/home/user/book/chapter13/recipe01.cpp:175:5: note: candidate:
'template<class T> client(interface<T>&)-> client<T>'
  175 | client(interface<T> &i) :
      |     ^~~~~~

...
```

The preceding error message is hardly useful, especially for a beginner. To overcome these issues, C++20 Concepts promises to provide a cleaner implementation of template programming moving forward. To best explain this, let's look at how we would implement the interface using C++20 Concepts:

```
template <typename T>
concept interface = requires(T t)
{
    { t.foo() } -> void;
};
```

As shown in the preceding example, we have defined a C++20 Concept called `interface`. Given a type `T`, this concept requires that `T` provides a function called `foo()` that takes no input and returns no output. We can then define `A` as follows:

```
class A
{
public:
    void foo()
    {
        std::cout << "The answer is: 42\n";
    }
};
```

As shown in the preceding code snippet, `A` no longer needs to leverage inheritance at all. It simply provides a `foo()` function given a normal C++ class definition. `B` is implemented the same way:

```
class B
{
public:
    void foo()
    {
        std::cout << "The answer is not: 43\n";
    }
};
```

Once again, inheritance is no longer needed. Clients of this interface are implemented as in the following:

```
template<interface T>
class client
{
    T &m_i;

public:
    client(T &i) :
```

```
        m_i{i}
    { }

    void bar()
    {
        m_i.foo();
    }
};
```

As shown in the preceding example, we have defined a class that takes a template type `T` and calls its `foo()` function. In our static polymorphic example earlier, we could have implemented the client the exact same way. The problem with that approach is that the client would have no way of determining whether the type `T` adhered to the interface. Static asserts combined with SFINAE, such as `std::is_base_of()`, could be leveraged to solve this issue, but every object that depends on the interface would have to include this logic. With C++20 concepts, however, this simplicity can be achieved without the need for inheritance or any complicated template tricks such as SFINAE. So, let's see what we can use instead of the following:

```
template<typename T>
```

The following can be used instead:

```
template<interface T>
```

The problem with C++ today with template programming is the fact that the `typename` keyword tells the compiler nothing about the type itself. SFINAE provides a means to solve this by defining certain characteristics about a type at a huge human cost as SFINAE is even more complicated to understand, and the resulting compiler errors when things go wrong are anything but useful. C++20 Concepts addresses all of these issues by defining the properties of a type, called a Concept, and then uses that concept in place of `typename`, providing the compiler with all of the information it needs to determine whether a given type adheres to the concept. When something goes wrong, the compiler can provide a simple error message about what the provided type is missing.

C++20 Concepts is an exciting new feature coming soon that promises to completely change how we program with C++ templates, reducing the overall human costs of working with templates at the expense of a more complicated compiler and C++ specification.

Working with Modules in C++20

In this recipe, we will learn more about a new feature coming with C++20 called Modules. This recipe is important as C++20 Modules removes the need for `#include` moving forward. C++ code today is usually divided between headers and source files. Every source file is compiled separately and must recompile the headers that it includes (and any headers the included headers include), resulting in slow compile times, dependency order issues, and the overuse of C-style macros. Instead, optionally, libraries will be included using C++20 Modules, changing the way we program even simple applications such as "Hello World".

Getting ready

Before beginning, please ensure that all of the technical requirements are met, including installing Ubuntu 19.04 or higher and running the following in a Terminal window:

```
> sudo apt-get install build-essential git cmake
```

This will ensure that your operating system has the proper tools to compile and execute the examples in this recipe. Once this is complete, open a new Terminal. We will use this Terminal to download, compile, and run our examples.

How to do it...

You will need to perform the following steps to try this recipe:

1. From a new Terminal, run the following command to download the source code:

    ```
    > cd ~/
    > git clone
    https://github.com/PacktPublishing/Advanced-CPP-CookBook.git
    > cd Advanced-CPP-CookBook/chapter13
    ```

2. To compile the source code, run the following command:

    ```
    > cmake .
    > make recipe02_examples
    ```

3. Once the source code is compiled, you can execute each example in this recipe by running the following commands:

```
> ./recipe02_example01
Hello World

> ./recipe02_example03
The answer is: 42
```

In the next section, we will step through each of these examples and explain what each example program does and how it relates to the lessons being taught in this recipe. It should be noted that examples 2 and 4 in the source cannot be compiled since, at the time of writing, C++ Modules is not yet supported by GCC.

How it works...

C++20 Modules provide a new way to include the definitions of APIs used in C++. Let's look at the following example of how to write a simple Hello World application in C++:

```cpp
#include <iostream>

int main(void)
{
    std::cout << "Hello World\n";
}
```

To write this same application using C++20 Modules, you would do the following:

```cpp
import std.core;

int main(void)
{
    std::cout << "Hello World\n";
}
```

Although the difference is subtle, under the hood, a lot has changed to make the preceding code possible. Let's look at a more complicated example, as follows:

```cpp
#include <string>

template<size_t number>
class the_answer
{
public:
    auto operator()() const
    {
```

```
        return "The answer is: " + std::to_string(number);
    }
};

#define CHECK(a) (a() == "The answer is: 42")
```

In the preceding code, we have defined a header file that defines a class template called `the_answer`. To implement this template, we must include the `string` library. We have also added a macro to this header to test our class. We can use this header as follows:

```
#include <iostream>
#include "header.h"

int main(void)
{
    the_answer<42> is;
    std::cout << is() << '\n';
}
```

As shown in the preceding code snippet, we include our header, create an instance of our template class, and use it to output a message. When executed, we get the following output:

Although this is a simple example showing a class template that implements a C++ functor, there are some issues with this code:

- The implementation of `the_answer` depends on the `string` library. This means that whenever you use `header.h`, you are not only including the definition of `the_answer`, but you are also including the complete definition of the `string` library, including all of its dependencies. This type of dependency chain results in large build time costs.
- The CHECK() macro is accessible to the client as well. In C++, there is no way to namespace a macro, resulting in the possibility of macro collisions.

- The preceding example is small, and therefore easy to compile, but suppose our header was 30,000 lines of template code mixed with several includes of its own. Now, suppose we must include our header in hundreds of source files. The result of this scenario would be extremely long compile times, as each time a source file is compiled, it must recompile the same huge header file, over and over and over again.

To understand how C++ Modules addresses these issues, let's look at how this same code would look using modules:

```
import std.string;
export module answers;

export
template<size_t number>
class the_answer
{
public:
    auto operator()() const
    {
        return "The answer is: " + std::to_string(number);
    }
};

#define CHECK(a) (a() == "The answer is: 42")
```

As shown in the preceding code snippet, our custom library includes a definition of string and then uses the `export` module to create a new C++ module called `answers`. We then define our class template with the `export` definition. Whenever a header is compiled (really, whenever any code is compiled), the compiler usually first converts that human-readable C++ syntax into something called an **Intermediate Representation** (**IR**). This IR is then converted into a binary assembly. The problem is that header files contain code (such as macros and includes) that cannot be converted into this type of representation, which means that, each time the compiler sees a header, it must convert the code into an IR and then into a binary every time.

C++ Modules provides a syntax and a set of rules that enables the compiler to convert a header into an IR and store the results of this IR with the rest of the resulting object files. The compiler can use this IR as many times as needed, removing the need to constantly perform the code for the IR conversion process, repeatedly. To see how the preceding code is used, let's look at the following:

```
import answers;
import std.core;
```

```
int main(void)
{
    the_answer<42> is;
    std::cout << is();
}
```

As shown here, we include both the definition of `std::cout` and our `answers` module. The difference is that the `main()` function doesn't have to convert the `answers` and `std.core` definitions from C++ syntax into the compiler's IR, decreasing the compilation time of the `main()` source file. The `main()` source file can also create a macro called `CHECK()` without colliding with the same macro in our `answers` module as macros cannot be exported.

Introducing std::span, a new view on arrays

In this recipe, we will learn how to use `std::span`, which is a new feature coming with C++20. This recipe is important as `std::span` is a descendant of the Guideline Support Library's `gsl::span`, which is a core component of the library used to ensure that your C++ is Core Guideline-compliant. In this recipe, we will not only introduce `std::span`, but we will also explain how to use it in your own code and why it helps to encapsulate an array with its size as well as provide a convenient API for working with arrays in general.

Getting ready

Before beginning, please ensure that all of the technical requirements are met, including installing Ubuntu 19.04 or higher and running the following in a Terminal window:

```
> sudo apt-get install build-essential git cmake
```

This will ensure that your operating system has the proper tools to compile and execute the examples in this recipe. Once this is complete, open a new Terminal. We will use this Terminal to download, compile, and run our examples.

How to do it...

You will need to perform the following steps to try the recipe:

1. From a new Terminal, run the following to download the source code:

```
> cd ~/
> git clone
https://github.com/PacktPublishing/Advanced-CPP-CookBook.git
> cd Advanced-CPP-CookBook/chapter13
```

2. To compile the source code, run the following command:

```
> cmake .
> make recipe03_examples
```

3. Once the source code is compiled, you can execute each example in this recipe by running the following commands:

```
> ./recipe03_example01
4 8 15 16 23 42

> ./recipe03_example02
4 8 15 16 23 42

> ./recipe03_example03
4 8 15 16 23 42

> ./recipe03_example04
4 8 15 16 23 42

> ./recipe03_example05
size: 6
size (in bytes): 24
size: 6
size (in bytes): 24
size: 6
size (in bytes): 24

> ./recipe03_example06
42
```

In the next section, we will step through each of these examples and explain what each example program does and how it relates to the lessons being taught in this recipe.

How it works...

In this recipe, we will explore what `std::span` is and why it is needed. In C++ (and even in C), to pass an array to a function, the following is implemented:

```
void foo(const int *array, size_t size)
{
    for (auto i = 0; i < size; i++) {
        std::cout << array[i] << ' ';
    }

    std::cout << '\n';
}
```

As shown in the preceding example, we have created a function called `foo()` that takes a pointer to an array as well as the size of the array. We then use this information to output the contents of the array to `stdout`.

We can execute this function as follows:

```
int main(void)
{
    int array[] = {4, 8, 15, 16, 23, 42};
    foo(array, sizeof(array)/sizeof(array[0]));
}
```

This results in the following output:

The problem with the preceding code is that it is not C++ Core Guideline-compliant. Specifically, we are forced to store the size of the array independently of the array itself. This can lead to issues if the array and its size become out-of-sync (something that is possible in large projects). The use of a pointer in relation to an array also prevents the use of ranged `for` loops, meaning we must manually traverse the array, which can also lead to potential stability issues if the `for` loop is not properly constructed. Lastly, we were required to calculate by hand the size of the array, an operation that, as shown, is prone to error, using `sizeof()`.

One way to solve this issue is to use a template function, as follows:

```cpp
template<size_t N>
void foo(const int (&array)[N])
{
    for (auto i = 0; i < N; i++) {
        std::cout << array[i] << ' ';
    }

    std::cout << '\n';
}
```

As shown in the preceding code snippet, we have defined a template function that takes a reference to an integer array of size N. We can then use N to traverse through this array. We can even use ranged `for` loops on the array since the compiler knows what the size of the array is at compile time. This code can be used as follows:

```cpp
int main(void)
{
    int array[] = {4, 8, 15, 16, 23, 42};
    foo(array);
}
```

As shown here, we have made several improvements. We are no longer passing around pointers that could lead to NULL pointer violations. We are no longer calculating the size of the array by hand using `sizeof()`, and we no longer need to store the size of the array independently of the array itself. The problem with the preceding code is that each time the size of the array changes, we must compile a completely different version of the `foo()` function. If the `foo()` function is large, this could be a problem. This code also doesn't support dynamically allocated arrays (in other words, whether the array was allocated using `std::unique_ptr`).

To solve this, C++20 has added the `std::span` class. Check out this example:

```cpp
void foo(const std::span<int> &s)
{
    for (auto i = 0; i < s.size(); i++) {
        std::cout << s[i] << ' ';
    }

    std::cout << '\n';
}
```

As shown in the preceding code snippet, we have created the `foo()` function using `std::span`, which stores an array of integers. Like most other C++ containers, we can get the size of the array, and we can use the subscript operator to access individual elements of the array. To use this function, we simply call it the same way we did using the template function, as follows:

```
int main(void)
{
    int array[] = {4, 8, 15, 16, 23, 42};
    foo(array);
}
```

Using `std::span`, we can now provide the same `foo()` function with arrays of different sizes, and we can even allocate the arrays using dynamic memory (in other words, `std::unique_ptr`) without having to re-implement the `foo()` function. Ranged `for` loops even work as expected:

```
void foo(const std::span<int> &s)
{
    for (const auto &elem : s) {
        std::cout << elem << ' ';
    }

    std::cout << '\n';
}
```

To use `foo()` with dynamic memory, we can do the following:

```
int main(void)
{
    auto ptr1 = new int[6]();
    foo({ptr1, 6});
    delete [] ptr1;

    std::vector<int> v(6);
    foo({v.data(), v.size()});

    auto ptr2 = std::make_unique<int>(6);
    foo({ptr2.get(), 6});
}
```

As shown in the preceding example, we ran the `foo()` function with three different types of memory created dynamically. The first time we ran `foo()`, we allocated memory using `new()`/`delete()`. If you are attempting to remain C++ Core Guideline-compliant, you are likely not interested in this approach. The second and third approaches allocated the memory using `std::vector` or `std::unique_ptr`. Both have their inherent disadvantages:

- `std::vector` stores its own `size()`, but also stores its capacity and, by default, initializes the memory.
- `std::unique_ptr` doesn't store its own `size()`, and it, too, defaults initialized memory.

Currently, C++ does not have an array type capable of allocating a dynamic array of uninitialized memory while also storing the array's size (and only its size). `std::span`, however, can be used with some combination of the preceding approaches to manage an array depending on your needs.

It should also be noted that when we created `std::span` in the preceding example, we passed it the size of the array based on the total number of elements, not the total number of bytes. `std::span` is capable of providing both for you, as follows:

```
void foo(const std::span<int> &s)
{
    std::cout << "size: " << s.size() << '\n';
    std::cout << "size (in bytes): " << s.size_bytes() << '\n';
}
```

If we run the preceding implementation of `foo()`, with the aforementioned dynamic memory examples, we get the following:

```
[~/book/chapter13/build]: ./recipe03_example05
size: 6
size (in bytes): 24
size: 6
size (in bytes): 24
size: 6
size (in bytes): 24
[~/book/chapter13/build]:
```

Finally, we can use the span to create additional sub-spans, as follows:

```
void foo2(const std::span<int> &s)
{
    for (const auto &elem : s) {
        std::cout << elem << ' ';
    }

    std::cout << '\n';
}
```

In the preceding `foo2()` function, we take a span and output all of its elements using a ranged `for` loop. We can then use the following to create sub-spans:

```
void foo1(const std::span<int> &s)
{
    foo2(s.subspan(5, 1));
}
```

The result of the `subspan()` function is another `std::span`. The difference is the fact that the pointer it stores internally has been advanced by 5 elements, and `size()` that the span stores is now 1.

Working with Ranges in C++20

In this recipe, we will learn how to use C++ Ranges, a new feature set coming with C++20. Ranges provides convenient functions for working with anything that mimics a range of objects or values. For example, 4, 8, 15, 16, 23, 42 is a range of integers. In C++ today, working with ranges can be cumbersome depending on what you are doing. This recipe is important as C++ ranges removes a lot of complexity associated with working with ranges, ensuring that your code is easier to read and maintain over time.

Getting ready

Before beginning, please ensure that all of the technical requirements are met, including installing Ubuntu 19.04 or higher and running the following in a Terminal window:

```
> sudo apt-get install build-essential git cmake
```

This will ensure that your operating system has the proper tools to compile and execute the examples in this recipe. Once this is complete, open a new Terminal. We will use this Terminal to download, compile, and run our examples.

How to do it...

To perform this recipe, perform the following steps:

1. From a new Terminal, run the following command to download the source code:

```
> cd ~/
> git clone
https://github.com/PacktPublishing/Advanced-CPP-CookBook.git
> cd Advanced-CPP-CookBook/chapter13
```

2. To compile the source code, run the following command:

```
> cmake .
> make recipe04_examples
```

3. Once the source code is compiled, you can execute each example in this recipe by running the following commands:

```
> ./recipe04_example01
1

> ./recipe04_example02
42

> ./recipe04_example03
42

> ./recipe04_example04
4 8 15 16 23 42

> ./recipe04_example05
4 8 15 16 23 42

> ./recipe04_example06
4 8 15 16 23 42
```

In the next section, we will step through each of these examples and explain what each example program does and how it relates to the lessons being taught in this recipe.

How it works...

C++ Ranges is a welcome addition to C++20 as it provides a simple means for working with any list of objects or values. To best explain how this works, let's look at the following example (note that, in these recipes, we will use Ranges v3 while we wait for GCC to support Ranges as v3 was the implementation adopted by C++20):

```
#include <iostream>
#include <range/v3/algorithm/count.hpp>

int main(void)
{
    auto list = {4, 8, 15, 16, 23, 42};
    std::cout << ranges::count(list, 42) << '\n';
}
```

As shown in the preceding code snippet, we have created a list of integers (in this specific case, we have created a simple initializer list). We then use the `ranges::count()` function to count the total number of times the value `42` shows up in the list, resulting in the following output:

Ranges can also be used for searching:

```
#include <iostream>
#include <range/v3/algorithm/find.hpp>

int main(void)
{
    auto list = {4, 8, 15, 16, 23, 42};
    if (auto i = ranges::find(list, 42); i != ranges::end(list)) {
        std::cout << *i << '\n';
    }
}
```

As shown in the preceding example, we have created the same initializer list of integers and we use ranges to return an iterator. This iterator can be used to traverse the list or get the located value. Initializer lists already support iterators, and one thing that Ranges does is extend this functionality to other types, including simple C-style arrays:

```
#include <iostream>
#include <range/v3/algorithm/find.hpp>

int main(void)
{
    int list[] = {4, 8, 15, 16, 23, 42};
    if (auto i = ranges::find(list, 42); i != ranges::end(list)) {
        std::cout << *i << '\n';
    }
}
```

The preceding example uses a C-style array instead of an initializer list and, as shown, Ranges provides an iterator to work with, in the C-style array, something currently not possible.

Ranges also provides some convenience algorithms. For example, consider the following code:

```
#include <iostream>
#include <range/v3/algorithm/for_each.hpp>

int main(void)
{
    auto list = {4, 8, 15, 16, 23, 42};

    ranges::for_each(list, [](const int &val){
        std::cout << val << ' ';
    });

    std::cout << '\n';
}
```

In the preceding example, we have created a list of integers. We then loop over the entire range of integers and execute a lambda on this list. Although this could be done using traditional loops, such as the range-based loops added in C++11, `for_each` could simplify your logic (depending on your use case).

Ranges also provides the ability to transform one list into another. Consider the following example:

```
#include <iostream>
#include <range/v3/view/transform.hpp>

class my_type
{
    int m_i;

public:
    my_type(int i) :
        m_i{i}
    { }

    auto get() const
    {
        return m_i;
    }
};
```

We will start this example by creating our own type. As shown in the preceding code snippet, we have a new type called `my_type` that is constructed with an integer and returns the integer using the `get()` function. We can then extend our previous examples to transform our list of integers into a list of our custom types, as follows:

```
int main(void)
{
    using namespace ranges::views;

    auto list1 = {4, 8, 15, 16, 23, 42};
    auto list2 = list1 | transform([](int val){
        return my_type(val);
    });

    for(const auto &elem : list2) {
        std::cout << elem.get() << ' ';
    }

    std::cout << '\n';
}
```

As shown in the preceding example, we create our initial list of integers and then convert this list into a second list of our custom types using the `ranges::views::transform` function. We can then iterate over this new list using a traditional range-based `for` loop.

Finally, Ranges also provides some actions that let you actually modify an existing range. For example, consider the following code:

```cpp
#include <vector>
#include <iostream>
#include <range/v3/action/sort.hpp>

int main(void)
{
    using namespace ranges;

    std::vector<int> list = {4, 42, 15, 8, 23, 16};
    list |= actions::sort;

    for(const auto &elem : list) {
        std::cout << elem << ' ';
    }

    std::cout << '\n';
}
```

In the preceding example, we use the `actions::sort` function to sort our list of vectors, resulting in the following output:

As shown in the preceding example, C++20 Ranges provides us with a simple means to sort `std::vector` using the pipe operator instead of having to use `std::sort`, explicitly defining our begin and end iterators.

Learning how to use Coroutines in C++20

In this recipe, we will take a brief peek into an upcoming feature in C++20 called Coroutines. Unlike some of the other features in being added to C++20, Coroutines are not possible in C++ today. Coroutines provide the ability to suspend the execution of a function and yield a result. Once the result is used, the function can be resumed where it left off to continue execution. This recipe is important as C++20 will be adding first-class support (that is, new keywords) to C++ to support Coroutines and it is likely that this new feature will begin to surface in libraries and examples in the near future.

Getting ready

Before beginning, please ensure that all of the technical requirements are met, including installing Ubuntu 19.04 or higher and running the following in a Terminal window:

```
> sudo apt-get install build-essential git cmake
```

This will ensure that your operating system has the proper tools to compile and execute the examples in this recipe. Once this is complete, open a new Terminal. We will use this Terminal to download, compile, and run our examples.

How to do it...

To try this recipe, please perform the following steps:

1. From a new Terminal, run the following command to download the source code:

   ```
   > cd ~/
   > git clone
   https://github.com/PacktPublishing/Advanced-CPP-CookBook.git
   > cd Advanced-CPP-CookBook/chapter13
   ```

2. To compile the source code, run the following command:

   ```
   > cmake .
   > make recipe05_examples
   ```

3. Once the source code is compiled, you can execute each example in this recipe by running the following commands:

   ```
   > ./recipe05_example01
   0 2 4 6 8 10
   ```

In the next section, we will step through each of these examples and explain what each example program does and how it relates to the lessons being taught in this recipe.

How it works...

As stated earlier, Coroutines provide the ability to suspend and resume the execution of a function. To demonstrate how this will work in C++20, we will briefly look at a simple example:

```
auto
even_numbers(size_t s, size_t e)
```

```
{
    std::vector<int> nums;

    if (s % 2 != 0 || e % 2 != 0) {
        std::terminate();
    }

    for (auto i = s; i <= e; i += 2) {
        nums.push_back(i);
    }

    return nums;
}
```

In the preceding example, we have created a function called `even_numbers()` that, given a range, returns `std::vector` of even numbers. We can then use this function as follows:

```
int main(void)
{
    for (const auto &num : even_numbers(0, 10)) {
        std::cout << num << ' ';
    }

    std::cout << '\n';
}
```

This results in the following output:

The problem with the preceding implementation is that this code requires the use of `std::vector` just to create a range of numbers to iterator over. With Coroutines, we will be able to implement this function as follows:

```
generator<int>
even_numbers(size_t s, size_t e)
{
    if (s % 2 != 0 || e % 2 != 0) {
        std::terminate();
    }

    for (auto i = s; i < e; i += 2) {
```

```
        co_yield i;
    }

    co_return e;
}
```

From the preceding code, we see the following:

- Instead of returning `std::vector`, we now return `generator<int>`.
- As we loop through each even value in our loop, we call `co_yield`. This causes the `even_numbers()` function to return with the value provided while saving its place.
- Once the `even_numbers()` function is resumed, it returns to where `co_yield` was originally executed, meaning the function can now continue its execution producing the next even number.
- This process continues until the `for` loop finishes and the Coroutine returns the last even number.

To use this function, our `main()` code doesn't change:

```
int main(void)
{
    for (const auto &num : even_numbers(0, 10)) {
        std::cout << num << ' ';
    }

    std::cout << '\n';
}
```

The difference is that we are not returning `std::vector` but instead returning the integer provided by the Coroutine.

Other Books You May Enjoy

If you enjoyed this book, you may be interested in these other books by Packt:

Hands-On Functional Programming with C++
Alexandru Bolboaca

ISBN: 978-1-78980-733-2

- Understand the fundamentals of functional programming
- Structure your code by understanding the building blocks of functional programming
- Compare design styles in functional programming and object-oriented programming (OOP)
- Use the concept of currying to create new functions in C++
- Become skilled at implementing design patterns in a functional way
- Get to grips with multithreading by means of functional programming
- Learn how to improve memory consumption when using functional constructs

Hands-On Design Patterns with C++
Fedor G. Pikus

ISBN: 978-1-78883-256-4

- Recognize the most common design patterns used in C++
- Understand how to use C++ generic programming to solve common design problems
- Explore the most powerful C++ idioms, their strengths, and drawbacks
- Rediscover how to use popular C++ idioms with generic programming
- Understand the impact of design patterns on the program's performance

Leave a review - let other readers know what you think

Please share your thoughts on this book with others by leaving a review on the site that you bought it from. If you purchased the book from Amazon, please leave us an honest review on this book's Amazon page. This is vital so that other potential readers can see and use your unbiased opinion to make purchasing decisions, we can understand what our customers think about our products, and our authors can see your feedback on the title that they have worked with Packt to create. It will only take a few minutes of your time, but is valuable to other potential customers, our authors, and Packt. Thank you!

Index

Printed in Great Britain
by Amazon